THE LEGENDS OF
NOTTINGHAM
FOREST
1865-2007

THE LEGENDS OF
NOTTINGHAM
FOREST
1865-2007

Dave Bracegirdle

First published in Great Britain in 2007 by
The Breedon Books Publishing Company Limited
Breedon House, 3 The Parker Centre,
Derby, DE21 4SZ. Reprinted 2007

Paperback edition published in Great Britain in 2012 by
The Derby Books Publishing Company Limited,
3 The Parker Centre, Derby, DE21 4SZ.

ISBN 978-1-78091-138-0

Printed and bound by Copytech (UK) Limited, Peterborough.

Contents

Foreword

by Lee Westwood

For as long as I can remember Nottingham Forest Football Club has played an important role in my life. Growing up, I became aware from an early age that the best team in Europe happened to be my local team – and it was natural that I should support them and follow their fortunes.

Years later, having enjoyed many 'highs' and had time to reflect on a few too many 'lows', they are still 'my team' and the thrill and excitement of watching them play has never left me.

Although I can't get to see them as regularly as I'd like to, I do enjoy the short breaks in my schedule when I am able to get to the City Ground to see them in action.

It's always amazed me how well known the club is around the globe. I've been fortunate that my golf has enabled me to travel to many places, yet whenever I'm asked to explain where I come from, Forest becomes a natural focal point for discussion.

This bears testimony to the many fine players and characters who have been associated with the club throughout its history. I've been privileged on occasions to meet and talk to a few of them, but for the majority their stories have either been forgotten or untold – until now.

The Legends of Nottingham Forest has been written and researched for everyone who has ever taken an interest in our story. I hope you enjoy reading it as much as I have!

Lee Westwood
Five-time member of the European Ryder Cup Team

Acknowledgements

So many people have helped me put together this tribute to *The Legends of Nottingham Forest* and my sincere thanks go out to them all.

First and foremost, I'm indebted to the many supporters who took time to send me suggestions or personal memories to be included in the book, particularly David Gibson whose catalogue of statistical records made research much easier than it would otherwise have been.

Once again, the knowledge and expertise of everyone at Breedon Books, particularly Steve Caron, Michelle Grainger and Sarah Allard, has been invaluable – everything comes to those who wait!

Both the *Nottingham Evening Post* and *Nottingham Football Post* have expertly covered Forest's fortunes over the years, and their help with confirming factual accuracy and providing most of the excellent photographs is very much appreciated.

Thanks are also due to Forest's Press Officer Fraser Nicholson, to Chubby Chandler and Sarah Harris at ISM, to Carly Bassett at Sky Sports, to the 'Flowserve Sunday Club' and, of course, to Lee Westwood for kindly agreeing to write the Foreword.

Love and thanks to Karen for her devoted support and hours of dedicated proofreading – and finally, to each and every one of the legends – I hope that I've been able to accurately portray your story.

I hope you all enjoy *The Legends of Nottingham Forest.*

Dave Bracegirdle, July 2007

Colin Addison

Date of birth: 18 May 1940, Taunton, Somerset

Nottingham Forest record:
Appearances: League 160, FA Cup 11, League Cup 3, Others 2
Goals: League 62, FA Cup 6, League Cup 1
Debut: 21 January 1961 v Cardiff City (h) won 2–1

Also played for: York City, Arsenal, Sheffield United, Hereford United
Managed: Durban City (South Africa), Newport County, Derby County, Celta Viga (Spain), Atletico Madrid (Spain), Hereford United, Merthyr Tydfil, Scarborough, Yeovil Town, Swansea City, Forest Green Rovers, Barry Town

Colin Addison has enjoyed a long and fruitful career as one of the most dependable lower League managers. For more than 30 years he has plied his trade, both at home and abroad, assisting any number of clubs where funds and playing abilities have often been in short supply. Any success has been due to a sharp footballing brain, developed after a lengthy playing career which included over five years spent at the City Ground.

He joined Forest in January 1961 after springing to prominence at York City. 'I'd signed professional terms for York on my 17th birthday after playing for their junior sides for a couple of years,' he recalls. 'I began to grab a few goals and a few clubs began to show an interest.'

Forest boss Andy Beattie tied up the transfer on a gentleman's agreement. 'A fee of around £12,000–15,000 was agreed between the two clubs but York didn't want me to leave until they'd been knocked out of the FA Cup. I remember we drew at home against Norwich City and then lost at Carrow Road. That was in the midweek – on the Friday Forest signed me on the way up to go and play a match at Newcastle. I went with them and watched them come back from 2–0 down to draw 2–2.'

Colin made his debut in the next match at home and suffered at the hands of an offside flag. 'I scored with a smashing header but it was disallowed!'

He did not have to wait long for his first goal in his new club's colours, netting both in a 2–1 win at West Brom. 'I managed to seize on a back pass from Graham Williams, took it round the 'keeper and slotted it in. We've been friends ever since, still meet regularly and I still remind him of that goal as often as I can!'

The new signing made a big impression at Forest and began to bang in a few goals. 'I played in the old-fashioned inside-forward position, ideally just off a big man, and usually wore number eight. I had a bit of pace in my younger days but gradually, over the years, I moved back into a more conventional midfield role.'

His eye for goal enabled Colin to top the club's scoring charts in three out of four seasons. All strikers like the satisfaction of bagging a hat-trick and he managed two for the Reds, both at home. 'My wife Jean and I got married on a Monday in 1964 and went to spend a few days in London together. I had to be back for training on the Friday, played against Birmingham the following day and scored three in our 4–0 win.'

Six months later Sunderland were soundly beaten on their trip to Nottingham and Colin again hit a treble. 'Two of the goals were just instinctive close-range efforts but one was a stunner – thrashed in from an angle, about 20 yards out.' Though spectacular, that strike does not match up to his favourite for Forest. 'It was against Leicester City – always a big game for the fans. Gordon Banks was in goal at the Trent End and I beat him from around 25 yards with a stunning half-volley.'

Eventually it was time for Colin to move on and begin a journey that was to take him right around the world as a player, manager and coach, but he admits to always following the fortunes of the Reds. 'I regularly go back to visit my wife's family and make sure I go to the City Ground as often as I can. Forest are a great club with a great tradition and have always tried to play football the proper way.'

For the last couple of seasons Colin has worked as a match summariser for BBC Wales, following the fortunes, principally, of Swansea City and Cardiff City. 'I enjoy talking about the game so much and this keeps me involved. It gives me the chance to travel up and down the country and meet up with so many of my old friends – particularly when I can get to Nottingham. There are still people there who remember me playing and I love seeing them all again. Forest will always be a big part of my life!'

Dennis Allsop

Date of birth: 13 February 1871, Derby
Died: 6 October 1921

Nottingham Forest record:
Appearances: League 206, FA Cup 27
Debut: 24 December 1892 v Wolverhampton Wanderers (h) won 3–1

Also played for: Derby Junction

The goalkeeper for Forest's 1898 FA Cup Final victory over Derby County was Dennis Allsop, a supremely agile shot-stopper who, ironically, had grown up supporting the Rams! Allsop had joined the Reds in the summer of 1892, as Forest were strengthening their squad ahead of the inaugural Football League season. William Brown began the campaign as the first-choice goalie, having already spent a year at the club, and he had the honour of playing in the club's first-ever League match – a 2–2 draw at Everton.

Newspaper reports of the day frequently described Brown's performances as 'erratic' and eventually Dennis was given his opportunity, making his debut on Christmas Eve. Forest had only won one of their previous nine contests, but a 3–1 success over Wolves heralded an upturn in fortunes and the start of a seven-year reign for Dennis.

Forest were regularly in the bottom reaches of the First Division, so invariably Dennis was a busy man. Many judges of the time felt he was a little unlucky not to gain any international recognition, yet he continued to serve Forest with total dedication. His reward, and that of his teammates, was the FA Cup success. Dennis kept clean sheets in three of the rounds, including the infamous semi-final replay against Southampton. After a drawn contest at Bramall Lane, the sides met again at Crystal Palace. In rapidly deteriorating conditions Forest scored twice in the closing minutes of extra-time, with a snow blizzard sweeping into the faces of the Saints. A protest was lodged by the losers, citing the opinion that the ground was unfit for play. An FA hearing was convened and, amid great controversy, the result was allowed to stand. Four years after Notts County's success, the city had another side in the Cup Final.

Opponents Derby County were huge favourites to win, but then the forecasters had not anticipated such a magnificent performance from Forest's goalkeeper. Playing again at Crystal Palace, Forest were hoping for some revenge against a side who had hammered them 5–0 in the League the previous week. They made the perfect start, with Arthur Capes putting them ahead, but they were soon pegged back by a powerful header from Derby's Steve Bloomer, the England international. The centre-forward was left unmarked to crash in a header off the underside of the bar and past Dennis's despairing dive.

Further goals gave the Reds a 3–1 advantage and they were seemingly on course for an easy victory, but then their opponents staged a remarkable onslaught upon Dennis's goal. Time after time he athletically foiled goal-worthy shots and headers. As his defenders grew more and more frantic, Dennis grew in stature and confidence. He would not be beaten and gobbled up crosses with ease as he turned in a match-winning performance. So rarely has a side triumphed in the Final and owed such a debt to their 'keeper; Dennis played the best 90 minutes of his life and fully deserved the accolades which followed.

Understandably, 16 April 1898 was Dennis's finest performance in a Forest jersey, but he remained hugely consistent the following season when he appeared in every game for his club. His big frame continued to foil opposition attackers and he took his tally of League appearances for the club beyond the 200 mark the following year. It looked for a while as though a repeat journey to the Cup Final lay in store as Forest again reached the semi-finals, but it was Bury who advanced after triumphing 3–2 in yet another replay.

With the emergence of Harry Linacre, another young promising goalie, Dennis began to wind down his career and he made the decision to retire after a humbling 8–0 defeat against West Brom on 16 April 1900 – exactly two years since his Cup Final heroics.

He retired to his Derby home and passed away in 1921, aged just 50. Not until Chick Thomson in 1959 would Forest have another FA Cup Final-winning goalkeeper.

Viv Anderson

Date of birth: 29 August 1956, Nottingham

Nottingham Forest record:

Appearances: League 328, FA Cup 23, League Cup 39, Others 40

Goals: League 15, FA Cup 1, League Cup 5, Others 1

Debut: 21 September 1974 v Sheffield Wednesday (a) won 3–2

Also played for: Arsenal, Manchester United, Sheffield Wednesday, Barnsley, England (30 caps)

Managed: Barnsley

Viv Anderson was very much a case of 'local lad done good'. A product of the Forest Academy, he played in both of the Reds' European Cup-winning sides, as well as achieving notoriety on the first occasion he pulled on an England shirt.

The young right-back had already had a brief taste of first-team involvement by the time of Brian Clough's arrival at the City Ground in early 1975 and he believes that the new manager inherited the basis of a decent squad. 'A lot of the players that went on to have great success under Cloughie were already at the club. He had the ability to look at a player and identify their strengths and weaknesses and always seemed to bring the best out of them.'

The first task for the Clough regime was to get the club out of the old Second Division and Viv remembers that the Forest lads were not even in the country when they heard they had been promoted. 'We'd already finished our fixtures and Cloughie took us away to Majorca. I can remember us celebrating on the beach when we heard that we'd been promoted!'

Forest took the top flight by storm and clinched two major trophies in their first season back up. 'We had good momentum going into the season and just kept plugging away. When we were there or thereabouts at Christmas we seriously began to believe that we could win the championship.'

By the time the League title had been won the Reds were already polishing the League Cup, claimed after a replay against Liverpool. Although the match was eventually decided at Old Trafford, Viv remembers the Forest fans coming out in force for the first match at Wembley. 'It was a great achievement for the club to get there and I was so pleased to be able to share the experience with so many of my family and friends. Much of the day passed me by. You just get carried away with all the emotion but hope you get through it and come out the other side which fortunately we did.'

Over the course of the next couple of seasons Viv formed a cornerstone of a Reds' defence that helped the club to a record-breaking stretch of 42 unbeaten League games. The young defender also rattled up a sizeable collection of medals and plaudits.

He was rarely absent, yet hit with a double-whammy in the spring of 1979 when suspension ruled him out of two important fixtures. 'I missed the League Cup Final against Southampton. I went to the FA to plead my case but the appeal fell on deaf ears.'

Viv then had to sit out the semi-final European Cup-tie at home to Cologne, but can still recall the build-up to the match. 'I lived in West Bridgford at the time and gave myself a couple of hours to get to the ground but only just made it. I'd never seen anything like it before – the atmosphere was amazing and everybody was out on the streets.'

By that stage of his career, Viv had innocently caused a bit of a stir when he was selected to play for his country for the first time. Lining up against Czechoslovakia at Wembley on 29 November 1978, he became the first black player to represent England. Considering the multi-cultural society we live in today it seems incredulous to believe the amount of newsprint devoted to the selection.

Understandably, Viv remains immensely proud of his achievement. 'I consider it a great honour to have been the first but many people forget that Laurie Cunningham had already played for the Under-21s.'

Viv confesses that it was teammate Garry Birtles who first came up with the nickname of 'Spider' for him. 'Again, it was in Majorca and I'd been jumping around from room to room looking for people and Garry said I was like a spider – I think the long legs were something to do with it!'

Those long legs were put to good use in more than 400 first-team games for Forest. He maintains his role in the side was easily defined. 'The manager liked you to play when the ball was on your side of the field. He hoped you would have the ability to do a bit of everything but, above all else, keep your winger quiet. Anything going forward was a bonus for the team.'

There were occasions when he did get forward to deliver and he recalls one match in particular. 'Playing at home to Middlesbrough I scored one with my right foot and one with my left – both in the first half. I'd never been on a hat-trick at half-time before!'

After cementing his place as one of Forest's all-time greats, 'Spider' later served Arsenal, Manchester United and Sheffield Wednesday with distinction before embarking on a brief stint as both player and manager at Barnsley.

It is clear that Forest's fortunes will always remain close to Viv's heart. 'They are still the first result I look for. I go back to the club from time to time and have always been made to feel very welcome. I still feel it was remarkable that a club like Forest could go on to achieve as much as they did and I'm proud to have played a part in it.'

Wally Ardron

Date of birth: 19 September 1918, Swinton-on-Dearne, South Yorkshire
Died: March 1978

Nottingham Forest record:
Appearances: League 182, FA Cup 9
Goals: League 123, FA Cup 1
Debut: 20 August 1949 v Brighton & Hove Albion (a) drew 2–2

Also played for: Denaby United, Rotherham United

For four consecutive seasons Wally Ardron was Forest's leading scorer and his haul of 36 in the 1950–51 campaign has never been bettered for the club.

Standing at just 5ft 9in tall, Wally was not a physically imposing man until he put on his football kit. Fast and strong, with a ne'er-say-die attitude, he terrorised defences and had the untrainable quality of being in the right place at the right time.

Hailing from South Yorkshire, the young Walter left school at 14 and took up employment at his local colliery until 1936, when he began working on the railways with LNER. A keen footballer, he was given the opportunity of joining Rotherham United but his shifts restricted his availability so the club released him after he had made just one League appearance.

Wally played for local side Denaby United and began scoring to such an extent that Rotherham paid £100 to get him back! He 'guested' for a number of sides during the war but on the resumption of League football he was very much a Miller and determined to make up for lost time.

His solitary League appearance before the war had been on 13 January 1939 and his second was played on 31 August 1946, a gap of seven years 228 days – an unusual and unprecedented record.

Over the course of the next decade Wally was the most prolific striker in English football. He became the first to score 200 post-war League goals and created individual scoring records at both Rotherham and then Nottingham Forest, whom he joined in the summer of 1949 for £10,000.

By the time he had left the Millers Wally had notched a total of 223 goals for them, 94 in the League and 122 in wartime matches. He claimed a record haul of 38 in the 1946–47 season and helped the side to the runners'-up berth of Division Three North in three consecutive years.

Forest were desperately keen to return to the Second Division when he joined them, having been relegated the year before. He netted on his debut, away at Brighton, and also on his City Ground bow a week later. Nevertheless, his 25-goal tally could only help the Reds into fourth place in the table.

If missing out on promotion was a blow, it only remained so for 12 months. In the 1950–51 season Forest swept all before them, winning the title by six points from Norwich City. The side hit 110 League goals, with Tommy Capel finishing on 23 – 13 goals adrift of Wally's record total.

Big wins were the order of the day – Wally hit hat-tricks against Aldershot, who were beaten 7–0, and Gillingham, who went down 9–2.

The impetus of a successful season was carried over and Forest challenged hard for a second promotion in 1951–52 before finishing fourth, just four points behind champions Sheffield Wednesday. Wally had netted a further 29 goals that year, including all in a 4–1 win at Hull City.

Legendary status was also guaranteed when the striker netted two in a derby win over local rivals Notts County, in front of a City Ground crowd which topped 40,000.

In total, Wally hit six hat-tricks for the Reds, equalling the feat set by Tom Peacock. His final one came against Leeds United on Christmas Day 1953 (the last Forester to achieve the feat on that day).

Having missed so much football during the war years, Wally's fitness enabled him to carry on playing until he was nearly 38. He had been an outstanding athlete earlier in his life, competing in national events up until 1939.

When time was eventually called on Wally's playing career he could look back on an aggregate of 221 League goals from just 305 matches.

He returned to Rotherham, taking up a job in the steelworks, but continued to be involved in professional football by working first as a trainer and physiotherapist for Doncaster Rovers and later as a scout for Carlisle United.

Ever-busy, he took a position at his local bank as well as setting up his own part-time business of physiotherapy and chiropody. Wally's love of the game enticed him to accept an offer to train Rawmarsh Welfare for several years during the 1960s, a side which contained his two sons.

A goal-grabbing hero at both Rotherham and Forest, Wally Ardron died in 1978, aged just 59.

Jack Armstrong

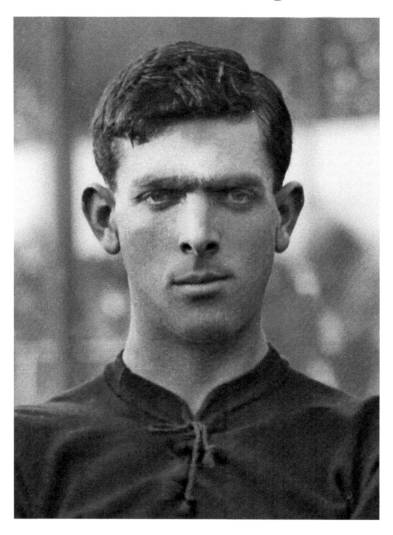

Date of birth: 4 February 1884, Willington, Derbyshire
Died: 9 November 1963

Nottingham Forest record:
Appearances: League 432, FA Cup 28
Goals: League 9, FA Cup 1
Debut: 23 December 1905 v Everton (h) won 4–3

Also played for: Keyworth United, Keyworth Town, Sutton Town

Jack Armstrong's tally of appearances for Nottingham Forest bears testimony to many years of devoted service he gave to the club. Only the illustrious names of McKinlay and Burkitt have appeared more often on League team sheets for the Reds, but their careers were not interrupted by a four-year cessation of fixtures.

Having played on the final afternoon of League football before World War One – a 0–7 trouncing by Arsenal – Jack's name appeared again 52 months later when football resumed.

Although he regarded himself as a wing-half, it is true he prospered in most positions. He was, undoubtedly, one of football's very first 'Mr Versatiles', appearing in every position, bar goalie, at some stage in his career – he would even volunteer to stand between the sticks in training sessions!

Jack had been spotted playing for his local side Keyworth United when Forest came calling. His debut for the Reds came in December 1905, a season that would end in relegation from Division One for the first time.

Life in the lower tier proved to be good for Forest and undoubtedly benefitted Jack at that stage of his career. He was one of only two ever presents in the side (full-back Walter Dudley being the other) as the Second Division title was won at a canter.

The Reds won 28 of their 38 League matches and remained unbeaten for the final 17 contests. Apart from his Championship medal, Jack could look back on a season that had also brought him his first couple of goals in League football. The first, at Clapton Orient, had been the decider in a scrappy 1–0 victory.

Never a prolific scorer, Jack was one of the Forest players who contrived not to get on the score sheet when Leicester Fosse were beaten 12–0 in 1909, the club's record-winning margin.

As the new century entered its second decade, Forest could no longer regard themselves as being one of the premier clubs in the land and they again endured relegation at the end of the 1910–11 season.

Many First Division clubs tried to lure Jack away from Forest at this time, most notably Aston Villa, but he remained loyal to the Reds and again set about the task of returning the club to its former status.

A devout teetotaller and confirmed non-smoker, Armstrong kept himself supremely fit and maintained an impressive turn of speed, which hardly diminished throughout his career.

This time, though, there was to be no immediate recovery for Forest. In fact, their decline intensified. Between 21 March and 27 September 1913, the club lost 14 consecutive League matches – a record which hopefully will never be broken!

Forest's fortunes were never at a lower ebb, on or off the field. They finished bottom of Division Two in 1914 and had to apply for re-election. They were only spared bankruptcy a year later thanks to a £50 grant from the League and, not for the last time, the generosity of their supporters.

With the world in the grip of terror and conflict, League football was understandably suspended. Ironically, the war years helped Forest to get back onto a firmer footing. Guest players helped the club compete in the various regional championships and by winning the Midlands Section they qualified to compete for the Victory Shield, beating Everton over two legs in May 1919.

League football resumed a few months later, with Jack skippering Forest on their return. He had played in 75 'unofficial' matches during the war years, and he continued to keep himself supremely fit while running his poultry farm at Keyworth.

Although his career was rapidly drawing to a close – he was in his late 30s – he helped the Foresters regain their top-flight status by collecting his second Division Two winners' medal at the end of the 1921–22 season, 15 years after his first. Following promotion Jack played just three more games for the club before bowing out, aged 38, after defeat at Burnley on 4 November 1922.

Jack Armstrong is listed in third place on Nottingham Forest's roll call of first-team appearances, such was his longevity with the club. He was actually the recipient of two benefit matches, nine years apart, against Huddersfield Town in 1913 and South Shields during his final season.

He retired to his farm, becoming one of the country's leading experts on poultry – although his name will always be more synonymous with the years of service he gave to Nottingham Forest.

Joe Baker

Date of birth: 17 July 1940, Liverpool, Merseyside
Died: 6 October 2003

Nottingham Forest record:
Appearances: League 118, FA Cup 8, League Cup 5, Others 4
Goals: League 41, FA Cup 5, Others 3
Debut: 8 March 1966 v Burnley (h) won 1–0

Also played for: Coltness United, Armadale Thistle, Hibernian (Scotland), Torino (Italy), Arsenal, Sunderland, Raith Rovers, Albion Rovers, England (8 caps)
Managed: Albion Rovers

Joe Baker was hugely popular during the three seasons he spent at the City Ground. He was idolised to the extent that the Forest fans dubbed him 'The King' and invented their own 'Zigger Zagger' chant in worship of his surging runs towards the opposition's goal. Although he was born on Merseyside, Joe's family were all Scottish and he was taken 'back home' when he was just a few weeks old.

His early club football was played in Edinburgh and he was taken on by Hibs at just 16. In four years at Easter Road he netted 159 goals, but he sought greater acclaim with an ambitious switch to Italian football with Torino. Sharing an apartment with Denis Law was a far from idyllic recipe for his employers and there were reports of several late-night scrapes, including a car crash with Joe at the wheel and Denis in the passenger seat. Most of his year in Turin was ruined by an injury of some sort or another but he did delight the fans with one magnificent strike that earned victory over bitter rivals Juventus.

The next stop on Joe's travels took him to north London and the red of Arsenal. Between 1962 and 1966 Baker brought up a century of goals for the Highbury club in just 152 games, a phenomenal strike-rate. His 'superman' persona took a bit of a knock one day, though, when he went between the sticks to replace injured goalie Jack McClelland in a match against Leicester City and conceded five! It was at the other end of the park in which Joe excelled: although short in stature, he was nippy, had excellent close control and was as brave as a lion.

Joe had joined Arsenal having already played international football during his time at Hibs, but not for his preferred Scotland. Despite his strong Scottish accent, the regulations at the time precluded a call-up for anyone but those whose country of birth was Scotland, so Joe reluctantly accepted his England call-up to become the first player to wear the Three Lions having not played English League football.

His impact was immediate – he netted on his debut in a 2–1 win over Northern Ireland in 1959. Joe played in the next four games but then remained in the wilderness until the 1965–66 season when Alf Ramsey recalled him into the set-up. An outstanding display against Spain in Madrid brought his second international goal, but after playing against Poland in the January he did not feature again. Many critics felt that Baker should have made the World Cup 22 – but who can argue with Ramsey's selection!

Forest manager Johnny Carey splashed out a then club-record fee of £65,000 to bring Joe to the City Ground in March 1966, with his side desperately close to the relegation trapdoor. The signing was inspired and reaped immediate dividends as his new striker scored five times in the run-in to help the Reds achieve safety by just three points.

The following season saw Forest transformed into serious challengers for both major domestic honours. In the League they finished as runners-up, just four points behind Manchester United, and in the FA Cup they reached the semi-finals before losing to Spurs. Joe's injury in the quarter-final success over Everton has always been cited as a significant factor in the Reds' failure to reach the Wembley Final.

He had scored a total of 19 League and Cup goals in his first full season at the City Ground and went two better the following year, including scoring the club's debut goal in European competition, away at Eintracht Frankfurt. Playing together, Joe and strike-partner Ian Storey-Moore netted more than a century of goals in three seasons between them. The partnership was prolific and the fans enjoyed watching them both, yet Matt Gillies, who had replaced Carey as manager in January 1969, sanctioned the sale of Baker to Sunderland later that year. Gillies was never forgiven.

The striker returned to Scotland to see out his playing career with Hibs, Raith and then Albion Rovers, for whom he later had two short stints as manager. Joe scored a total of 294 League goals in his career, from just short of 500 matches. He later ran a pub in Lanarkshire and was a popular matchday host at Hibs for many years.

Tragically, Joe died of a heart attack while playing in a charity golf tournament in 2003. He was 63 – long live 'The King'!

John Barnwell

Date of birth: 24 December 1938, High Heaton, Tyne and Wear

Nottingham Forest record:
Appearances: League 180, FA Cup 13, League Cup 5, Others 3
Goals: League 22, FA Cup 2, League Cup 1
Debut: 21 March 1964 v Sheffield Wednesday (h) won 3–2

Also played for: Bishop Auckland, Arsenal, Sheffield United
Managed: Peterborough United, Wolverhampton Wanderers, AEK Athens
(Greece), Notts County, Walsall, Northampton Town

Forest's side of the mid-1960s came so close to achieving domestic success thanks to the squad assembled by manager Johnny Carey. Among those brought in to play a key role was midfielder John Barnwell, recruited from Arsenal. 'I was 24, going on 25 and had been at Highbury since I was 16,' he recalls. 'Consecutive managers had failed to make any significant progress and I really couldn't see us winning things. I wanted a fresh challenge.'

Freedom of contract had recently been introduced into football and John began negotiating a transfer. 'I'd spoken to Manchester City and all but agreed a move but the Arsenal Chairman, Dennis Hill-Wood, asked me if I'd do him a favour and speak to Nottingham Forest. When I asked why, he said, "Because they'll look after you."'

A deal was soon arranged, but John's Forest debut suddenly came under doubt when he trapped a nerve in his back. 'The doctor gave me a cortisone injection – not the wisest thing to do on reflection – but it enabled me to get through my first match.' Soon afterwards he registered his first goal for the club, a memorable decider in a 3–2 win at West Brom. 'Colin Addison got to the byline, pulled it back and from just outside the box I hit home a screamer of a half-volley.'

The following season, 1964–65, John scored 12 times in 40 League appearances. 'I was given free range to get as far forward as I wanted because the manager knew I was likely to get him a goal or two.'

Good stamina coupled with the ability to pick out a decisive pass were John's key strengths and he was an integral part of the side that took Forest to within touching distance of glory in 1966–67. 'They were exciting times,' he recalls. 'We had a good side, with plenty of height in defence and skill and pace further forward. The game which sticks out most in my mind is the Everton FA Cup tie – and not just for Ian Storey-Moore's hat-trick. It was a fierce Cup tie between two evenly matched sides, played on a wet top. There were tackles flying in that you wouldn't get away with today.'

The 3–2 win over the Goodison Park outfit propelled Forest into the last four – but at a cost. 'Joe Baker was injured against Everton and unable to play in the semi-final against Spurs. I remember the despair of losing and will always believe that with Joe in the side we'd have won that day.'

The Forest players had to endure more disappointment when they finished up as League runners-up, four points behind champions Manchester United. 'We'd had two great games with them that year – winning 4–1 at home and playing really well at Old Trafford before Denis Law scored a winner for them right at the death.'

Although the season had brought plenty of joy to Forest supporters, it ended in misery for John. 'We ended the season with a friendly against Barcelona at the Nou Camp. Although we won fairly easily someone stood on my heel. Despite a summer of rest I still could hardly run during pre-season training. I missed several months of the season but then got hurt again in a match against Everton. Alan Ball and I jumped for a ball. As we landed we collapsed in a heap and one of his studs caught in my ankle. The final whistle went then and I had to be stretchered back to the dressing room.'

An injury-laden 18 months followed. Patched up, John joined Sheffield United in 1970 but the injuries had taken their toll and heralded the end of his playing days. Coaching then management was a natural progression and, 10 years after leaving the City Ground, John inflicted pain on his old side by leading Wolves to a 1–0 League Cup Final win over Brian Clough's side. That result was particularly sweet for 'Barny', who'd fought his way back from a car crash which had left him with a fractured skull and fighting for his life.

Between June 1987 and December 1988 John was back beside the Trent as manager of Notts County. He later worked at Walsall, Northampton Town and Grantham Town in a variety of roles before becoming chief executive of the League Managers' Association in 1996.

Although he has overseen many changes in our national game, John has no regrets about his own career. 'I consider myself to be very fortunate to have played when I did because football was fun back then. It gave me lots of very happy memories and I enjoyed my time, particularly at Forest.'

Colin Barrett

Date of birth: 3 August 1952, Stockport, Cheshire

Nottingham Forest record:
Appearances: League 69, FA Cup 5, League Cup 10, Others 10
Goals: League 4, League Cup 1, Others 3
Debut: 13 March 1976 v Fulham (h) won 1–0

Also played for: Cheadle Town, Manchester City, Swindon Town

Colin Barrett's role in the emergence of Nottingham Forest can never be overstated. Arriving at the City Ground as something of an unfulfilled talent, he filled the role of utility defender as the Reds bridged the gap from Second Division lightweights to European champions. Having made just over 50 League appearances for Manchester City, he initially joined Forest on loan towards the end of the 1975–76 season. 'Cloughie was there on his own at the time and I really enjoyed my few weeks at the club. So much so, that in the summer I was happy to make the move permanent.'

With the Forest manager doing the negotiating, Colin recalls the deal was far from straightforward. 'He signed me for £29,000, refusing to go to the asking price of £30,000!'

Peter Taylor had joined the club around the same time and the promotion push began to take full swing as the season progressed. Nominally a left-back, Colin's versatility came to the fore as Forest picked up their first trophy for 17 years – the Anglo-Scottish Cup. 'We got through to play Orient in the Final and drew 1–1 in the first leg,' he recalls. In the home return, he was pushed into midfield and marked the move with a couple of scintillating strikes. 'The first was from a free-kick and I drove home the second after a fine cut-back from Ian Bowyer. At the time I wondered what I was doing that far up the field but it was still nice to get a couple in a Final.'

Injury restricted Colin's League appearances that season – one of many he was to sustain at Forest – but he more than played his part as the Reds swept to the First Division title in their initial season back in the top flight. 'I played in something like 35 of the League games – filling in at left-back, right-back or in the middle, but I missed out on a League Cup Final spot through a stress fracture.'

The title brought additional rewards. Colin made his Wembley debut in the Charity Shield win over Ipswich Town and then looked forward to the side's first European Cup adventure. 'We couldn't believe it when we were pulled out of the hat to play Liverpool – we were anticipating trips to some sunnier climes!' The first leg was in Nottingham and

a decent result was imperative. 'The manager prepared us properly and we got the early goal through Gaz Birtles. We knew then how important it was to shut them out and take that lead to Anfield.'

With the clock ticking, a moment came that Forest fans who were present will never forget. 'I've seen the goal many times over,' says Colin. 'I charged down a ball in the middle of the park and released Gaz [Garry Birtles] down the left. I just carried on running as the cross came in and was there as Tony Woodcock nodded it down. I just hit it as sweetly as I could with my right and it flew in. At that point I knew we were home and dry and it had knocked the stuffing out of Liverpool.'

Colin was in and out of the side as it progressed towards its first European Final and suffered the disappointment of missing out on the day itself, but he did end up with a replica medal. 'They only gave out 16 medals on the night and after the match Cloughie instructed that they all be put on a table. He handed them out again to those that had played and took away the rest. I know the others were distributed to some of the backroom staff but the club did get replicas made for those of us that had played in the previous rounds.'

By then Colin had collected a League Cup-winners' medal of his own, having played against Southampton as the holders retained their trophy. 'It was a satisfying feeling to play in a Wembley Final. I'd missed out on two at Manchester City and been injured the previous year against Liverpool so I really enjoyed the occasion, even though we had to weather a late storm as they came back to 3–2.'

Injuries continued to disrupt Colin's career and he was allowed to leave the Reds in the summer of 1980 for a brief stint at Swindon Town. Since hanging up his football boots the former defender has kept a close eye on his old club, working as a painter and decorator in the Southwell area. 'Call me an interior designer, they get paid more,' he laughs. His sporting passion has continued with regular rounds of golf but, invariably, his return to the clubhouse often meets with a request to describe 'that goal' against Liverpool.

Chris Bart-Williams

Date of birth: 16 June 1974, Freetown, Sierra Leone

Nottingham Forest record:
Appearances: League 207, FA Cup 14, League Cup 17, Others 9
Goals: League 30, FA Cup 2, League Cup 3
Debut: 12 September 1995 v Malmo (a) lost 1–2

Also played for: Leyton Orient, Sheffield Wednesday, Charlton Athletic, Ipswich Town, APOEL Nicosia (Cyprus), Marsaxlokk (Malta)

Forest have not had too many completely 'versatile' footballers throughout their history, but the name of Chris Bart-Williams would come into that category in recent times.

'Bart', or 'The Bartman' (for obvious reasons), was an underestimated talent for most of his five years at the City Ground. Yet, by the time of his departure he had played in most outfield positions, assumed the mantle of penalty taker, worn the skipper's armband and finished as the club's top scorer.

Born in Sierra Leone but raised in North London, Chris made his full League debut for Leyton Orient while still a 16-year-old trainee. He turned professional a year later and had made 36 appearances for the O's when Sheffield Wednesday signed him for a fee of around £275,000. He appeared for the Owls in their FA Cup Final sides of 1993 (as a substitute), as well as scoring a Premier League hat-trick for them against Southampton.

With 16 England Under-21 caps to add to those won at Youth level, he was seen as being quite an acquisition for Forest when Frank Clark bought him from the Hillsborough club for £2.5 million. Clark, as manager of Orient, had first-hand knowledge of the youngster's ability.

Chris made his Forest debut in the UEFA Cup, coming on as a sub in a first-round game in Malmo but then settling into his favoured central-midfield role for the rest of that first season at the club.

A good all-round player, he looked comfortable in the top flight where his competitive nature and sheer will to win soon endeared him to the fans. Often misused wide on the left, and occasionally as an emergency full-back, Chris had to wait until his second season before notching his first goal for Forest, scored in a 2-0 home win over Chelsea.

Sadly that year the Reds were relegated, but Chris played his part in getting them straight back up. He contributed four goals – two of them being match-winners – against Oxford United early on and then against Reading at the business end of the season.

Forest's yo-yo existence, plus Bart's willingness to play in any position, scuppered his hopes of a full England cap, especially as the team were soon relegated again. Under David Platt's management he was appointed club captain and moved into a defensive midfield role. Tinkering further, the gaffer tried out a 3-5-2 formation for a while, with Chris playing as a sweeper.

This move instantly paid off, with a 5-0 thumping of Burnley. Admittedly, there was no confusing Chris with Franco Baresi, but he did look at home in this position and scored two of the goals – one from the spot.

As a penalty taker, he proved to be as reliable as any around, netting 10 of the 11 he took for the club – his only miss coming against Sheffield United in April 2000. His prowess from 12 yards was instrumental in his finishing the 2000–01 season as the club's top scorer with a total of 16 goals – eight of them having come from the spot. Deservedly, the Forest faithful voted overwhelmingly for the Bartman as their Player of the Year.

Despite this, Chris yearned to get back into the Premiership and submitted a transfer request. Negotiations between club and player soured somewhat, with Forest in need of a cash injection and Bart turning down alleged £1 million bids from Birmingham City and Southampton.

Eventually he left to join Charlton Athletic – initially on loan, but later the deal was made permanent with Forest resigned to letting him move for free in order to remove him from their wage bill.

Having made just 29 League appearances for the Addicks, Chris joined Ipswich Town in December 2003. He was released at the end of the season, though, and moved abroad, playing in both Cyprus and Malta before a back injury brought a premature halt to his playing career. He then moved to the US, taking up a coaching role at one of the many soccer schools on the east coast.

The unsavoury manner in which Chris parted company from Forest left a bitter taste in the mouths of many, but the commitment he showed every time he pulled on the Garibaldi shirt can not be questioned.

Dave Bassett

Date of birth: 4 September 1944, Stanmore, Middlesex

Nottingham Forest record:
Manager: February 1997 (initially as general manager) – January 1999

Played for: Hendon, Walton and Hersham, Wimbledon
Also managed: Wimbledon, Crystal Palace, Watford, Sheffield United, Barnsley,
Leicester City

Midway through the 1996–97 season things were getting so bad at the City Ground that the Forest board might have considered sending for International Rescue or the legendary American firefighter Red Adair.

Instead, with the team stranded at the foot of the Premiership, they opted to recruit Dave Bassett. The street-wise Londoner, known throughout the game as 'Harry', was brought on board to assist caretaker manager Stuart Pearce and try to turn the tide on the club's misfortunes. 'The Forest board asked me if I'd be interested in coming,' he recalls. 'I think they were a little bit concerned that Stuart wouldn't be able to stay in a player–manager role at that level for too long. It was such hard work and any help I could give him would make life easier all round.'

Dave was brought in too late to halt the slide into the lower division but was entrusted with the task of masterminding an immediate return after being given the manager's job full-time when Stuart elected to concentrate on his playing career. 'Stuart had the opportunity of staying in the Premiership as a player [with Newcastle United], so I was happy to take on the Forest job with the priority of taking the club straight back up.'

One of Dave's first moves when he arrived at Forest was to persuade the board to sign Pierre van Hooijdonk from Celtic, but he could not be accused of not doing his homework before completing the deal. 'I knew all about him,' says Dave. 'As a bloke he was disruptive, selfish and arrogant and had fallen out with everybody wherever he'd been. He wasn't a team player at all but he could score goals. He was a good player in a good team. I knew we'd get no more than a year to 18 months out of him – top whack – but I felt he'd get us goals and so it turned out.'

The task of returning Forest to the top flight could not have begun better. The club won all of their first six matches for the first time in 120 years and the manager still recalls each and every one of them. 'We made hard work of it against Port Vale, hammered Norwich and QPR, got away with it at Oxford and then beat Doncaster home and away in the League Cup.'

Van Hooijdonk scored seven goals in those early matches but it was another player that caught his manager's eye. 'Kevin Campbell was the catalyst behind many of the goals. He really played well that season and was brought down so many times for penalties and free-kicks.'

As well as winning promotion at the first time of asking, Dave had also set about revamping the youth set-up at the club and recruited what he felt was the right man for the job. 'I brought Paul Hart in from Leeds to run the academy but the best day's work I did at Forest was advising the board to buy the land at Wilford to ensure the club had a proper training facility for the youngsters.'

He wonders if other managers might have acted more selfishly. 'I could have had that money to develop the team – not that there was a great deal – but it was better spent on improving the club's facilities. The purchase was the right thing to do and I think that decision bore fruit – look at the players that have come through the academy since then, the likes of Williams, Prutton, Jenas, Reid, Dawson, Harewood and plenty of others.'

Plotting for the Reds' return to the top flight, Dave suddenly found his budget had been drastically amended. 'I'd been promised £8 million to spend if I got them back up. I did that – but what happened instead? They decided we needed to raise £2.5 million and sold Campbell behind my back. Van Hooijdonk then went on strike and the morale we'd built up was destroyed.'

Understandably, he remains angry at the change of events. 'I still don't think Pierre got enough stick for what he did. Ultimately his behaviour and the board's decisions got the club relegated and me the sack. Even if we'd kept Kevin and sold Pierre we'd have been all right.'

Dave was dismissed partway through the 1998–99 season with the club heading for its second drop in three years and he remains philosophical about how things turned out. 'I've still got a warm affection for the club. It's a shame how it all turned out. I believe we should have gone back up and consolidated in the Premiership. I still speak to Forest fans and I think they accept I had to try and do a job there with both arms tied behind my back.'

During his early days as a player, Dave skippered Walton and Hersham to FA Amateur Cup success at Wembley and his managerial career will always link him with Wimbledon's rapid rise through the Football League. His achievements at Forest should not be overlooked, though, and he still believes there is unfinished business for him at the City Ground. 'Ever since I left the place I've always felt that I would end up back at Forest one day,' he says. 'Who knows?'

Garry Birtles

Date of birth: 27 July 1956, Nottingham

Nottingham Forest record:
Appearances: League 212, FA Cup 11, League Cup 31, Others 29
Goals: League 70, FA Cup 3, League Cup 15, Others 8
Debut: 12 March 1977 v Hull City (h) won 2–0

Also played for: Long Eaton Rovers, Long Eaton United, Manchester United, Notts County, Grimsby Town, Ilkeston Town, England (3 caps)
Managed: Gresley Rovers

There is no question that the emergence of Garry Birtles could not have been timed any better by Forest's management. The young striker brought zest, vibrancy and, most importantly, goals to a side that had won the League title, yet still sold their joint top scorer.

'When Peter Withe left the club I wasn't even first choice to succeed him,' reveals Garry. 'Steve Elliott was the gaffer's preferred option and rightly so, because he'd been banging in goals for fun in the reserves and deserved his chance but in the first team he was really unlucky, hitting the post, the 'keeper, everything.'

Garry had been at Forest for a couple of years and had made just one League appearance during the club's promotion season. He had to bide his time for another opportunity but was brought into the team for a League game against Arsenal and kept his place for the eagerly anticipated first-round European Cup tie against Liverpool. It was essential that Forest seized the initiative, which they did through Garry's first goal for the club. 'Tony Woodcock did brilliantly for me. He just ran and ran with the ball – as Ray Clemence advanced, Tony just squared it to me at the edge of the box and allowed me just to stroke it home.'

The goal lifted the spirits of all at the City Ground, except in the minds of their opponents. 'Phil Thompson kept saying, "One won't be enough to take to Anfield", stuff like that.'

Late on, the youngster played his part in conjuring up the perfect response. 'I wrapped my foot round the ball and crossed for Tony to set up Colin Barrett's great volley for our second. I went over to Thompson and said, "Will two be enough?" I was out of order really, cheeking one of the great defenders of the time, but I just couldn't resist!'

That match confirmed to the football world that Forest had arrived as serious contenders to challenge for the major prizes. It also helped establish Garry as an integral part of the side and he responded with a stunning goal against Middlesbrough the following week.

'That was one of the best goals of my career – no question. I picked up the ball just inside their half, pushed it round the side of one defender, did the same to the next then hit a left-footed screamer straight into the top of the goal at the Bridgford End from about 25 yards.'

To complete a fairy-tale first full season he scored 25 times, played in all of the European Cup matches and turned in a match-winning performance on his Wembley debut in the League Cup Final against Southampton. 'I scored two goals that day – but felt I should have had four,' he reflects. 'The first one they disallowed for offside was marginal – very, very tight. I then scored a couple and thought I should have had a third. I actually took the ball on, went round the keeper and stuck it in before the linesman put his flag up. I'd have really liked to have scored a hat-trick at Wembley as not too many people have ever done that!'

The young striker's emergence had been spectacular. He had pace and power, a brutal shot and was dominant in the air. His manager was fulsome in his praise at the end of Garry's first full season with the Reds and admitted that the club had been desperate to find someone who could find the net so consistently.

The pair had spent plenty of time together, with Garry frequently being summoned to report to Cloughie. 'I would often get a call at the end of training to get myself over to the squash courts because the manager wanted a game. Off I'd go, caked in mud, and we'd play for hours. I enjoyed spending time with him – after all he was one of the greatest goal scorers ever and if I couldn't learn from him then I didn't deserve to be playing football.'

Garry's impact on the game was phenomenal as Forest extended their reign as European champions. An England call up arrived and with it a trip to the European Championships. A big money move to Manchester United followed.

The goals dried up at Old Trafford, though, and a return to the City Ground ensued – confirmation of his affinity with the club. 'I have always been a Forest fan and always will be,' he emphasises. Garry's work as a leading radio and television pundit has caused him to question the club on occasions and he acknowledges that may have upset a few fans. 'People who know me are aware of how much the club means to me – they know how much I care about Forest'.

Ian Bowyer

Date of birth: 6 June 1951, Little Sutton, Cheshire

Nottingham Forest record:
Appearances: League 445, FA Cup 34, League Cup 47, Others 38
Goals: League 68, FA Cup 7, League Cup 13, Others 8
Debut: 20 October 1973 v Blackpool (a) drew 2–2

Also played for: Manchester City, Leyton Orient, Sunderland, Hereford United
Managed: Hereford United

One of the unsung heroes of the successful Reds side of the late 70s and early 80s was the flame-haired Ian Bowyer. The hard-working midfielder became one of the most respected players in his position thanks to the accuracy of his passing and the lung-busting bursts he would make to support either defence or attack.

In an association with the club which eventually spanned four decades, a couple of Ian's clearest Forest memories occurred during the FA Cup run in his first season at the City Ground. 'The Manchester City game was very special for me,' he recalls. 'They were my old club and the one that I still had a lot of affection for. I was lucky enough to grab a couple of goals but it will always be remembered as "the Duncan McKenzie game". They just couldn't handle him. He was too much for them on the day.'

Forest's victory enabled further progression in a competition from which they eventually departed in controversial fashion. 'We were 3–1 up at Newcastle in round six when a couple of hundred fans ran on the pitch and disrupted play.'

Once order was restored and play was able to resume, the home side fought back to win 4–3 but the FA ordered that the match be replayed at a neutral venue. 'If the match hadn't been stopped then we'd have won easily, maybe four or five goals to one – but the incident shook up a few of our lads. They ordered a rematch but it's always disappointed me that the FA didn't have the foresight to throw Newcastle out of the competition. It surely would have prevented any other fans from ever wanting to run on again.'

There was more controversy when the rematch at Goodison Park was drawn – they insisted on another game at the same venue, much to Forest's disbelief. 'We played them three times yet didn't get a home match – how can that be right? After the drawn game we should have had a replay back in Nottingham but our appeals fell on deaf ears. Looking back it's still very disappointing because we'd have been through to a semi-final against Burnley, which I feel we'd have won.'

The midfielder finished as the club's top scorer during the 1975–76 season, although he does reveal that several of his 16 goals were scored while helping out as a striker.

Forest's fortunes really took off following the arrival of Brian Clough and Ian was very much an integral part of all the success that arrived at the club. He scored in the Anglo-Scottish Cup Final in the promotion season and then made major contributions in the domestic and European campaigns that followed.

Many regard Ian's goal in the semi-final win over Cologne as being one of the most important ever scored by the club, but he states that the players expected to win. 'Having drawn 3–3 at home we knew what we had to do out there and when we arrived in Germany we saw travel agents already booking trips to the Final in Munich – that was better motivation for us than any team talk. The goal came from a Robbo [John Robertson] corner, Garry [Birtles] flicked it on and I was just in the right place to head it in.'

The goal was enough to secure Forest's passage to the first of their back-to-back European Cup Finals, a feat that even now seems beyond belief. 'To get to the first Final was very special,' recalls the man known throughout football as 'Bomber'. 'Many of the same players had stayed together for a journey that had taken us from the Second Division to the biggest stage in European football.'

Ian's knack of popping up with an important goal served him right through his Forest career and he can look back on vital contributions towards each of the Reds' successes. He even scored twice in the European Super Cup Final against Valencia in November 1980.

In January 1981 he briefly severed his tie with the City Ground by signing for Sunderland, but within 12 months he was back to add to his appearance tally and, a year later, claim the club captaincy.

His 564th and final match for Forest was on 20 April 1987 at home to Norwich City. Only Bobby McKinlay has made more appearances for the club and his 96 goals equals that of Garry Birtles in joint-seventh place on the all-time list of Reds goal scorers.

After leaving the City Ground Ian joined Hereford United as a player before becoming their manager. In April 1990 he appeared in the same Bulls line up as his son Gary, one of the very rare occasions this has happened in an English League match.

Since then Bomber has worked on the coaching staff of a number of clubs, including spells under former Forest teammates Peter Shilton (at Plymouth Argyle) and Trevor Francis (Birmingham City), before returning to the City Ground during the Paul Hart era – a welcome return for one of the club's greatest-ever servants.

Jack Burkitt

Date of birth: 19 January 1926, Wednesbury, West Midlands
Died: 12 September 2003

Nottingham Forest record:
Appearances: League 464, FA Cup 37, League Cup 2
Goals: League 14, FA Cup 1
Debut: 30 October 1948 v Coventry City (a) won 2–1

Also played for: Darlaston FC (Staffs)
Managed: Notts County

Nottingham Forest's captain in the 1959 FA Cup Final was Jack Burkitt, the very definition of a leader – respected, brave and proud. He was tough and tenacious – and a Red through and through!

For many Forest supporters 'of a certain age', the image of Her Majesty the Queen handing over the Cup to Jack is the pinnacle of their lifetime's involvement with the football club.

There would be the euphoria of the European Cups and the League Cup successes but the 1959 team will always hold a special place in the hearts of those interested in the fortunes of the Garibaldis.

John Orgill Burkitt hailed from Staffordshire, where he was spotted playing local football and invited to Forest for trials. He signed as a professional in May 1947 but had to wait almost 18 months before being handed his opportunity in the first team.

Having played all of his early football at centre-half, Jack found himself switched to left-half. His enthusiasm was infectious. Keen to learn from experienced pros around him, such as Horace Gager and Bill Morley, his development was rapid and his contribution to the club's half-back line increased with every appearance. Dependable in the tackle and strong in the air, it was clear that the newcomer had all the qualities needed to succeed in the professional game.

A first goal for the club, the winner at home to Blackburn in January 1949, was an additional tonic to the young pro. Although goalscoring was not his primary role, Jack chipped in with some invaluable strikes throughout his career. In 1950–51 Forest romped to the Third Division South title – and Jack was fully deserving of his Championship medal, having played in all but four of the League matches.

Over the course of the next half-a-dozen seasons a seemingly constant availability, allied to consistently high performances, ensured that Jack would be regarded as the best player of his type in the Second Division.

Almost having taken ownership of the number-six jersey he was an ever present in three of those campaigns, including the joyous 1956–57 season when Forest were edged out of the title by local rivals Leicester City but nevertheless claimed promotion back to the top flight.

After a gap of 32 years Forest, under the leadership of Jack, kicked off a season in the First Division. If the first year back was all about consolidation, then the following year will always be synonymous with the Cup adventure. Led by their inspirational captain, Forest survived eight tough matches before cementing their place at Wembley. If their skipper had any nerves about the big occasion he certainly did not show them as he introduced his players to the royal party and exchanged pennants with Syd Owen, the Luton captain.

On an afternoon of heroes none had risen above Jack Burkitt, leading his beloved Reds through adversity to triumph. In a tireless individual performance he provided the perfect example, as he cajoled and encouraged those around him after Forest had been numerically handicapped through Roy Dwight's injury.

Jack was 33 years of age at the time of the Cup success and played on for another couple of seasons before appearing in his 503rd and final game for the Reds, away at Manchester City, in October 1961. His tally puts him in sixth place on Forest's list of all-time appearances, although of those above him only Bobby McKinlay (with 614) has played in more League matches.

In recognition of his services to Forest, the club granted him a testimonial and Malmo provided the opposition at the City Ground in November 1961.

After hanging up his boots, Jack joined the coaching staff at the City Ground before being accepted for the vacant managerial position at Notts County in March 1966. The appointment was short-lived and he was given leave of absence nine months later through nervous exhaustion caused by overwork.

Later he joined Brian Clough and Peter Taylor at Derby County as the first-team trainer, before becoming a sub-postmaster in Oakdale Road in Nottingham.

Jack later retired to Yorkshire, where he sadly passed away in 2003. He will always be remembered for his consistency and leadership – and as the only Forest captain to lift the FA Cup in the 20th century.

Kenny Burns

Date of birth: 23 December 1953, Glasgow, Scotland

Nottingham Forest record:
Appearances: League 137, FA Cup 14, League Cup 25, Others 20
Goals: League 13, League Cup 1, Others 1
Debut: 20 August 1977 v Everton (a) won 3–1

Also played for: Glasgow Rangers, Birmingham City, Leeds United, Derby County, Notts County, Barnsley, FC Elfsborg (Sweden), Sutton Town, Stafford Rangers, Grantham Town, Gainsborough Trinity, Ilkeston Town, Oakham United, Scotland (20 caps)
Managed: Sutton Town

It seemed an unlikely alliance when Kenny Burns, a player who had fostered a reputation for being an awkward customer to handle, linked up with Brian Clough's Nottingham Forest in the summer of 1977. 'I wasn't as bad as it was made out,' confesses the Scot. 'I'd been moved up front at Birmingham and a lot of it was due to frustration at not getting the ball or because others weren't doing their jobs properly. Most of my bookings were for swearing at either teammates or referees. I knew it wouldn't happen at Forest and Cloughie didn't have a problem with me at all.'

Kenny had begun his career in his home city with Glasgow Rangers but had to move south to join Birmingham City before being given an opportunity to prove himself at League level.

Having begun as a central defender, he was pushed into attack to try to find some goals for the Blues and responded with 20 goals in the First Division. Despite his prowess in front of goal, manager Clough had a different role in mind when he signed Kenny. 'He just told me I was playing at the back and that was it!'

Although not a towering defender, Kenny was rarely beaten in the air and possessed the priceless quality of being able to read a situation long before it happened.

The 1977–78 campaign ended with Forest becoming League Champions for the first time. Additionally, the Reds also lifted the League Cup – an occasion which brought immense pride for Kenny. During the drawn first match at Wembley, skipper John McGovern had been injured and was ruled out of the replay.

'No one gave much thought to the issue of who would be captain,' recalls Kenny. 'Before extra-time at Wembley Larry Lloyd had gone up for the toss of the coin and I presumed it would be him, but just before we went out at Old Trafford the gaffer threw the ball at me and said I was to do it!'

A couple of hours later, in his stand-in role, Kenny held aloft the first major trophy of the Clough era. 'It was great for the club – but I remember thinking, what was I doing winning something like this?'

Collecting silverware became a very pleasant habit for the Forest players over the next couple of seasons and Kenny knew that his efforts had been appreciated when he was awarded the Professional Footballers' Association Player of the Year Award in 1978. Shortly afterwards he left for Argentina as a member of Scotland's World Cup squad.

Apart from missing the League Cup Final against Southampton in 1979 due to a cartilage injury on his right knee, he helped Forest to Charity Shield success, two European Cup wins and a host of other Finals, including the Super Cup success over Barcelona.

'We'd won the home leg 1–0 but then had to contend with almost 100,000 screaming fans in the Nou Camp for the return. The atmosphere was unbelievable, more so after they scored from a penalty. Then Robbo [John Robertson] put over a corner, Larry [Lloyd] flicked it on and I powered home the header – it was a routine we practised time and time again – and I knew that we'd won the Cup then.'

Working under Brian Clough at such close quarters, Kenny remembers many examples of his unorthodox methods, not least when the players went to Japan for the World Club Championship against Uruguay's Nacional. 'The night before the game the manager told us to go out for a drink and relax. We didn't want to abuse the offer and all came back before 11, but Cloughie told us we needed to keep our body clocks on UK time so sent us back out again until 3am!'

Forest lost the match the next evening but, according to Kenny, it was nothing to do with the previous night's celebrations. 'We murdered them – really were all over them. They had one shot and scored – it really was a bit of a travesty!'

With the passing years Kenny has one big regret from his time at the City Ground. 'I actually asked for a transfer,' he says, still shaking his head. 'I thought the team were starting to break up and that I could make a few bob by signing for Leeds. It was the worst thing I ever did'.

His best days having been spent at the City Ground, he moved clubs with great regularity towards the end of his career, plying his trade at a number of other League and non-League clubs with varying success.

Despite these affiliations Kenny has always followed the fortunes of the Reds and for many years has been a popular and outspoken member of the media, commenting on the club's fortunes with the same passion and belief he always displayed as a player.

'I have to tell the truth – tell it as I see it. I know some people don't like what I have to say sometimes but you can only say what you feel. I've retained a soft spot for Birmingham but Forest will always be my team'.

Kevin Campbell

Date of birth: 4 February 1970, Lambeth, London

Nottingham Forest record:
Appearances: League 80, FA Cup 11, League Cup 2, Others 3
Goals: League 32, FA Cup 3
Debut: 19 August 1995 v Southampton (a) won 4–3

Also played for: Arsenal, Leyton Orient (loan), Leicester City (loan), Trabzonspor
                   (Turkey), Everton, West Bromwich Albion, Cardiff City

Kevin Campbell was a much-underrated talent who helped Forest return to the Premiership at the first time of asking. True, he had been a graduate of Arsenal's academy and was a member of the FA Youth Cup-winning side, but few outside Highbury's Marble Halls knew just how good he really was!

Between 1988 and 1995 Kevin made 166 League appearances for the Gunners, scoring 46 times, but he was very rarely afforded the luxury of a lengthy run in the first team, especially during the early part of his career.

Loan spells at both Leyton Orient and Leicester City broadened his ambitions and it was at the former that he first worked under Frank Clark. The O's boss wanted to sign the raw young striker but Arsenal would not sell him.

Four England Under-21 caps and an appearance for the England B side gave testimony to his potential and Kevin became a force to be reckoned with, scoring important goals as his club won the League and Cup double in the spring of 1993.

A year later he added a Cup-winners' Cup medal to his already impressive tally of honours, but the likes of Ian Wright, Dennis Bergkamp and John Hartson were also contenders for his starting place.

Six years after first bidding for him, Frank Clark eventually prised Kevin away from North London. A fee of £3 million brought him to Nottingham, with the Reds coming off the back of a season in which they had finished third – nine places and 26 points better off than Arsenal!

Crucially, though, Stan Collymore had just been sold and the hidden suggestion was that Kevin would be able to replicate the achievements of the Liverpool-bound international. In a season of UEFA Cup combat Forest slipped to ninth in the Premiership, with Kevin scoring six times. His first goal for the Reds came in just his fourth outing – away at his old stamping ground in a 1–1 draw against Arsenal.

The following year was one of extremes. It began in spectacular fashion for Kevin and for the team – a 3-0 win at Coventry City, with the muscular frontman grabbing all of the goals. Sadly, his season was then wrecked by injury and his lengthy absence was critical. The goals dried up and Forest suffered relegation for the second time in four years.

Dave Bassett took over as manager and was able to call upon a front pairing of a fit-again Kevin with the 'Flying Dutchman' Pierre van Hooijdonk. The duo combined magnificently and fired on full cylinders for the whole term. Opposition defences could not cope with either man, let alone their combined talents, and there were smiles once again on Trentside as the fans had a season to enjoy.

Although the margin between themselves and runners-up Middlesbrough was only three points, Forest had looked odds-on for the title for much of the season. Fifty-two goals of Forest's League total of 82 came from their two strikers and, although Pierre contributed slightly more with 29, many were from free-kicks and penalties usually conceded for fouls on his rampaging partner.

Among Kevin's 23 League strikes was his second hat-trick for the Tricky Trees, away at Crewe Alexandra in March 1998, helping to set up a 4–1 win.

Amid the jubilation was a statistic not lost on Forest fans – many of the Londoner's goals came at crucial stages of the campaign. On five occasions, against Port Vale, Stoke City, West Brom, Birmingham City and Ipswich Town, he hit the winner in narrow 1–0 successes.

The title secured and a medal won, Kevin then left these shores to try his hand in Turkish football with Trabzonspor but returned after just seven months to help steer Everton clear of the relegation trapdoor with a 'nine goals in eight games salvo'.

He remained on Merseyside for almost six years, hitting 45 League goals from 145 outings before joining West Bromwich Albion. A further switch to Cardiff City came 16 months later.

Kevin spent the 2006–07 season on the books of the south Wales club but his appearances became increasingly infrequent. A substitutes appearance against former club West Brom came shortly after his 37th birthday and may have been his League swansong, with the Bluebirds releasing the striker at the end of the campaign.

Of the 143 goals Kevin scored in English League football, the Forest faithful will always be grateful for the 23 he scored in his final season at the City Ground to help cement promotion back to the top flight.

Tommy Capel

Date of birth: 27 June 1922, Chorlton, Greater Manchester

Nottingham Forest record:
Appearances: League 154, FA Cup 8
Goals: League 69, FA Cup 3
Debut: 5 November 1949 v Crystal Palace (h) won 2–0

Also played for: Droylesden, Manchester City, Chesterfield, Birmingham City, Coventry City, Halifax Town, Heanor Town

Tommy Capel was a key figure as Nottingham Forest freed themselves of life in the old Third Division by helping them to the League title in the 1950–51 season. While Wally Ardron took most of the goalscoring plaudits for his 36 League goals, the contribution of Tommy was nevertheless equally important.

A Mancunian by birth, Tommy had served with the Royal Marines in Sri Lanka during World War Two and guested for Manchester City on his return home. He stood out as a player with a good turn of speed, a powerful shot and tricky, dribbling skills, and forced his way into City's first team.

Further moves to Chesterfield (where he played alongside his brother Fred) and, very briefly, Birmingham City preceded his move to Forest, with manager Billy Walker paying £14,000 to secure his services – a club-record fee. His debut coincided with a 2–0 home win against Crystal Palace on Bonfire Night 1949, but the real fireworks did not materialise that season as the Reds could only finish fourth.

Forest's fans were subdued for much of the campaign. They had expected a swift return to Division Two – almost as a divine right – but matters were compounded by the success of the side on the other bank of the Trent.

Notts County were enjoying a spirited period in their history and brushed most of the opposition aside on their way to the Division Three South Championship. Both local derbies were tight, tense affairs and although the Magpies claimed bragging rights after each, both clubs emerged with a lot of credit. Tommy actually scored in the opening encounter, a 1–2 defeat at the City Ground. The return at Meadow Lane was witnessed by a ground-record attendance of 46,000, but as hard as Tommy and his teammates tried they could not prevent County from getting the win they needed to secure promotion.

The Championship trophy did not have far to travel at the end of the following season, though, as the Reds made sure at the second time of asking.

Goals being the most priceless commodity in football, Forest were indebted to a pair of strikers who scored 59 League goals between them. Playing at inside-right, Tommy enjoyed the best season of his career, notching up 23 goals from just 35 appearances with a further contribution coming against Rotherham in the FA Cup.

His most prolific afternoon in a red shirt came on 18 November 1950, when he scored four of the goals in Forest's crushing 9–2 home victory over Gillingham. That same afternoon Ardron scored three times, making it the first time two players from the club had scored hat-tricks in the same match.

It looked as if Forest might complete successive promotions for much of the 1951–52 campaign but they eventually finished fourth, just two points behind second-placed Cardiff City. Injury restricted Tommy to just 32 appearances, from which he bagged 10 goals.

As his career developed he became renowned for good, close ball control. He was extremely difficult to dispossess and would think nothing of a spot of showboating to delight the fans. He developed a style of running which he termed 'The Bicycle Trick', whereby he would confuse defenders with a series of outrageous step-overs and dummied back-heels.

In an era where the 'professional foul' was rarely punished, Tommy would get more than the occasional whack from a disgruntled opponent, but he would continue undeterred and became a great crowd favourite.

Ardron missed much of the 1953–54 season through injury so extra responsibility fell on the shoulders of Tommy and his new partner, Alan Moore. The result was another fourth-placed finish, with Tommy grabbing 18 League goals – one behind Moore.

Among his haul were two against their city rivals, one in the 5–0 thrashing at home and then Forest's single goal in the drawn return at Meadow Lane. He also hit his second hat-trick for the club in a 4–1 home win against Fulham on 13 February 1954.

At the end of that season Tommy's stint at the City Ground drew to a close with Coventry City making a joint purchase, signing both him and Colin Collindridge, Forest's pacy left-winger.

Tommy played just 36 times for the Highfield Road club, scoring a more than respectable 19 times. He ended his League career with Halifax Town before winding down his playing days at non-League Heanor Town.

Although he was never an out-and-out striker at the City Ground, Tommy Capel's haul of 72 goals in 162 first-team outings for the Reds has ensured he will always be remembered as a true Forest legend.

Arthur Capes

Date of birth:	23 February 1875, Burton-upon-Trent, Staffordshire
Died:	26 February 1945

Nottingham Forest record:

Appearances:	League 168, FA Cup 23
Goals:	League 33, FA Cup 9
Debut:	5 September 1896 v Derby County (a) drew 1–1
Also played for:	Burton Wanderers, Stoke City, Bristol City, Swindon Town, England (1 cap)

The name of Arthur Capes will forever be synonymous among Forest fans for his achievement in scoring twice in the 1898 FA Cup Final. Not only did his goals help the Reds to their first-ever success in the competition, but it was also recorded at the expense of fierce rivals Derby County.

Arthur joined Forest from his local side, Burton Wanderers, at the same time as his brother. It was said that the club were much keener on acquiring Adrian, the elder of the two, but 'neither would sign without the other'. In the end, Adrian remained for only one year before going off to enjoy a long and successful career with Port Vale. Capable of playing as an out-and-out centre-forward, as a deeper lying inside-forward or out on the wing, Arthur's versatility proved an immediate asset to Forest. During his first season at the club he only netted six times (brother Adrian was joint top scorer with eight), but his all-round game drew admiration and respect.

Capes opened the 1897-98 season with Forest's goal as the city derby against Notts County finished 1–1. Wins were proving elusive, though, as the first five League matches brought four draws and a defeat. If the season was to bring any reward it would have to be in the FA Cup, a competition in which very little success had been accrued thus far. Arthur's first goal in the competition helped see off Grimsby Town in round one and further victories over Gainsborough Trinity and West Bromwich Albion took Forest through to their first semi-final.

Southampton provided the opposition and, after a draw at Bramall Lane, Forest won the replay 2–0 at Crystal Palace, also to be the venue for the Final. The win was overshadowed by protests from the Hampshire club. The match was played in a snow blizzard and they felt the conditions were not suitable. An appeal was eventually overruled by the FA and the result stood. As it was, on 16 April 1898 Forest were through to their first Final but were assessed as huge underdogs to overcome a spirited Derby County side that paraded the great striker Steve Bloomer, who had been in the very sharpest of good form.

This day was to belong to Forest, though – with Arthur Capes standing up to the challenge. It was Arthur who opened the scoring in the 19th minute, collecting a free-kick from Billy Wragg to fire low beyond Fryer in the Derby goal. After Bloomer had brought the scores level, Arthur struck again, just before the interval, driving home a rebound after the goalkeeper had failed to hold a shot from Sammy Richards.

Amid great scenes of jubilation, both at the venue and back home in Nottingham, Forest added a third to clinch the win. While all the team were fêted as heroes, special praise was heaped upon the shoulders of Arthur for his two strikes which had blunted the spirit of their opponents.

During the subsequent close season Forest moved home, taking up residence at the City Ground for the first time. A 1-0 reversal to Blackburn Rovers was a poor way to mark the opening of a new ground, but a fortnight later Arthur's goal helped earn a 1-1 draw against Sunderland and put him in the record books as the first Forest player to score at the new headquarters.

During his time with the club, 'Sailor', as he was known, helped the Reds to two more FA Cup semi-finals. Although both ended in defeats, he did score in the original 1900 match against Bury and the losing replay a few days later. After six years and almost 200 appearances he was tempted by the challenge of a move to Stoke in 1902. The switch was soon vindicated when the England selectors called him up for the annual joust against the Scots, although it was to be his only international appearance.

Arthur later played for both Bristol City and Swindon Town before retiring to his home town of Burton-upon-Trent, where he lived right up to his death shortly after his 70th birthday.

Johnny Carey

Date of birth: 23 February 1919, Dublin, Republic of Ireland
Died: 19 August 1995

Nottingham Forest record:
Manager: July 1963–December 1968

Played for: Manchester United, Northern Ireland (7 caps), Republic of Ireland (29 caps)
Also managed: Blackburn Rovers, Everton, Leyton Orient

In terms of winning silverware, the years between Billy Walker and Brian Clough remained barren for a succession of Nottingham Forest managers. One man came so close to completing the historic double, though – Johnny Carey.

Johnny's own playing days had been spent entirely with Manchester United. Having crossed the Irish Sea in 1936 to join the Old Trafford club, he made his debut a year later as an inside-forward and helped his new side to the runners'-up spot in the Second Division.

After the war Matt Busby, the United manager, converted Johnny to left full-back and also made him captain of the club. As leader, he was able to climb the Wembley steps and receive the FA Cup after his side had defeated Blackpool in the 1948 Final.

Individual honours accrued, with the Footballer of the Year award in 1949 and the Sportsman of the Year accolade arriving 12 months later. There was to be further team success when Johnny led United to the First Division title at the end of the 1951–52 season.

His international career was somewhat unusual in that he turned out for both Northern Ireland and the Republic of Ireland. Indeed, it was so chaotic that he played for both sides within the space of three days in 1946 – both times against England.

He won 36 caps in all, 29 of them for the Republic for whom he also netted his only three international goals. A further recognition of Johnny's status within the game arrived when he was selected to captain the Rest of Europe side in 1947, in a match against a Great Britain XI.

After a playing career that had seen him turn out for United on 346 occasions, Johnny could not wait to try his hand at management and he took over the reins at Blackburn Rovers in 1953. His appointment at Ewood Park brought steady progression to the club and they achieved promotion to the top flight at the end of the 1957–58 season.

Everton had been watching Johnny's development as a manager carefully and they stepped in with an offer to tempt him to Goodison Park. His three years on Merseyside were not wholly successful, though, and the Toffees cruelly dismissed him on Christmas Eve 1961.

A move to Leyton Orient brought Johnny a place in their Hall of Fame after guiding them into Division One at the end of his first full season with the club. Although they were relegated just as quickly, the O's had experienced life in the top flight of the English game for the only time in their history.

Johnny's next appointment brought him to the City Ground to succeed Andy Beattie. Forest had underachieved since the break up of Billy Walker's Cup-winning team, but some astute purchases brought about a fifth-place finish in his second season at the club.

Nottingham Forest celebrated their centenary in 1965 but the year after brought even more reasons for the Reds' supporters to enthuse about with the team coming so close to winning the League Championship, something they had never achieved before. All year long they pushed Johnny's old club, the eventual champions Manchester United, to the wire.

Johnny even had the satisfaction of turning over Matt Busby's star-studded team in comprehensive fashion with a 4–1 win at home. Winger Chris Crowe scored a hat-trick that day in a match watched by 49,946, still a City Ground record.

Forest's title ambitions fell short by just four points, a second blow for the supporters to swallow in the space of just a few weeks. Many felt that the Garibaldis were heading for another Wembley Cup Final but they were defeated at the semi-final stage, going down 2–1 to Tottenham Hotspur at Hillsborough.

The standards set by Forest in the 1966–67 campaign could not be maintained over the next 18 months and a slide down the table led to the board dismissing Johnny in December 1968.

He returned to Blackburn Rovers, initially in an administrative position but he took over again for the 1970–71 season. Sadly, Johnny's inspirational powers deserted him and he bowed out of professional football after the side suffered relegation to Division Three.

Johnny Carey – Forest's 'nearly man' – died in 1995, aged 76.

Sammy Chapman

Date of birth: 18 August 1946, Aldridge, West Midlands

Nottingham Forest record:
Appearances: League 359, FA Cup 32, League Cup 19, Others 12
Goals: League 17, FA Cup 2, League Cup 1, Others 3
Debut: 18 January 1964 v Stoke City (h) drew 0–0

Also played for: Notts County, Shrewsbury Town, Tulsa Roughnecks (US), Burton
Albion, Keyworth United

With more than 400 first-team appearances for the club, Sammy Chapman was a gloriously loyal servant to Forest. As a solid, uncompromising defender or a hard-working midfielder, he remained faithful to the City Ground cause for around 15 years.

Robert Dennis Chapman (but known as Sammy to one and all) was signed from Staffordshire football as a young goal scorer, though he made his Forest debut up front in 1964.

At just 17 years and five months of age he became the youngest player to appear for the club at that stage – although the match was less memorable, a tame goalless draw!

Displaying some early leadership potential, Sammy skippered the youth team in international tournaments in France and the Netherlands while waiting to make an impact on the first team, although opportunities at the highest level were scarce. It was to be more than three years – and over 20 appearances – before he got his name on the score sheet and then, like London buses, along came two at once! Appropriately his goals came in the capital, a couple of headers inspiring Forest to a 3–2 win at Fulham. An end of season tour of Spain then saw Sammy feature in both of Forest's matches, against Barcelona and Valencia.

In the 1967–68 season he began to feature more often and scored in Forest's brief Inter-Cities Fairs Cup adventure, against Eintracht Frankfurt of Germany.

Following Terry Hennessey's departure and an injury crisis at the club, Sammy moved back into a central-defensive role with great effect. Between 29 November 1969 and 18 March 1972 he appeared in 113 consecutive League and Cup matches for the Reds – great testimony to his consistency and also to the regulations in force at the time. On 27 November 1971, playing at home against Leeds United, Sammy became the first Forest player to be sent off in a League match for 32 years. No suspension was imposed!

Despite maintaining his own form and fitness, Forest's fortunes began to wane and at the end of the 1971–72 season they were relegated down to Division Two after 15 seasons of playing their football in the top flight.

Sammy scored his first FA Cup goal in the 1973–74 season, helping the Reds overturn a late 3–2 deficit to beat Bristol Rovers. Having advanced to the sixth round, all hopes of a Wembley Cup Final evaporated after an unsavoury pitch invasion by Newcastle United fans, dispirited at the sight of their heroes losing 1–3 to Forest. Two replays later, both at the neutral venue of Goodison Park, saw the side from the North East emerge victorious.

One year on, Forest's next FA Cup adventure coincided with the arrival of a new manager. Brian Clough took over at the City Ground 48 hours before a third-round replay away at Tottenham Hotspur. Cloughie's first decision was to appoint Sammy as 'club captain' – an inspirational choice, with the defender turning in one of his finest performances to get BC's reign off to a winning start.

While Sammy did not go on to win a host of medals and international caps, his commitment and loyalty to Forest did not go unnoticed. Nearly 11,500 fans turned out for a testimonial match in his honour in April 1975. England manager Don Revie brought a Select XI to the City Ground and a Forest side featuring many former favourites, like Joe Baker and Duncan McKenzie, won the match 3–2.

As his time as a Forester began to draw to a close, Sammy did experience a couple of highs in his final season at the City Ground. He scored a goal in a Cup Final – albeit the Anglo-Scottish affair – and more than played his part in helping the Reds win back promotion with their third-placed finish in the spring of 1977. Against Millwall on the final day of that season, Sammy played his 422nd and final first-team game for the club – only 11 men have played more.

He joined Notts County from the Reds and later played for Shrewsbury Town and in the US before returning to become a licensee in the Nottingham area and to play in local non-League circles.

Still a regular and popular visitor to the City Ground, Sammy is also an enthusiastic club cricketer and his son Bobby has played for Nottinghamshire.

Steve Chettle

Date of birth: 27 September 1968, Nottingham

Nottingham Forest record:
Appearances: League 415, FA Cup 36, League Cup 52, Others 23
Goals: League 11, League Cup 1, Others 2
Debut: 5 September 1987 v Chelsea (a) lost 3–4

Also played for: Barnsley, Walsall, Grimsby Town, Burton Albion, Ilkeston Town

There have been very few Nottingham Forest players that have endured as many highs and lows as Steve Chettle. During an affiliation with the club that spanned 15 years, he played in winning and losing Cup Finals as well as participating in three relegations and two promotions!

'The highlight for me,' says Steve, 'was the 1990 League Cup Final win at Wembley. I'd sat on the bench the previous year for the Luton game, had got a medal and went round on the lap of honour but it felt a bit false because it was the other players that had run their socks off and deserved their moment. Against Oldham I felt I'd had a good game. We kept a clean sheet and won the match and that's what professional football is all about.'

Steve had been under no illusion what life would be like as a Forest player. His apprenticeship had been rewarding, as well as a little unorthodox.

'Once a month the apprentices had to go and do Cloughie's garden – and it was a big garden! I usually ended up sweeping the leaves but by the time you'd finished a load more had fallen so you had to start again – it was a bit like painting the Forth Bridge. The highlight was lunch time when he brought us out some soup that he'd made himself!'

The central defender's debut was not exactly as he had expected either. 'I came on as a sub at Chelsea to replace Lee Glover and was asked to play on the left wing!'

Steve found himself playing in a variety of positions during the early stages of his career and was at right-back on the opening day of the following season. 'I scored my first goal for the club away at Norwich. Steve Hodge had been poleaxed going for a free-kick and I came in behind and headed it in at the far post. It was our first goal of the season – so for the first and last time in my career I was the leading goalscorer!'

Forest lost that match 1–2 and Steve says there was usually a common theme whenever he scored. 'We usually lost when I got a goal. My best strike for the club was at Derby – beating Shilton from 25 yards – but we lost, and we were also beaten when I scored perhaps the most high-profile goal of my career.'

In Munich's Olympic Stadium he scored Forest's goal in a narrow first-leg defeat to Bayern in a 1996 UEFA Cup match.

'The goal actually came from a training ground routine. David Phillips was meant to take the free-kick, I would peel off at the back post and head it back across the face for someone to nod in. I connected with it all wrong and it spun off the side of my head and went in. I've seen photos of it and I was practically off the pitch when it went in.'

The defender, known to one and all as 'Chet', admits that his game was based on doing what he could do best. 'I realised I was never going to be like Des [Walker] but you need somebody to work alongside people like him or Colin Cooper. I was pretty good in the air and a good reader of the game but I'd like to think my best attribute was giving everything I could every time I played.'

His biggest disappointment as a Forest player was the 1991 FA Cup Final defeat to Spurs.

'The build-up was very special, getting measured for the suits and all that sort of thing. Our training had gone well and we were very confident. I got a good night's sleep in and everything seemed to be going well in the match for us. At half-time everything was pointing to us winning, so we were so distraught when things turned against us. There was absolute desolation afterwards. We'd perhaps believed all the talk that "our name was on the Cup". We'd really wanted to win it for Cloughie but fate came and slapped us in the face.'

Chet was an ever present in Frank Clark's side that won promotion and was later appointed club captain by Dave Bassett. 'I'd done it a few times before but took over on a full-time basis when Colin Cooper left for Middlesbrough. "Harry" [Dave Bassett] asked me and it didn't take me too long to answer. I regarded it as a great honour – all I'd wanted to do growing up was play for Forest, score for Forest and then captain Forest!'

Steve's marathon stint at the City Ground ended in November 1999 when he joined Barnsley on a free transfer. His total of 526 first-team appearances for Forest has only been bettered by three players – testimony to his unstinting loyalty. He felt the manner of his departure could have been handled better, though.

'I was upset at the circumstances as I felt I was almost forced out. The new manager [David Platt] had brought a lot of new faces in and mine obviously didn't fit.'

Chet is now back, helping out as a coach at the Forest academy and is quite rightly regarded as something of a legend by the youngsters he works with. 'Over 500 games for the club – I must have been doing something right!'

Frank Clark

Date of birth: 9 September 1943, Rowlands Gill, Tyne and Wear

Nottingham Forest record:
Appearances: League 117, FA Cup 12, League Cup 13, Others 15
Goals: League 1
Debut: 16 August 1975 v Plymouth Argyle (h) won 2–0
Manager: May 1993–December 1996

Also played for: Crook Town, Newcastle United
Also managed: Leyton Orient, Manchester City

Frank Clark achieved great success at Forest as both player and manager. Brought to the club supposedly in the twilight of his career, he ended his playing days as a European Cup winner. 'I jumped at the chance to join Forest,' recalls Frank. 'I'd been given a free transfer by Newcastle and didn't have too many other options, to be honest.'

Over the next two years Frank was an ever present at left-back, a statistic that he is proud of. 'Newcastle cited one of the reasons for getting rid of me was that I was injury-prone!'

An Anglo-Scottish Cup winner with the Reds and a member of the team that achieved promotion back to the top flight, Frank reveals that it was the first game of the new season that put things into perspective for the club. 'We won 3–1 at Everton on the opening day and that convinced us all that we could cope with life in the First Division. Everyone kept saying we would "blow up" at some point but we never did and were worthy champions.'

The season also brought success in the League Cup competition and Frank could not help but smile as he collected his medal after beating Liverpool in the replay. 'It was presented by Lord Westwood, President of the Football League – the bloke who'd been Chairman at Newcastle and agreed that I could leave the club!'

On a personal front, the campaign also featured an unusual event – Frank's only Forest goal.

'The circumstances were quite bizarre really,' he remembers. 'It was a midweek game away at Ipswich just after we'd sewn up the title and it was their final match before the FA Cup Final on the Saturday. Understandably it was poor! I was on the bench but at half time Cloughie told me he was putting me on for Peter Withe and wanted me to play up front – I'd never heard Larry Lloyd laugh so loudly!'

The switch paid off, though. 'Our front two were myself and Archie Gemmill – what a fearsome duo. Anyway, a corner dropped at my feet – five yards out and even I couldn't miss from there.'

Injuries and the form of Colin Barrett restricted Frank's appearances the following year but he still picked up a couple more medals. 'I was fortunate that I got in when others were injured and played in the successes over Southampton and Malmo. People say it must be great to play at Wembley – it is – but it's better to win at Wembley!' says Frank about the League Cup triumph.

The European Cup Final win in 1979 marked the end of his playing career, and he spared a thought for a couple of players who were left out. 'On the morning of the game I knew that only one of Martin O'Neill, Archie Gemmill or myself were going to play and was fortunate that I was selected – I did feel for the other two guys though.'

Fourteen years later, after serving as assistant manager, manager and then managing director at Orient, Frank returned to the City Ground to succeed the retired Brian Clough.

'The club was in disarray when I went back,' he confesses. 'Apart from just being relegated, I'd got a number of senior players who were all unsettled and were hoping for transfers back to the Premier League, there was a bung enquiry going on, the *World in Action* team had camped outside hoping to get some dirt on the club and the police were investigating some alleged irregularities in the ticket office.'

Despite all of those distractions, Frank turned Forest's fortunes around almost immediately. 'Above all else, there were some lovely people who worked at the club. They had all become a bit demoralised by events but they were a pleasure to work with and made my job a lot easier.'

Promotion was secured at the first time of asking and then Frank's side achieved a third-placed finish in their first season back at the highest level, an achievement that earned the manager some well-deserved recognition. 'I won the LMA Manager of the Year Award. To receive this after being nominated by my fellow members was a great honour – one of my proudest moments in football.'

The following year Forest finished ninth, but the campaign featured over 60 League and Cup matches and Frank admitted that the club did not have the resources to cope.

'It was a strange set-up at the time,' recalls Frank. 'Forest were run by a board of directors who were all elected shareholders. Nobody in their right mind would invest any money because they never knew if they would get elected back in or not. Eventually, the bank became very nervous amidst talk of a takeover and I couldn't get the backing I needed to do the job properly.'

In December 1995 Frank resigned his position at Forest and began a two-year tenure at Manchester City several months later. He continues to serve the game with great distinction as vice-chairman of the League Managers' Association.

Brian Clough

Date of birth: 21 March 1935, Middlesbrough
Died: 20 September 2004

Nottingham Forest record:
Manager: 1975–1993

Played for: Middlesbrough, Sunderland, England (2 caps)
Also managed: Hartlepools United, Derby County, Brighton & Hove Albion, Leeds United

It is particularly difficult to be innovative when describing Brian Clough's contribution to Nottingham Forest. Quite simply, his was the singular most successful contribution to the club's history.

Brian was unquestionably one of the greatest English managers of all time and for more than two decades was one of the most instantly recognisable faces in the sporting world.

For 18 glorious seasons he enabled Forest fans to 'live the dream' – scaling heights that seem even more incredulous with every passing year.

During his own playing career Brian had been a phenomenally successful forward, scoring 251 times in just 274 League games for Middlesbrough and Sunderland – his only two clubs. Despite this impressive strike rate, he was only selected to play twice for his country, against Wales and Sweden in 1959. His career ended prematurely after a knee injury sustained against Bury on Boxing Day 1962. After failed attempts to return to full fitness, Brian turned to coaching before accepting his first managerial appointment in October 1965, when he took over at Hartlepools (as they were then known) United. At just 30 he was the youngest manager in the League and he soon made what he described as 'the best signing of my life' when he recruited Peter Taylor to become his assistant.

The Clough and Taylor partnership moved on to Derby County, where they secured promotion to the First Division in 1969 and took the club to their first League title three years later. Fallouts with the board resulted in Brian's resignation in October 1973. Short stints at Brighton and then Leeds (just 44 days!) were unproductive before another East Midlands club found themselves in urgent need of guidance.

In January 1975 the Nottingham Forest board installed Brian Cough as the new City Ground manager, replacing the sacked Allan Brown. The club was languishing in the second tier of the domestic game when he took over, yet within five years he had turned them into League champions and European Cup winners. With his own unique style of man-management and the shrewd eye of Taylor to spot a player who might benefit the cause, Clough moulded together a side that achieved promotion and then took the top flight by storm.

Forest won the Football League Championship by seven points, remaining unbeaten from 19 November 1977 until the end of the season. The run was stretched until 9 December 1978, a sequence of 42 matches – a record which would stand for more than 25 years.

Apart from the title win, Forest also lifted the League Cup in 1978; the first of four such wins under their mercurial manager. As League winners, the Reds embarked on their first European Cup adventure that climaxed with victory over Malmo in the Final. The following year they defended their crown, this time with success over Hamburg. Cloughie's team had become two-time European champions – the fans were in heaven!

Apart from enjoying phenomenal success as a manager, Brian was also treated with the utmost respect for the way his sides conducted themselves. Referees would be the first to compliment Forest for the disciplined way they accepted decisions – dissent was never an option under Cloughie. Principled and proud, he had strong beliefs – and fair play was one of them.

In his early years at Forest he had a board erected facing the fans at the Trent End. It said, simply, 'Gentlemen – No Swearing Please! Brian.' There were occasions when it seemed that he may be lured away to take on another challenge. On one such occasion, the fans responded with their own message: 'Brian – No Leaving Please! The Gentlemen.'

If he should have gone anywhere then the England job seemed most likely, according to every football fan in the country – but not the FA. 'They thought if they took me on and gave me the job, I'd want to run the show,' he once reflected. 'They were shrewd because that's exactly what I would have done.'

Lesser competitions such as the Simod Cup and Zenith Data Systems Cup were also lifted but the FA Cup was to always elude Brian, with a 1991 Final defeat to Spurs the nearest he came. In 1993 he announced his retirement, sadly coinciding with the club's first relegation under his stewardship.

During his reign Brian signed many great stars and introduced a vast number of youngsters into the squad, although privately his proudest moment would surely have been when he handed a first-team debut to son Nigel in 1984.

Brian was awarded the OBE in 1991, heralding another of his famous one-liners when he announced it stood for 'Old Big 'Ead'! It is inconceivable, though, that his achievements were not recognised with a knighthood, and even after his tragically early death from stomach cancer in 2004 there were calls for a posthumous award.

The City Ground's largest stand is now called 'The Brian Clough Stand', and a bronze bust of the legend has pride of place in the club's main reception area.

In gratitude of the success he brought to them, Brian was given the Freedom of both Nottingham (in 1993) and Derby (10 years later), and following his death the A52 linking the two cities was renamed 'Brian Clough Way'.

There will never be another quite like him – thank you BC!

Nigel Clough

Date of birth: 9 March 1966, Sunderland, Tyne and Wear

Nottingham Forest record:
Appearances: League 324, FA Cup 28, League Cup 46, Others 14
Goals: League 102, FA Cup 6, League Cup 22, Others 1
Debut: 26 December 1984 v Ipswich Town (h) won 2–0

Also played for: Heanor Town, Liverpool, Manchester City, Stoke City, Burton Albion, England (14 caps)
Managed: Burton Albion

Nottingham Forest were extremely blessed that they had sufficient connections among their backroom staff to persuade Nigel Clough to play for them!

It can not have been easy for Nigel to play for the side that was managed by his father, but once the City Ground regulars had observed the young forward in action they knew that his selection would be down to sheer footballing ability and nothing else.

From the outset, it was clear that he possessed outstanding natural ability, as well as the family trait for sticking the ball in the net – in eight full seasons with the Reds, 'young Cloughie' finished as the top scorer on six occasions.

Nigel made his League debut at home to Ipswich on Boxing Day 1984, and made a few sporadic appearances that season before bagging his first goal for the club in a home draw with Watford.

Technically gifted, and with the intuition and vision to pick out a defence-splitting pass, Nigel was a difficult footballer to label correctly. He certainly was not a target man or a mere goal-poacher. He liked to make himself available and pull the defenders around – yet however tightly he was marshalled he would always seem to appear at the right moment to convert a half-chance.

Twice a League Cup winner with the Reds, Nigel scored twice in the 1989 Final against Luton Town – one from the penalty spot to inspire a 3–1 victory. He also pocketed winners' medals in the Simod Cup and Zenith Data Systems Cup competitions, as well as playing in the 1991 FA Cup Final defeat to Tottenham Hotspur.

The League Cup competition was particularly kind to Nigel – no Forest player has scored more than his 22 goals in the tournament and he could have had another couple of victories as well.

He played in the losing Final against Manchester United in 1992, a year after Forest's exit in an extraordinary tie against Coventry City. Defending the silverware after beating Oldham Athletic the year before, the Reds found themselves 4–0 down early on. Nigel led a rousing fightback with a stunning hat-trick and a Garry Parker goal levelled it at 4–4 – all before the break. Disappointingly, the home side scored again to win by the odd goal in nine!

Nigel scored one other hat-trick for the club – again in unusual circumstances, with all three goals coming in the space of four minutes against Queen's Park Rangers and all in the last nine minutes of the match.

Emulating his father, Nigel became a full England international. After playing in 15 Under-21 games, an England B match and an appearance for the Football League XI, he made his senior bow against Chile at Wembley Stadium in 1989.

Over the course of the next three or four years, he flitted in and out of the selection process without ever being given an extended opportunity to convert his club form into the international arena. His tally of 14 caps failed to produce a single goal – more a reflection of the system he was asked to adapt to rather than any shortcomings on Nigel's part.

At the end of the 1992–93 season, after Forest's relegation and the retirement of his father, Nigel moved to Liverpool on a £2.75 million transfer. With Ian Rush and Robbie Fowler usually the preferred options, Nigel was used sparingly.

He later joined Manchester City and even spent a brief period back on loan at Forest in the 1996–97 season – notching up a further 13 appearances for the club. A persistent heel injury finally put paid to his involvement at the highest level.

Since 1998 Nigel has been the inspiration and driving force behind Burton Albion. As player-manager he helped steer them into the Conference as champions of the Northern Premier League.

The Staffordshire outfit came under the media spotlight on 8 January 2006 when Nigel's side held Manchester United to a goalless draw in the FA Cup before succumbing bravely in the Old Trafford replay.

One of the most popular players ever to have represented the club, Nigel is one of only five Foresters to have registered a century of League goals – and his 131 in all competitions puts him second behind Wally Ardron on the all-time list.

Stan Collymore

Date of birth: 22 January 1971, Stone, Staffordshire

Nottingham Forest record:

Appearances: League 65, FA Cup 2, League Cup 9, Others 2

Goals: League 41, FA Cup 1, League Cup 7, Others 1

Debut: 24 August 1993 v Crystal Palace (a) lost 0–2

Also played for: Wolverhampton Wanderers, Stafford Rangers, Crystal Palace, Southend United, Liverpool, Aston Villa, Fulham (loan), Leicester City, Bradford City, Real Oviedo (Spain), England (3 caps)

Fans of Stan Collymore – and he accumulated a huge galaxy of admirers – still feel slightly cheated that he did not go on to become one of England's all-time great international strikers. Injuries, depression and assorted personal problems all prevented the powerful centre-forward from making a real success in the game, despite an assortment of high-profile big-money transfers.

Whereas Stan left both Liverpool and Aston Villa without creating the impression those clubs had hoped for, the City Ground supporters certainly have no cause for complaint about his performances for Forest.

Forty-one League goals in just 65 appearances is a return that would be perfectly acceptable to anyone, particularly in that Stan was bought to help get the Reds straight back into the top flight – a target he achieved with style.

Frank Clark signed Stan from Southend United for a fee that eventually rose to £2.75 million. An ulcerated mouth prevented him from playing in the opening three matches of the 1993–94 season and his debut, against one of his former sides, ended in a 2–0 defeat at Crystal Palace.

Stan's next outing brought his first Forest goal – bizarrely in the Anglo-Italian Cup Preliminary phase – at home to Notts County. Having broken his duck for the club, he then set off on a scoring spree and notched eight goals in seven games – including a hat-trick against Wrexham in the League Cup.

It was not just the quantity of goals that made him a delight to watch for Forest supporters – it was the nature of them. He would frequently set off on an unstoppable gallop towards the opposition box before unleashing a thunderbolt of a shot past a startled 'keeper.

Physically, Stan was impressive. Strong and muscular, he had genuine pace, excellent ball control, and heading and shooting accuracy that mere mortals could only wonder about!

Nevertheless, his first season at the City Ground had begun indifferently for Forest and it was largely due to Stan's consistency in and around the penalty area that hauled the Reds back into contention for a promotion berth.

A hamstring injury then threatened to derail the charge – with Stan forced to sit out eight important matches. His return was greeted like the Second Coming by the anxious fans but arrived like an uncertain helping of 'sweet and sour' against Bolton Wanderers. After scoring what turned out to be the match winner, Stan's impetuosity led to a red card and an early bath. Nothing ever seemed to run smoothly for the Forest faithful.

Fortunately it all came good in the end – and fittingly the big striker's left-footed drive at Peterborough United clinched promotion with a couple of matches to spare. Twenty-five goals, of which 19 were scored in the League, confirmed that Frank Clark had not wasted a penny of Forest's money in signing Stanley Victor Collymore.

Back in the top flight Forest opened the campaign away at Ipswich without Stan, who had picked up an ankle injury, but he returned to score a magnificent 25 yarder against Manchester United, the reigning champions.

If anyone had cause to question whether he could maintain his form at the highest level, that goal would have dispelled it. Like Clough's side 17 years earlier, Forest made an immediate impact in their first season back in the big time. A third-place finish represented an unbelievable turnaround in the club's fortunes and much of it was down to the goalscoring prowess of Stan, who recorded another 25-goal contribution – this time with 22 of them coming in the League.

Speculation began to link Stan with a number of clubs and also with an international call-up. He made his first two England appearances (against Japan and Brazil) in June 1995 while still a Forester, but shortly afterwards he signed for Liverpool in a transfer valued at £8.5 million – a British record at the time.

There is no doubt that Stan was sorely missed at the City Ground – his goal output was not really replaced and the club were relegated again a couple of years later. A career that could have taken him anywhere brought him an FA Cup Final appearance for Liverpool and a further England cap while at Villa – but ended far too prematurely.

Turning his hand to acting, Stan made an appearance in *Basic Instinct 2* (with Sharon Stone) in 2006. If the first rule of show business is 'Always leave them wanting more', then this is a maxim that he certainly applied to much of his footballing career.

At Forest, though, he left 50 'goalden' memories for the fans to enjoy!

Kris Commons

Action Images

Date of birth: 30 August 1983, Mansfield, Nottinghamshire

Nottingham Forest record:
Appearances: League 99, FA Cup 6, League Cup 4, Others 5
Goals: League 23, FA Cup 4, Others 1
Debut: 25 August 2004 v Scunthorpe United (h) won 2–0

Also played for: Stoke City

As a young Nottingham Forest supporter it is easy to imagine Kris Commons daydreaming about playing for the club and helping them to win some silverware. By the end of the 2006–07 season Kris was being called upon to re-evaluate schoolboy ambition alongside solid career progression.

As Forest slumped to a Play-off semi-final exit to Yeovil Town, the prospect of another season in Division One – the third tier of English football – was a bitter pill for all Reds supporters to swallow. It was equally heartbreaking for Kris, who many believe has enough talent to play at the highest level.

Mansfield-born Kris was educated at Quarrydale School in Sutton-in-Ashfield and, but for uncertainty by Notts County, may well have started his League career on the opposite bank of the Trent. He played for the Magpies junior sides from the age of 10 up until he was about 15, but indecision about offering him a YTS contract forced the youngster to try his luck elsewhere.

Kris played for Chesterfield in a match against Stoke City's youngsters and later revealed that 'I played quite well and the Stoke scout approached me afterwards and within a week I'd signed YTS forms for them. I stayed for three years – one on YTS terms and two as a professional.'

The youngster made his debut for the Potters in a League Cup tie at Blackpool in October 2001, but did not get a run in the League side until the following term. He had made just 41 League appearances for Stoke before Forest paid £300,000 to sign him in July 2004. Initially, he faced competition on the left side of midfield from Andy Reid, but once the Irishman had left to join Spurs the Reds supporters soon realised that they had a ready-made replacement on hand who was equally capable of producing stunning shots and bewildering close-ball control.

Like Reid, the former Stoke player enjoyed being given a licence to roam. 'I like to start on the left but enjoy getting the opportunity to drift inside in a free role,' he reveals.

The first goal Kris scored for Forest was of the highest calibre – a spectacular 40-yard lob at QPR, in the FA Cup. The competition always seemed to bring the best out of him and a stunning display at White Hart Lane against Spurs earned him the accolade of the FA Player of the Fifth Round.

Kris's first season at Forest ended with the disappointment of relegation and the battle to bounce back into the Championship proved to be far more difficult than most supporters had imagined.

Forest just missed out on the Play-offs in the spring of 2006 but, under Colin Calderwood's management, it looked as if they were 'nailed on' to achieve promotion a year later. A hamstring injury sustained against Tranmere Rovers ruled Kris out for two months of the season and forced him to miss high-profile FA Cup ties against Charlton Athletic and Chelsea. More importantly, he was forced to miss several crucial League fixtures, which ultimately may have had a bearing on Forest's final League placing.

A fully fit and rejuvenated Kris could have done no more in the closing weeks of the season, illuminating his displays with some stunning long-range goals – particularly against Bournemouth when he scored with a couple of thunderbolts, one with each foot!

Third in the final standings, Forest had to take their chance in the end of season Play-offs and managed to defeat Yeovil Town away in the opening leg of the semi-final.

Kris rolled in a first-half penalty to convert his 13th goal of the season – a personal best – but the Somerset side overturned their two-goal deficit to end Forest's season a week later with an extra-time victory at the City Ground.

Instead of heading off to Wembley to play for his club, Kris could only accept an invitation from the FA to attend the Chelsea versus Manchester United Cup Final, a prize won for again securing a Player of the Round award.

In the first round of the 2006–07 competition Kris had scored his first Forest hat-trick against non-Leaguers Yeading and he later admitted feeling particularly nervous before converting his final goal. 'I was only three or four yards out but so many things went through my mind before scoring it. I'd never scored a hat-trick before and it was a great feeling.'

Forest will clearly be desperate to hang on to their creative playmaker for the 2007–08 season and were quick to offer him a contract extension ahead of the new campaign.

With 99 League appearances for the Reds under his belt, the Forest faithful will be desperately keen that Kris does not just complete his century of outings for the club but elects to remain with them for many, many more seasons.

Colin Cooper

Date of birth: 28 February 1967, Sedgefield, County Durham

Nottingham Forest record:

Appearances: League 180, FA Cup 12, League Cup 14, Others 7

Goals: League 20, FA Cup 1, League Cup 2

Debut: 15 August 1993 v Southend United (a) drew 1–1

Also played for: Middlesbrough, Millwall, Sunderland (loan), England (2 caps)

Colin Cooper was a classy central defender who was brought to the City Ground to help get Forest back into the Premiership – and he ended up doing it twice.

In the immediate post-Clough era there was rebuilding work to do for new boss Frank Clark, and he quickly identified his targets. 'I understand he listed a central defender and a striker as being his priority signings to get Forest straight back up,' says Colin. 'He signed myself and Stan Collymore, so it was clear what we were meant to achieve!'

Considered to be among the pre-season favourites for promotion, Colin says their early form made the bookmakers' odds laughable. 'By November time no one fancied our chances but then things began to happen. One or two of us had had slight niggling injuries that cleared up and suddenly we had the right blend, the right people in the team – and, of course, Stan [Collymore] found a bit of form!'

Composed under pressure and an intelligent reader of the game, Colin complemented his defensive qualities by adding nine goals to the cause – seven of them in the League. 'Super Cooper' chants became commonplace. 'The most important thing about many of them was that they came late on to either win us a game or save us a point.' One strike, in particular, stands out. 'It was a free-kick against Derby County at the Baseball Ground. I just put my foot through it – full throttle as usual – and it flew in. A goal against Derby is a great way for any new Forest player to help cement a relationship with the fans!' By May it was mission accomplished, with Forest comfortable in second spot ensuring it had been just a one-season stay at the lower level. There was no thought of resting on any laurels, though. 'We hit the Premiership running and were unbeaten after the first 11 matches. We had a fantastic season and played some decent football. Stan got his goals but I felt we all played our part.'

Colin's progress at the highest level had been monitored and a call up to the national side followed, when he was included in Terry Venables's squad for the four-team Umbro Cup. 'I was perhaps a little fortunate that one or two of the regular squad members weren't available but it's an experience I'll never forget. I was on the bench against Japan but played against Sweden at Elland Road and Brazil at Wembley.' The second of those matches was made even more special for Colin. 'Stuart Pearce played alongside me and even though we'd appeared together for Forest on so many occasions, the fact that he was there really made the day for me.'

The new season brought a new adventure, as Forest returned to European football after a gap of 11 years. 'The UEFA Cup run was very enjoyable. We got through against Malmo, Auxerre and Lyon pretty much by the skin of our teeth, but, although we weren't turning teams over, we were very difficult to beat.'

But for a disputed decision Colin believes the Reds might have made further progress. 'I was suspended for the first leg of the quarter-final away against Bayern Munich but we brought them back home trailing by only one goal. Early on I scrambled in a rebound after Kevin Campbell's header had been parried but it was disallowed for a very dubious offside. They went on to beat us quite convincingly but had that early goal stood, who knows what might have happened?'

Forest's fortunes then took another backward step. Inexplicably, the club was relegated again at the end of the next campaign, with manager Clark not being around to see the end of it. 'As players we all felt we'd let Frank down.' The arrival of Dave Bassett at the club coincided with Colin's appointment as skipper. 'It was a great honour to lead the team but I was disappointed that at the end of the season we never had the opportunity of parading the Championship trophy to our fans. We clinched the title at West Brom but had to wait until a civic reception to receive it. Although we showed it off in the Market Square later, it wasn't the same.'

Just before the big kick-off to a season that would again feature Forest in the Premier League they lost their captain, who signed for Middlesbrough for a fee of £2.5 million. 'I just couldn't see myself leaving at all,' confesses Colin. 'But I'd started at Middlesbrough as a kid and had a bit of a tie with them. I know it upset a lot of the Forest fans but 'Boro were the only club I'd have gone to.'

Of his relationship with the Forest faithful, he has nothing but praise. 'I think they are magnificent. I'd like to think that every player knows the history of the club when they pull on the shirt and realise what it means to the supporters.

'On a personal note, I've never really had the opportunity of being able to properly thank the Forest fans – and many other people from Nottingham – for all the flowers, cards and hundreds of kind messages that were sent to me and my family following the death of our son Finlay – they were all very much appreciated. Thank you.'

Gary Crosby

Date of birth: 8 May 1964, Sleaford, Lincolnshire

Nottingham Forest record:

Appearances: League 152, FA Cup 21, League Cup 30, Others 11

Goals: League 12, FA Cup 3, League Cup 6, Others 4

Debut: 16 January 1987 v Charlton Athletic (h) drew 2–2

Also played for: Lincoln United, Lincoln City, Grantham Town, Grimsby Town (loan), Huddersfield United, Rushden & Diamonds, Burton Albion

Gary Crosby was a nippy right-winger who won two Wembley winners' medals with Forest, as well as cunningly scoring one of the City Ground's most comical goals.

Playing against Manchester City on 3 March 1990 Gary found himself 'goal-side' of the visiting 'keeper Andy Dibble. Had the events that followed occurred in the festive season then Andy might have expected a pantomime roar of 'He's behind you!' from either supporters or teammates. That did not happen, so, holding the ball in the palm of his right hand, the startled City custodian suffered total indignity as the alert and stealth-like Gary took him unawares to head the ball free and roll it into an empty net. Appeals to the referee proved fruitless. The goal stood and to add to Dibble's embarrassment it proved to be the only score of the contest!

Gary had begun his career in Lincolnshire non-League circles but was helped on his way by a former Forester. Martin O'Neill, Gary's manager at Grantham Town, alerted the Forest scouts that he had a wide player worth keeping an eye on. Just a few short weeks later (and a transfer fee of around £20,000), Gary had swapped life as a 'Gingerbread' for the more exalted trappings of the professional game.

He made his debut as a sub in a home draw against Charlton but then started a couple of weeks later and, christened a fine performance with his first senior goal in a 3–2 victory over Chelsea.

Like a duck to water, Gary took an instant shine to playing at the highest level of the English game and, just four months into his first season at Forest, he appeared for them in an FA Cup semi-final – Liverpool winning the match 2–1.

The following season he was very much on the fringes of the first XI and did not play in any of the side's big Cup matches – the League Cup and Simod Finals or the abandoned FA Cup semi-final at Hillsborough.

Few Forest players have accumulated as many 'terrace' nicknames as Gary. They usually contained a reference to his physical stature and were often along the lines of 'Little Fly', 'Mighty Flea' and 'the ilk'. Less imaginatively, he was often referred to simply as 'Bing'.

During the 1989–90 campaign Gary really established himself as a first-choice selection and weighed in with a high tally of nine goals, including a strike in a 2–1 win over Derby County – a scenario guaranteed to raise his profile among the Reds followers.

His first major Final resulted in victory, with Forest beating Oldham Athletic to retain the League Cup. It was back to Wembley a year later for the FA Cup Final against Spurs, where Gary played a major hand in helping the side get through to their date at the Twin Towers after an eventful afternoon against West Ham United at Villa Park in the semi-final.

With the game still awaiting its first goal, the winger ran on to a through ball only to become the victim of a mistimed challenge from Tony Gale. Although the Forest man did not appear to be running directly towards goal, referee Keith Hackett sent off the Hammers defender. The joy Gary later experienced in scoring the first goal in Forest's win more than compensated for the undeserved abuse he had been subjected to by disgruntled fans of the claret and blue.

Apart from his jinky dribbling skills and exhaustive work rate, Gary became known as the 'King of the Cut-Back'. Unlike many other wingers, his percentage of wasted crosses was few. Having beaten his man and advanced to the byline, Gary could usually be relied on to accurately cut the ball back enabling an on-rushing midfield colleague to cash in.

He played in the Zenith Data Systems Cup Final of 1992 against Southampton and also another League Cup Final the same year – Forest losing by one goal to nil against Manchester United.

Nippy and direct, Gary was a firm favourite at the City Ground but became one of the casualties after relegation from the top flight in the spring of 1993. Initially he moved to Grimsby Town on loan and then played a handful more matches for Forest under Frank Clark before sealing a permanent switch to Huddersfield Town. Later he linked up with his former clubmate Nigel Clough at Burton Albion, firstly as a player but then later as assistant manager.

Still very much a Red, Gary often turns out for his old club in testimonials and charity games and remains a firm favourite with the fans.

Mark Crossley

Date of birth: 16 June 1969, Barnsley, South Yorkshire

Nottingham Forest record:
Appearances: League 305, FA Cup 32, League Cup 41, Others 20
Debut: 26 October 1988 v Liverpool (h) won 2–1

Also played for: Millwall (loan), Middlesbrough, Stoke City (loan), Fulham, Sheffield Wednesday (loan), Oldham Athletic, Wales (8 caps)

If there was one area of the field in which Brian Clough was more fastidious than any other, it would be over his choice of goalkeeper. The successful years with Peter Shilton were followed by Steve Sutton's lengthy stint, giving way eventually to the man who would join a very small and exclusive club of FA Cup Final goalkeepers and who would serve Forest proudly for more than a decade.

Mark Crossley served his apprenticeship at the City Ground and learnt well, but his first-team debut, at home against Liverpool, arrived totally out of the blue. 'I'd come in to do my apprenticeship duties, clean out the away dressing room and all that stuff. Cloughie then appeared and said, "Young man, come here. I want to see you – get your boots on – you're playing."'

There was not time for Mark to let family members know about his imminent debut, but he found out that his manager had taken care of things. 'Cloughie had rung my mum and dad, told them I was playing, got them down to the club and then wined and dined them at Antonio's restaurant – all without me knowing!'

The 'keeper enjoyed a winning start to his professional career but still had to wait a couple of years before being given an extended run in the side. Indeed, he was a paying spectator on the Kop on the day of the Hillsborough semi-final disaster in April 1989.

According to Mark, it was his teammate Stuart Pearce who was responsible for first giving him the nicknames of 'Norman' or 'Big Norm', monikers that have stuck for many years. 'A few people thought it was because of the guy in *Cheers*, but Pearcey always felt I looked like the former Manchester United player Norman Whiteside!'

Big Norm's moment of Wembley immortality occurred in the 1991 FA Cup Final. Referee Roger Milford awarded Tottenham their spot-kick after Mark was adjudged to have brought down Gary Lineker. 'I've always said that I'd got a slight touch on it but after seeing the replays I can understand why it was given. Now, years later, I'm so pleased he did because it gave me the chance to save it but at the time I was worried that I might get sent off because that was the year when referees started to punish goalkeepers more.'

Lineker's spot-kick went to Mark's left. 'As soon as the kick was given I'd made my mind up which way I wanted to go. Gut feeling – instinct – I don't know. At the time people said it was a decent height to save but I've watched it again and I think he hit it quite well – I really do think it was a decent save. It was certainly a great feeling to keep it out.' The save enabled him to join an elite list of just two goalkeepers who have saved a penalty in an FA Cup Final. 'It's strange how Dave Beasant ended up playing for Forest as well.'

Another penalty stop also earned Mark some plaudits. 'I'm the only 'keeper to save from Southampton's Matt Le Tissier – I think he scored 48 out of 49 penalties but I saved one at the Dell. I went the other way this time, to my right!'

Mark maintains that the best form of his career came during Forest's UEFA Cup campaign in the 1995–96 season. 'That run of matches sticks out in my mind as being very special. I was Man of the Match against Malmo away and in both legs against Auxerre. I felt I could have done a little better with Ziege's free-kick against Bayern Munich but overall I was pleased with my contribution throughout those matches.'

It was that level of consistency that eventually brought international representation. The big, Yorkshire-born 'keeper had played for England Under-21s earlier in his career but was as proud as anyone from the Valleys when he was capped at full senior level by Wales. 'My mother's father was Welsh,' he explains.

During his time at the City Ground, Mark experienced two relegations and a promotion and clocked up an impressive total of 398 first-team appearances, but his years in the game have enabled him to notice a change in defensive responsibilities.

'I regularly kept 15 or 16 clean sheets a season and would have been upset if I hadn't – nowadays only the top three or four sides are doing that. Mind you – I did have decent defenders in front of me – Pearcey, Des, Chet at his best and Lawsy were very good defenders.'

During the 2006–07 season – his 18th in the game – the big goalie managed to do something he had never managed before. On loan to Sheffield Wednesday and playing against Southampton, he had gone forward for a late corner and headed in an equaliser.

'All 'keepers fancy themselves as strikers. The only time I scored for Forest was in Pearcey's testimonial when he pushed me up front – I'm pleased to have done it in a proper League game though!'

Chris Crowe

Date of birth:	11 June 1939, Newcastle-upon-Tyne, Tyne and Wear
Died:	May 2003

Nottingham Forest record:

Appearances:	League 73, FA Cup 3, League Cup 2
Goals:	League 12, FA Cup 2, League Cup 1
Debut:	22 August 1964 v Birmingham City (h) won 4–3
Also played for:	Leeds United, Blackburn Rovers, Wolverhampton Wanderers, Bristol City, Walsall, Auburn (Australia), Bath City, England (1 cap)

Many footballers have their entire career defined by an outstanding performance in one single game. While it was not necessarily true in Chris Crowe's case, Forest fans will always associate him best with the events of Saturday 1 October 1966.

Manager Johnny Carey was in the process of assembling a side capable of challenging for domestic honours and in that 1966–67 season he came mighty close to winning some silverware, with a runners'-up spot in the League and a place in the FA Cup semi-finals.

Early on, though, there was little to suggest that the Forest fans would be enjoying their most successful season since the 1959 Cup win. They had lost their opening two League matches against Stoke City and Chelsea, gone out of the League Cup and won only four matches before the end of September.

In addition, Chris Crowe had become frustrated. A former England international, who had been pretty much a regular at his previous clubs, he was now in competition with teammates and fellow wingers Alan Hinton and Ian Storey-Moore for a place on the Forest flanks. Three into two would not go – and Chris had been placed on the transfer list to allow him to try to seek first-team football.

Nevertheless, after missing the early weeks of the season, he had been recalled to the side for a League Cup tie against Birmingham City and had tucked away a penalty in the replay, which Forest had lost 2–1.

His form had impressed sufficiently and he was selected to start against Manchester United, a side managed by Matt Busby and brimming with some of the most talented individuals in the land, including Bobby Charlton, George Best and Denis Law.

United would go on to win the title – pipping Forest – and would confirm their quality by lifting the European Cup 12 months later, but on that balmy City Ground afternoon they were torn to shreds by Chris Crowe in front of almost 42,000 spectators.

Whether he felt there was something to prove or he was just lifted by the intensity of the occasion, Chris was unstoppable as he teased and tormented the United defenders on his way to scoring three of the goals – one of them a penalty – in Forest's 4–1 win. Curiously, it was the only hat-trick he would

register for the club and they also turned out to be his final goals for the Reds, as he was allowed to sign for Bristol City shortly afterwards.

Born in the North East, Chris had joined Leeds United straight from school and made his League debut for them aged just 17. He went on to play 95 League matches for the Elland Road club, scoring a very acceptable 27 times from the wing.

Blessed with plenty of pace, he was snapped up by Blackburn Rovers in March 1960 for £25,000. He spent two years at Ewood Park and then slightly longer at Wolves, with whom he won his only England cap when he played against France in a drawn European Nations Cup qualifier at Hillsborough.

Chris arrived at the City Ground in the summer of 1964 and made his debut on the opening day of the campaign in a thrilling 4–3 win over Birmingham City. Playing wide on the right, the fair-haired newcomer quickly endeared himself to the Forest faithful. He had to wait until October before opening his goal account for the Reds but he grabbed both in a 2–2 home draw against Chelsea.

On Tuesday 28 September 1965 Spanish giants Valencia arrived at the City Ground to provide the opposition for Forest's centenary celebrations. Fittingly, the match ended all square and it was Chris who tucked home the Forest goal from the penalty spot after just five minutes. Unusually, he played inside-right against the Spaniards and many Forest fans feel he should have been given an extended run in that position.

Towards the end of his playing career, after joining Bristol City, came an incident which some of the older fans at Ashton Gate still recall. A dog ran onto the pitch, interrupting a game, and no one could catch it as it ran around playfully. Eventually Chris got down on all fours and began barking at the animal – whether he had any 'Doolittle' qualities in him we will never know, but the creature trotted over to the winger and gave himself up for capture.

It has been said that 'every dog has its day'. Well, no one barked louder in a Forest shirt than Chris Crowe on that amazing afternoon against Manchester United.

After ending his playing days Chris settled in Bristol, where he sadly died in 2003.

Peter Davenport

Date of birth: 24 March 1961, Birkenhead, Merseyside

Nottingham Forest record:
Appearances: League 122, FA Cup 9, League Cup 10, Others 12
Goals: League 54, FA Cup 1, League Cup 1, Others 2
Debut: 1 May 1982 v Liverpool (a) lost 0–2

Also played for: Cammell Laird, Manchester United, Middlesbrough, Sunderland, Airdrie, St Johnstone, Stockport County, Southport, Macclesfield, Congleton Town, England (1 cap)
Managed: Bangor City, Macclesfield, Southport

Forest's knack of unearthing raw talent and moulding it into a top-class First Division player was never illustrated better than with Peter Davenport. Twice in the mid-1980s the big, strong Merseysider finished as the club's top scorer.

Peter had spent 14 months at Everton, playing in their A and B sides in the Lancashire League before being released. His dreams apparently crushed, a family member gave a helping hand. 'In March 1981 Everton released me and I went back to play for Cammell Laird. Unbeknown to me, my brother Paul had written to Forest recommending they look at me.'

Intrigued by the approach, the Forest management requested that Peter's credentials be checked out. 'Peter Taylor had passed on my details to the north-west scout who came to watch me a few times. I was scoring a lot of goals for Cammell at the time and Forest asked me to play in a reserve-team match against Sheffield United at Bramall Lane. From then on, Forest acted quickly. I scored in our 2–0 win and did well in a few more reserve games and then they offered me a professional contract.'

It was not long before Peter was knocking on the first-team door and, appropriately enough, his debut came a few miles from home. 'I'd been in the squad the week before against Aston Villa but didn't get on. The manager obviously wanted to have a look at me and told me a couple of days before we were due to face Liverpool that I would be starting at Anfield.'

Despite a heavy presence of family and friends, Peter could not crown his debut with a goal but he made enough of an impression to remain in the side. 'I played in the final five games of the season and they were against the five top teams in the table so it gave me confidence that I'd done well against them.'

Peter opened his scoring account for the club in a 2–0 home win over Spurs and then, in just his fifth match for Forest, he hit all the goals in a 3–1 win at Ipswich Town. 'I've still got the match ball from that game. The signatures are all a bit faded now but I can still make out the writing: "Be Good – Brian Clough".'

Over the next four years the hard-working frontman learned his trade well and became a productive goalscorer, finishing with 17 in both the 1983–84 and 1984–85 seasons. Despite his haul of goals, he played for the Reds during the barren period when major silverware was absent from the

City Ground. 'No, we didn't win anything during my time at Forest,' he reflects. 'But we came pretty close, particularly in the UEFA Cup.'

Peter remains utterly disappointed by the manner of Forest's semi-final defeat at the hands of Anderlecht – a result later confirmed as having being fixed by a corrupt match official.

In March 1985 Peter won his only England cap, appearing as a sub for Mark Hateley against the Republic of Ireland at Wembley. 'I was in pretty decent form and then got injured, pulling a hamstring. Just before then I'd been measured for a suit to go on England's summer tour to Mexico, where a pre-World Cup tournament was taking place. I was with the gaffer when he rang the England manager to tell him I was unavailable. "Young Robert [Bobby Robson]," he said, "Peter's not going to make it!"'

Peter's second and third Forest hat-tricks both came at home, against Sunderland in August 1984 and against Arsenal 14 months later, but he remembers a couple of other goals with even greater affection. 'My best Forest goal was against PSV Eindhoven. I got it on the halfway line, wide on the left and kept running forwards, I cut inside and hit it in right footed from the edge of the box. The other favourite was from the other side of the field against Spurs, cutting in to score off the post past Ray Clemence.'

In March 1986 Peter signed for Manchester United for a fee of £570,000. 'I wanted to stay at Forest in many ways but felt it was perhaps the right time to move on and try something new.'

The striker spent two and a half years at Old Trafford, scoring 26 times for the first team, but then began to move clubs with greater frequency towards the latter end of his playing career. While with Sunderland in 1992 he appeared in the FA Cup Final defeat to Liverpool.

Peter spent the second half of the 2006–07 season as boss of Southport and remembers fondly his association with one of the all-time great managers. 'Cloughie was absolutely brilliant towards me and my family. He was a fabulous manager to play for – I deeply regret that I didn't see him too much towards the end of his life.'

And as for his former club? 'Forest were great to me. I've always wanted them to do well and hope they're soon back playing at the level they should be.'

Michael Dawson

Date of birth: 18 November 1983, Northallerton, North Yorkshire

Nottingham Forest record:
Appearances: League 83, FA Cup 2, League Cup 4, Others 1
Goals: League 7
Debut: 1 April 2002 v Walsall (h) lost 2–3

Also played for: Tottenham Hotspur

Tall and elegant, Michael Dawson broke the hearts of many Forest fans when he left the City Ground at the end of January 2005 in search of Premiership football. While no one would deny that 'Daws' deserved to be playing at the highest level, most hoped he would be the inspirational leader who helped the Reds back to the top.

A native of North Yorkshire, Michael attended the Wensleydale School and was soon under the watchful eye of the Forest scouts, who were well aware of the footballing pedigree of the Dawson family. Elder brothers Andrew and Kevin were already attached to the Forest academy and both made it into the first team (Andrew, one League Cup match in 1998; Kevin, 12 first-team outings between 1999 and 2002).

Daws had signed schoolboy forms at 14 and moved to Nottingham two years later. While his brothers went on to further their careers at other clubs, Michael had learned carefully under the watching eye of academy director Paul Hart, whose later appointment as first-team manager was clearly beneficial to the crop of young stars he had helped nurture through the academy.

Towards the back end of the 2001–02 season, Michael's rapid development was considered worthy of closer scrutiny and he was handed a first-team debut at home to Walsall. While Des Walker's return to the Forest fold that summer provided competition for the defensive berth that Michael craved, he could not have had a better role model. Watching, training and eventually playing alongside the former England great was as good a grounding as was possible for the youngster. Walker's ability to spot and snuff out any potential danger clearly began to rub off on his young apprentice.

Once firmly installed in the team, Michael played in 38 of the final 40 League matches of the season, helping the Reds into a sixth-placed finish and a spot in the dreaded end-of-season Play-offs.

At 6ft 2in tall he possessed natural authority in the air but his composure on the ball marked him down as a player with a very bright future ahead of him. That initial season in the Forest ranks was also garnished with five goals, the first coming at Stoke City in just his fifth start for the club.

All was going well – and hopes were high of a return to the top flight – when Sheffield United visited the City Ground for the first leg of those semi-final Play-offs. Forest's hopes were hit hard, not only by the 1–1 scoreline but also with Michael being harshly dismissed for a challenge on Steve Kabba which forced him to miss the second leg – a tie that eventually swung the way of the Yorkshire side.

A call-up to play for the England Under-21 side provided a welcome distraction from the disappointment, but while away on international duty Michael contracted glandular fever which caused him to miss the first few matches of the following season.

The team struggled, despite replacing Hart with Joe Kinnear. Michael missed other games with groin and hamstring problems but when available he began to captain the Reds on a regular basis, having first worn the armband when just 19 – one of the youngest Forest players ever to do so.

A further new manager, Gary Megson, failed to trigger another promotion push in the 2004–05 season and speculation began to link Michael with a number of other clubs.

On January's deadline day Tottenham Hotspur came in with an undisclosed bid, reputed to be around the £8 million mark, to whisk Michael and his teammate Andy Reid off to White Hart Lane.

No longer eligible for the England Under-21s (after playing 13 times, many as captain), a full cap would seem to be edging ever closer for the former Forester.

Both Sven-Göran Eriksson and his successor, Steve McClaren, have summoned Michael to train with the national side on a number of occasions and he came on as a substitute for the England B side in a friendly international against Belarus at Reading in May 2006.

After more than 18 months at Tottenham, Michael eventually scored his first goal for the club in a historic win over reigning champions Chelsea in November 2006.

Johnny Dent

Date of birth: 31 January 1903, Spennymoor, County Durham
Died: 6 November 1979

Nottingham Forest record:
Appearances: League 196, FA Cup 10
Goals: League 119, FA Cup 3
Debut: 3 October 1929 v Bradford Park Avenue (h) drew 1–1

Also played for: Spennymoor Rangers, Durham City, Tow Law Town, Huddersfield Town, Kidderminster Harriers

Johnny Dent was one of the most prolific strikers ever to play for Nottingham Forest. Between 1929 and 1937 he hit 119 League goals in just 196 appearances. Among his haul were five hat-tricks, four of them in the League.

Hailing from the North East, Johnny played for a couple of local sides before being given his first taste of League football with Durham City, then a Third Division North side. After netting 26 goals from just 47 matches, he moved to Tow Law for the 1925–26 season but returned to the League a year later, becoming a professional with Huddersfield Town.

His spell at Leeds Road was tinged with disappointment when he did not make the starting line up for the 1928 FA Cup Final, having played in the semis. After three years with the Terriers he headed south to join Forest for a transfer fee of £1,500.

Although Dent did not join the Reds until three months into the 1928–29 season, he comfortably managed to top score for the side and blasted 15 goals from the remaining 24 League matches, which included a scoring spree of goals in six consecutive games. In addition, he hit his first treble for the club, notching three of the Reds' goals in the 5–0 FA Cup third-round demolition of Rotherham United.

Johnny's will to win and all-out endeavour made him popular with teammates and supporters alike, although he was unable to propel Forest into the challenging positions for promotion from Division Two.

A similar story emerged during the following campaign. Johnny was outstanding and again topped the scoring charts with 23 in the League, but the squad was not strong enough and finished nearer the bottom than the top of the table.

Towards the end of the campaign, Forest undertook a rare overseas sortie and played a Netherlands Select XI in Rotterdam. Johnny's converted penalty helped secure a 3–1 win for the English side.

Goals continued to flow for the powerfully-built striker and he enjoyed fruitful partnerships with both Bill Dickinson and then Tom Peacock, but promotion remained just a pipe dream for the City Ground regulars.

There were high spots during the 1930s, of course, most of which featured goals from Johnny. He twice scored important goals against Notts County, a feat guaranteed to earn him a drink or two in the red half of the city.

The 1933–34 season was his most plentiful, knocking in an amazing 27 goals from just 36 League outings. Forest actually scored more goals than Preston, who finished in second place in the table, but their leaky defence contributed to a lowly 17th-place finish.

During March 1935 Johnny hit a real purple patch in front of goal, notching back-to-back hat-tricks in matches against Oldham and Burnley and bringing up his 100th League goal for the club in the process.

The following season he was still performing to the highest level and netted twice in a 9–2 demolition of Port Vale, but time and injuries were slowly catching up with Johnny. He only featured five times during the next campaign, with his last appearance coming against Leicester City in December 1936. With a total of 119 League goals to his name for the Reds he brought his City Ground days to a halt by signing for Kidderminster Harriers at the end of the season.

He continued to play for them until the outbreak of World War Two, when he was called upon to serve in the Royal Air Force. After peace was declared Johnny returned to Nottingham and played cricket in West Bridgford for many years.

Right up until his death in 1979, he remained in the area and closely followed Forest's fortunes. He remains one of only five players to score a century of League goals for the club, with only Wally Ardron and Grenville Morris ahead of him.

Roy Dwight

Date of birth: 9 January 1933, Belvedere, Kent
Died: 9 April 2002

Nottingham Forest record:
Appearances: League 44, FA Cup 9
Goals: League 21, FA Cup 6
Debut: 23 August 1958 v Wolverhampton Wanderers (a) lost 1–5

Also played for: Hastings United, Fulham, Gravesend & Northfleet, Coventry
City, Millwall
Managed: Tooting and Mitcham United

Injury and a famous family connection have ensured that the name of Roy Dwight will not be forgotten among football supporters, particularly Forest fans.

Roy achieved what most schoolboys dream of doing by netting in an FA Cup Final at Wembley Stadium. Sadly, although his goal helped set his side up for victory, he was unable to climb the famous steps to the Royal Box to collect his winners' medal. Instead, he was in a hospital bed by the end of the match, having his broken leg treated.

The 1958–59 season began, as it ended, on something of a sweet and sour note for Roy. Having just joined the Reds from Fulham, he had scored on his debut, although the team lost heavily away at Wolves.

Although a right-winger by trade, Roy had the happy knack of cutting in from the flanks, either to shoot for goal himself or help create space for others. In terms of productivity he had an enviable goal-scoring record, claiming around 50 goals from 80 starts for Fulham. Forest boss Billy Walker was looking for a similar return from his new acquisition and could not have been happier as his new number seven continued to find the back of the net.

Nottingham Forest's progression to the Cup Final had been lengthy and not without obstacles. By the time they had confirmed their place beneath the Twin Towers the Reds had already played eight ties, which included five goals from Roy. His tally included a City Ground goal in the third-round replay against Tooting and Mitcham and then four against Birmingham City. The initial fifth-round clash at St Andrews had been drawn and the replay in Nottingham was just as tight until the visitors went ahead in extra-time, but a late leveller, scored by Roy, preserved Forest's interest in the competition.

Considering how even the first two matches had been, it was somewhat surprising that the second replay turned out to be as conclusive as it did. Forest swept their opponents aside by five goals to nil with Roy achieving a hat-trick – and creating a statistical oddity at the same time. The match was played at Leicester City's Filbert Street ground and just 86 days earlier he had scored all three of Forest's goals there in a 3–0 win over the Foxes – a case of 'horses for courses'.

By the time of the FA Cup Final Roy had scored 25 goals for Forest in his first season at the club. Within nine minutes of the start, he had added his 26th, crisply converting a well-placed pass from Stewart Imlach.

Less than a quarter of an hour later, with Forest 2–0 up, the so-called 'Wembley hoodoo' struck. During the 1950s the FA's showpiece occasion had been ruined several times with a serious injury disrupting the Final. An innocuous-looking challenge by Brendan McNally, the Luton right-back, left Roy on the ground. Although he rose to his feet and tried to hobble, the injury was clearly serious. In the cruellest of circumstances he had to leave his teammates and was taken to Wembley hospital.

Despite his pain, Roy was delighted to find that the match was being shown on a hospital television and he insisted on watching the closing minutes and seeing his captain climb the steps to accept the Cup.

X-rays confirmed that Roy's right tibia had been broken, but his spirits were lifted later that evening when the Forest manager and players were able to visit his bedside and bring along his medal and the FA Cup itself.

The healing process was slow and it took 10 full months before Roy was able to make his return to the Forest colours, which he celebrated by netting in a home draw against Preston North End.

Sadly, he was never the same player after the injury and he only played twice more for the club before being allowed to leave. Stints at Gravesend, Coventry and Millwall followed, all serving as proof that the leg break had severely interrupted what could have been an outstanding career.

Roy's love of the game did not diminish, though, and he sought fulfilment in a near seven-year stint as manager at Tooting and Mitcham – the non-League club that he had scored against on Forest's road to Wembley.

After leaving Tooting, Roy switched sports to become racing manager at Crayford Greyhound Stadium until ill-health forced his retirement, and he was only 69 when he sadly died in 2002.

Memories of Roy's exploits in the 1959 Final were revived 25 years later when his nephew, Reg (better known as pop superstar Sir Elton John), went to Wembley as chairman of 1984 finalists Watford.

Frank Forman

Date of birth: 23 May 1875, Aston-upon-Trent, Derbyshire
Died: 4 December 1961

Nottingham Forest record:
Appearances: League 223, FA Cup 33
Goals: League 23, FA Cup 5
Debut: 16 March 1895 v Bolton Wanderers (h) drew 3–3

Also played for: Aston-upon-Trent, Beeston Town, Derby County, England (9 caps)

It could be argued that no one served Nottingham Forest with any greater distinction than Francis (Frank) Forman. After joining them from Derby County in December 1894, he remained with the club as player, committee member and life member until his death in 1961. An FA Cup winner with Forest in 1898, he also represented his country on nine occasions, appearing in three of those matches alongside his brother and club teammate, Fred. Indeed, the Formans were the last pair of brothers to line up for England until Jackie and Bobby Charlton 66 years later. A third Forman brother, Thomas, also played for Forest on a handful of occasions in the early 1900s before going on to achieve more considerable success with Barnsley and Spurs.

Frank had played local non-League football until joining Derby County in March 1894. Nine months later he moved to Forest but had to bide his time before being handed a debut in March 1895. Apart from their Division One commitments, Forest's first team also competed in the United Counties League and it was in this competition that Frank registered his first goal for the club, netting in a 3-0 home win over Notts County. Over the course of the next couple of seasons, he matured into one of the finest half-backs in the land. Positionally sound and an accurate passer of the ball, he rapidly gained the respect and admiration of his teammates. Standing at just under six feet tall he was an imposing physical presence on the field but a quiet, unassuming character off it.

During the 1898 FA Cup run Frank was a dominant force as the Reds swept past Grimsby Town, Gainsborough Trinity, West Bromwich Albion and Southampton to reach their first Final. On the big day itself, Forest needed their star player to perform to his full potential and he did not disappoint, either in defence or attack, as favourites Derby County were overwhelmed by three goals to one.

The Cup win rounded off a successful couple of months for Frank as he had just forced his way into the England side, making his debut in March 1898 against Ireland in Belfast. With so few internationals being played in those days it is hardly surprising that he made just nine appearances for his country over the space of a five-year period. England won seven and drew two of the matches in which Frank played and he achieved a couple of noteworthy milestones.

His third England appearance also came against the Irish, at Roker Park, and saw him line up alongside brother Fred for the first time. Both siblings marked the occasion by getting on the score sheet in a convincing 13-2 hammering. In 1902, also against Ireland in Belfast, Frank was afforded the accolade of skippering his country for the only time and he led them to a slender one-goal victory.

By this stage of his career, Frank had succeeded John MacPherson as club skipper and switched to a centre-half position. He had also assumed the mantle of penalty taker and his powerful, accurate shooting began to accumulate a steady tally of goals from open play.

During the 1901–02 season there was optimism that Forest were going to repeat their FA Cup triumph as Frank scored in every round to help the side to the semi-finals for the third time in four years. This time there was to be no fairy-tale ending, though, as the Reds were overcome by Southampton, relieved no doubt to have gained revenge for their defeat at the same stage four years earlier.

Frank's long and successful playing career drew to a close in 1905 with a 2-1 win over Small Heath, his last League game, although he made a couple of Cup appearances later. With brother-in-law Jimmy Linacre, the former Forest goalkeeper, he worked professionally as a building contractor in and around the West Bridgford area of Nottingham but his loyalty to Forest remained undiminished and unquestionable as he gave the club more than half a century of devoted committee work.

Trevor Francis

Date of birth: 19 April 1954, Plymouth, Devon

Nottingham Forest record:
Appearances: League 70, FA Cup 8, League Cup 6, Others 9
Goals: League 28, FA Cup 5, Others 4
Debut: 3 March 1979 v Ipswich Town (a) drew 1–1

Also played for: Birmingham City, Detroit Express (US), Manchester City, Sampdoria (Italy), Atalanta (Italy), Glasgow Rangers (Scotland), Queen's Park Rangers, Sheffield Wednesday, England (52 caps)
Managed: Queen's Park Rangers, Sheffield Wednesday, Birmingham City, Crystal Palace

Stored among the great memories for all Nottingham Forest fans is the moment when Trevor Francis threw himself forward to connect with John Robertson's cross to head home the winning goal in the 1979 European Cup Final.

Trevor's arrival at the City Ground could not have been more timely, arriving as he did in a blaze of publicity towards the end of the 1978–79 season. Brian Clough splashed out a British record fee of £1 million to get his man and then selected him for an A-Team fixture against Notts County 48 hours later! 'The media made that into more of a story than it actually was,' recalls Trevor. 'When I joined Forest I hadn't played for a while so I was just grateful for a chance to get some match practice in.'

Almost 25, Trevor joined the Reds as a seasoned international and with a wealth of experience behind him. Many felt he would never leave St Andrews, but Trevor admits to yearning for some silverware. 'Forest were one of the top teams in the country and certainly the only side who looked capable of challenging Liverpool for domestic honours. That was a key factor because I wanted to win things.'

The first few weeks at Forest were frustrating for Trevor, as he was ineligible to play as his new side lifted the League Cup and the timing of his signing meant that he was not available for either the quarter-final or semi-final matches in the European Cup. Nevertheless, the manager selected him for all of the League matches and his new acquisition soon began to find the net regularly in the build-up to the Final in Munich against Malmo. 'I consider myself very fortunate that my debut in European competition was in a Final and that I was able to score the winner – at least I felt I'd played some part in the success.'

Of the goal itself, Trevor is full of admiration for the way it was created. 'The thing that I most remember is the quality of Ian Bowyer's ball out to find John Robertson. When it was played I was only just in the attacking half of the field and quickly realised that John was very likely to beat his man and whip in a cross. I knew I had to make up a lot of ground to get there!'

Predictably, almost telepathically, Robbo's cross came in as expected. 'I was able to time my run just right to connect with the header and score.'

The 1979–80 season again saw Forest challenging both domestically and in Europe. Trevor was not to complete the season but he netted 14 League goals from 30 appearances as the Reds finished fifth. Among his haul was a hat-trick at home to Manchester City.

He played in both legs of the European Super Cup win over Barcelona and in the League Cup Final at Wembley, but Forest appeared to be losing their grip on the European Cup when they lost the first leg of their quarter-final at home to Dynamo Berlin by a single goal.

Before the second leg there was the additional disappointment of the League Cup Final defeat, but fortunes were turned round with what many believe was Trevor's best performance in Forest's colours. 'We arrived in Berlin needing to pick ourselves up after losing at Wembley. It was about eight degrees below freezing at kick-off – I'm sure it was the coldest I've played football anywhere but we performed so well in that first half. We were 3–0 up and knew we were through already.'

Trevor had scored twice in the win against Berlin and notched another in the semi-final win over Ajax. Just 10 days later, though, he suffered a major setback, rupturing his Achilles tendon against Crystal Palace. 'We were 4–0 up with about 10 minutes to go when it happened. It meant I was out of the Final and also the forthcoming European Championships with England.'

The injury forced him to miss the first half of the 1980–81 season, although he was back to play against Valencia in the Super Cup and Nacional in the World Club Championship in Tokyo. 'I thought we were desperately unlucky to lose as we'd dominated the match throughout.'

Just as Forest fans were looking forward to seeing the best of their 'million-pound man', the unthinkable happened in September 1982 – he was sold! 'I'd started the new season well but then there was lots of conjecture about me moving to Manchester City. Things gained momentum and the deal was quickly done. Looking back, I do think my time at Forest ended prematurely and I wished I'd had longer there.'

Although brief, Trevor's time at the City Ground was historic – he scored better goals in his career but none as important as the goal that won the European Cup.

Horace Gager

Date of birth:	25 January 1917, West Ham, London
Died:	March 1984

Nottingham Forest record:

Appearances:	League 258, FA Cup 10
Goals:	League 11
Debut:	28 February 1948 v Leicester City (h) won 1–0

Also played for: Vauxhall Motors FC, Luton Town

Despite not arriving at the City Ground until he had passed his 31st birthday, Horace Gager is still regarded as being one of the finest centre-halves ever to play for Forest. Billy Walker had signed him from Luton Town in February 1948 where he had been on the staff at Kenilworth Road since 1937, having been spotted playing for his works team Vauxhall Motors. However, he had not really been given the opportunity to establish himself before the outbreak of World War Two.

Horace was sent to serve in Northern Ireland during the war, where he guested for a Glentoran side featuring a former Forest favourite, Dave Martin. Most of his best footballing years had been lost during the conflict, but he rejoined Luton afterwards and scored twice in 62 outings for the Hatters.

The switch to Forest gave him the chance to resurrect a career, but he had moved to a club where defeats were becoming an all-too-familiar occurrence. After slotting into the Reds' defence, Horace played in a dozen matches towards the end of the season and helped his new side keep their heads just above water, with a final finishing spot of 19th in the Second Division standings.

It was a sad sign of things to come as far as Forest were concerned, and relegation ensued 12 months later. Despite all the doom and gloom around the ground, the fans knew that their manager had bought wisely in securing Horace's services and he gave solidity and presence to a backline guilty of shipping too many soft goals before his arrival.

Hopes were high that Forest would bounce straight back at the first time of asking. These hopes were misplaced; although the Third Division South Championship Shield did come to Nottingham at the end of the 1949–50 season, sadly for Forest it was Notts County, fierce local rivals, who took the crown in an exciting season for the city.

Forest finished fourth – nine points behind the Magpies – but, crucially, only a couple of points from a promotion position. Obvious disappointment soon gave way to optimism and the 1950–51 campaign was a joyous one for all

connected with the club. By now, Horace had succeeded Bob McCall and been elevated to club captain, and the wisdom of the appointment was very evident as he enjoyed the most consistent season of his career. He was an ever-present figure at the heart of a defence that was the most miserly in the League.

Skippering Forest to the title was an immensely enjoyable experience for Horace, watching his sharp-shooters Wally Ardron and Tommy Capel lead the way to more than a century of goals and 70 points – a record at the time.

Horace was such a commanding figure that he was even talked about as a possible England candidate, but the thought was always unlikely given his advancing years. He did receive some positive recognition, though, by being selected to play alongside Billy Wright in an FA Representative XI in a match against Cornwall.

In more than 250 League matches for Forest the defender only got forward to convert one single goal from open play – at Brentford in January 1953 – but, apart from his leadership skills and defensive qualities, Horace was useful to the team for his calmness from the penalty spot. During his time at Forest he converted 10 out of 11 penalties, with only a miss at home to Millwall in 1950 blotting his copybook.

Among his successful conversions was one against Notts County in a crushing 5–0 win in October 1953 – confirmation that the balance of power had firmly switched back to the Reds.

The emergence of Bobby McKinlay gradually began to have an effect on Horace's appearances and he was to play only five times in the 1954–55 campaign, his final outing for the club coming in a 2–0 home victory over Plymouth Argyle on 12 March 1955 – two months after his 38th birthday!

League football came relatively late in life for Horace Gager, but he will always be remembered for helping turn around a club that had dropped into the third tier and were badly in need of leadership and drive to reverse the trend. Nottingham Forest have a lot to thank him for.

Archie Gemmill

Date of birth: 24 March 1947, Paisley, Renfrewshire, Scotland

Nottingham Forest record:
Appearances: League 58, FA Cup 7, League Cup 7, Others 8
Goals: League 4, Others 1
Debut: 1 October 1977 v Norwich City (h) drew 1–1

Also played for: St Mirren, Preston North End, Derby County, Birmingham City,
                 Jacksonville Teamen (US), Wigan Athletic, Scotland (43 caps)
Managed: Rotherham United (co-manager with John McGovern),
                 Scotland Under-19s

At his best, Archie Gemmill was one of the most fiercely competitive midfielders around. A tenacious tackler, his primary role was to win the ball and give it but that belied his other qualities. Capable of rounding off a lung-bursting surge upfield with a shot at goal, he also possessed dribbling skills to make any winger go green with envy.

Indeed, one particular Archie goal has been replayed more than any other Scotland has ever scored. The 1978 World Cup Finals in Argentina ultimately saw the ritual early flight home for the Scottish, but not before Archie had twisted and turned, dribbled and weaved his way past a mesmerised Dutch defence to convert one of the truly great international goals of all time. In most polls, only Carlos Alberto's strike for Brazil in the 1970 Final or Diego Maradona's solo effort in 1986 against England come close to rivalling it.

Forest fans would argue that they did not see that sort of prodigious finishing too often during his two-year stint at the City Ground, but few would disagree with the claim that Archie was an integral cog in the title success of 1978.

When signing the Scottish international, Brian Clough certainly knew what he was getting. Gemmill had played for him at Derby County, where he had picked up two Championship medals. He spent seven years at the Baseball Ground, having previously played for Preston North End and, earlier, St Mirren, for whom he had made a statistical mark by becoming the first-ever substitute to appear in the Scottish League (against Clyde in August 1966).

Although he did not arrive at the City Ground until a month into the Championship season, his contribution was essential. Thirty-four appearances and three vital goals – a winner against Manchester United, a point-earning equaliser against Liverpool and the second in a 2–0 win over Arsenal.

Archie was not eligible to play in the League Cup competition, having appeared for the Rams in an earlier round, but he did experience two successful Wembley outings with the Reds in his second season at Forest.

His tigerish determination was a key factor in helping overwhelm FA Cup holders Ipswich Town in the Charity Shield and later in the campaign he played against Southampton in the successful defence of the League Cup competition.

In the first leg of the European Cup quarter-final against Swiss side Grasshoppers, Archie scored Forest's third – like all his other goals for the club it came at the City Ground – and helped ensure safe progress into the semi-finals. There, Forest met German opposition and their last four battle with Cologne on 11 April 1979 is regarded as one of the most nail-biting matches ever witnessed on Trentside. The final outcome was a 3–3 draw, but, although he did not know it at the time, Archie was not to play a competitive game again for the club. A hamstring injury ruled him out of the second leg and the remaining League fixtures. Although he had a 20-minute run out in a County Cup tie against Mansfield Town, manager Clough decided he was not fit enough to play in the European Cup Final against Swedish champions Malmo. Archie was deeply disappointed by the decision, despite qualifying for a medal as an unused substitute.

The midfielder moved to Birmingham City in the close season, but he later returned to Forest after hanging up his boots, initially as coach and then as the reserve-team manager.

During his time on the club's backroom staff he oversaw the emergence and development of his own son Scot, who went on to appear in over 300 matches for Forest.

Aided and abetted by his former midfield partner John McGovern, Archie then spent a couple of seasons at Millmoor as joint manager of Rotherham United in the mid-1990s.

He continues to give much back to the game – being employed by the Scottish FA to look after their Under-19 set-up – but Archie remains deeply passionate about Forest's fortunes and is always assured of a regal welcome whenever he returns to the club.

Scot Gemmill

Date of birth: 2 January 1971, Paisley, Renfrewshire, Scotland

Nottingham Forest record:
Appearances: League 245, FA Cup 21, League Cup 31, Others 14
Goals: League 21, FA Cup 1, League Cup 3, Others 4
Debut: 30 March 1991 v Wimbledon (a) lost 1–3

Also played for: Everton, Preston North End (loan), Leicester City, Oxford United,
New Zealand Knights, Scotland (26 caps)

For almost eight years Scot Gemmill held down a midfield berth in the Forest first team. Like his father Archie, Scot experienced some of football's highs during his days at the City Ground and he also experienced first hand what it was like to work for Brian Clough.

Speaking many years after leaving the City Ground, Scot admitted that his father's influence on his career had been crucial. 'Realistically, I was only given an opportunity to be an apprentice at Forest because of the relationship between my dad and Cloughie.'

The 'it's not what you know but who you know' maxim can only work so far in football, though. Underachievers are quickly found out and it is important to emphasise that Scot's career blossomed due to his own talent rather than by family connections. In truth, like teammate Nigel Clough, it is probably accurate to say that he had to work harder than his contemporaries to eliminate any accusations of bias when it came to team selection.

His introduction to the first team came just before the 1991 FA Cup Final with a couple of starts and another couple of appearances from the bench as Cloughie rested some of his regulars ahead of the big day. Scot was just a spectator as Forest lost to Spurs, but he was to create his only piece of Wembley history the following season.

Having held down a first-team place for most of the 1991–92 campaign – and scored goals at a healthy rate, his first of a very-respectable total of 12 coming against Oldham Athletic – he played in two Cup Finals at the Venue of Legends in a fortnight.

Despite it coming so early in his Forest career, Scot ensured himself of a place in his club's Hall of Fame by scoring twice at Wembley in the Zenith Data Systems Final. With a goal at either end of the pitch, his contribution helped defeat Southampton 3–2.

Contrasting emotions were very evident two weeks later when the youngster left the pitch in tears after Forest had lost in the League Cup Final to Manchester United. There were plenty more tears on Trentside a year later as Cloughie's final

term in charge ended with relegation. Although the club bounced straight back, Scot remarked that it did not erase the sadness of the previous season.

His role in the Forest side was essential – a 'fetch and carry man' who was happy to link defence with attack, a role that is neither spectacular nor eye-catching but essential nonetheless. Like his father, Scot could pick a pass – long or short – and possessed a decent shot from distance.

Comparisons with Archie were inevitable but ultimately futile. They played for Forest at different ends of their careers – and whereas visually Scot was much taller, he certainly had more hair than his father! The common ground was that they both possessed great stamina and were appreciated for the energy and drive they gave with every performance.

On 21 May 1995 Scot made his international debut, appearing against Japan in Hiroshima. He was to play for Scotland on 26 occasions, 13 of them as a Forest player, and he was included in the squads for both the 1996 European Championships and the World Cup Finals two years later, although he did not get on the pitch in either tournament.

By that stage of his career he had experienced a further drop into the second tier and another immediate 'bounce-back' as part of Dave Bassett's Division One title-winning side. Having played in 44 of the 46 League contests, Scot deserved his medal.

The 1998–99 season was also hurtling towards a catastrophic conclusion and Forest reluctantly agreed to part with the long-serving midfielder, accepting a bid of £250,000 from Everton.

Later he returned to the East Midlands to join Leicester City and then had one appearance for Oxford United before being tempted by the opportunity to play his football in New Zealand.

Although he was just regarded as 'Archie's son' when he began at the City Ground, Scot Gemmill matured into a Forest legend in his own right and scored their final Wembley goal of the 20th century.

Tommy Graham

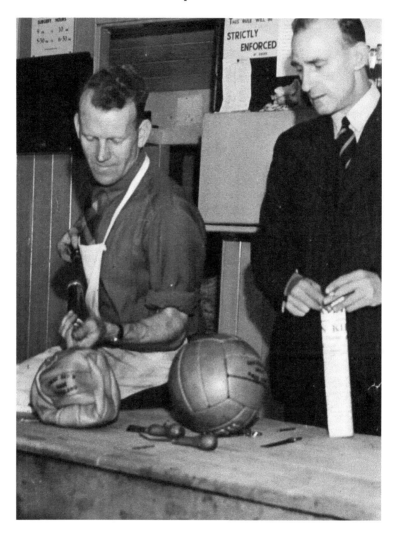

Date of birth: 5 March 1907, Hamsterley, County Durham
Died: 29 March 1983

Nottingham Forest record:
Appearances: League 372, FA Cup 18
Goals: League 7
Debut: 7 April 1928 v Bristol City (a) drew 0–0

Also played for: Hamsterley Swifts, Consett Celtic, England (2 caps)

Tommy Graham devoted most of his life to Nottingham Forest Football Club. From the time of his first practice match with the Reds in 1927 to his death over half a century later, he was linked to the Reds in a variety of roles.

He was a skinny youngster – of that there is no doubt – and football was an alien concept to him until he was persuaded at 15 to muck in with some of his mates and join Hamsterley Swifts, a side with associations to the local colliery. Having not played the game at school he had some catching up to do, but football quickly became the be-all and end-all for Tommy and he revelled in his new unfamiliar pastime.

He joined another north-eastern amateur side, Consett Celtic, and even attracted the attentions of Newcastle United, who invited him for a trial. Although nothing came of it, Tommy's appetite had been sharpened by the prospect of making a career out of the game. The young wing-half began to attract the attention of a number of League clubs, but it was Nottingham Forest who took a punt on his potential and signed him in the summer of 1927.

Tommy had to wait until the latter stages of his first season at the club before being given a chance in the first team. Injuries enabled him to play at either left-half or left full-back during his first couple of years at the City Ground, but eventually he was switched, with great success, to centre-half.

The feature of the 1929–30 season for Tommy and his teammates was an FA Cup adventure that ended in a sixth-round replay at Hillsborough, in front of a crowd of 59,205.

Despite playing in Division Two throughout his entire career, Tommy's talent was unquestionable and the England selectors fulfilled their duty by calling him into the international fold, albeit for two matches only, during 1931.

His debut resulted in a 5–2 mauling by France in Paris, but his other appearance met with a happier outcome, ending in a 6–2 England victory over Ireland at Windsor Park, Belfast.

The defensive side of Tommy's duties was paramount to him, and he had played well over 100 League games for Forest before he ventured far enough upfield to register his first goal for the club – a home winner against Port Vale in March 1932.

In truth, the 1930s were one of Forest's most non-descriptive decades. At no time could they ever have been described as promotion candidates, although they did have a couple of close shaves with the relegation trap door. At the end of both the 1937–38 and 1938–39 seasons they only survived in Division Two courtesy of having a superior goal average than their closest rivals.

Tommy played his 372nd and final League match for the Reds in April 1939 – only eight other players have appeared more often for Forest. He did turn out a few times in war-time friendlies, but more often than not he chose to concentrate on his new position as the club's trainer, a position he would hold for over 20 years under Billy Walker. In 1957 the club granted him a testimonial match against an All Stars XI in recognition of his years of service.

Tommy was never busier than on 2 May 1959, at Wembley Stadium. While the players deservedly took the plaudits for the FA Cup Final success, the trainer also earned his money that day. He was called into action on any number of occasions to administer the magic sponge and smelling salts to stricken bodies. Sadly, not even his first-aid skills and words of encouragement could prevent Roy Dwight being taken from the action with his broken leg.

Ill-health finally forced Tommy to give up his position in 1961, but he continued to work with the club's youngsters and to scout for the first team right up until his death in 1983.

Frank Gray

Date of birth: 24 May 1927, Dinnington, Tyne and Wear

Nottingham Forest record:
Appearances: League 201, FA Cup 17, League Cup 2, Others 3
Goals: League 28, FA Cup 5
Debut: 24 August 1957 v Preston North End (h) won 2–1

Also played for: Dinnington Colliery, Wolverhampton Wanderers, Gateshead, Leyton Orient, Chelsea, Burnley, Millwall
Managed: Millwall, Brentford, Notts County

One of Forest's FA Cup-winning heroes of 1959, Billy Gray came to the City Ground as a proven First Division performer and notched up more than 200 first-team appearances before leaving to embark on a successful managerial career.

William Patrick Gray was born in the North East and worked at his local colliery after leaving school. His footballing talent began to flourish and during the war years he played for both Wolves and Gateshead as an amateur before earning a professional contract with Leyton Orient in May 1947. Further transfers took him to Chelsea and then Burnley. Playing predominantly as a right-winger he had one England B cap, against Switzerland in 1950, while on the staff at Stamford Bridge and had twice appeared in losing FA Cup semi-final teams.

His luck in that competition was about to change with a move to Forest. Manager Billy Walker converted his new charge to the inside-left position and was immediately rewarded with the winning goal on his debut.

Billy's goal tally in the 1957–58 season reached nine but it was bettered the following year, with five of his 12 strikes coming in FA Cup ties as the Reds marched triumphantly towards their first Wembley Final.

His first goal en route to the Twin Towers is widely regarded as being one of the most important in the club's history. Away at Isthmian League side Tooting and Mitcham, Billy Walker's side were just 15 minutes away from one of the most embarrassing defeats ever recorded in the competition until Billy converted a penalty-kick to salvage a 2–2 draw for Forest and a replay back in Nottingham.

A couple of goals followed in each of the next two rounds, at home to Grimsby Town and against Birmingham City in the fifth-round second replay match, which was played at the neutral venue of Filbert Street.

It was third-time lucky as Billy advanced beyond the semi-final stage for the only time in his career to proudly line up in his first Cup Final. In front of a capacity 100,000 crowd the early stages of the match went unbelievably well for Forest, with two goals in the first 14 minutes – and the number 10 was involved in both goals. Billy played a key pass in the build up to Roy Dwight's opener and then supplied the inch-perfect cross from the left, from which Tommy Wilson headed the second goal.

While that would remain the biggest match of Billy's life, he continued to play for the Reds for four more seasons and was involved in several important chapters in the club's history.

He participated in the Charity Shield match against Wolves which acted as the curtain-raiser for the following season, played in Forest's first-ever League Cup tie – a home win against Halifax on 6 October 1960 – and also took part in the Reds brief European debut, appearing in both legs of the Inter Cities Fairs Cup defeat to Valencia in 1961.

By that stage of his career Billy had switched to the left-back position but continued to perform consistently well and rack up a healthy tally of appearances. He played in his last game for Forest just a month short of his 36th birthday before leaving to join Millwall as their player–manager.

While at the Den he achieved a couple of promotions with the Lions and also had managerial spells at both Brentford and Notts County, as well as a coaching stint at Fulham, before returning to the City Ground as groundsman.

Billy Gray

Date of birth: 27 October 1954, Castlemilk, Glasgow, Scotland

Nottingham Forest record:
Appearances: League 81, FA Cup 8, League Cup 14, Others 15
Goals: League 5, FA Cup 1, League Cup 2
Debut: 18 August 1979 v Ipswich Town (a) won 1–0

Also played for: Leeds United, Sunderland, Darlington, Scotland (32 caps)
Managed: Darlington, Harrogate Town, Farnborough Town, Grays Athletic,
            Woking

Frank Gray moved to Forest in the summer of 1979 to enjoy being part of their success story – and became a European champion to make up for earlier disappointments. He had broken into the Leeds team at just 17 and scored on his debut, but he faced stiff competition at left-back from senior international defenders Terry Cooper and Trevor Cherry.

Forced to sit and watch as the Elland Road side had lost in the FA Cup Final and the European Cup-winners' Cup Finals of 1973, he was selected to start in the European Cup Final two years later. Sadly for Frank, German champions Bayern Munich overcame a sticky start to win 2–0.

Brother of Eddie, the legendary Leeds and Scotland left-winger of the 60s and 70s, Frank had been on the staff at Elland Road for around seven years, making almost 200 League appearances in that time. Included among the managers that he had played under was Brian Clough, who spent a high-profile 44 days in charge of the Yorkshire club. It is believed that Frank was one of the players that had impressed his boss during that short stint and Cloughie went back to his former club to snap him up for £500,000 when his need for a left-back intensified.

So, hungry for success, Frank jumped at the opportunity to link up with Forest, who were in need of a replacement for the recently retired Frank Clark. The stylish Scot stepped straight into Forest's back four and for two seasons hardly missed a fixture, turning in solid performances week after week. Winning silverware was one of the motivations behind his move and the gamble – if that is what it was – paid off handsomely!

Frank was able to pocket a European Super Cup-winners' medal after the Reds had defeated Barcelona over two legs and then played in the 1–0 success over Hamburg in Madrid to become the first player to appear for two different English sides in a European Cup Final.

Apart from these outstanding successes, he also appeared in three more Finals where the result did not go Forest's way. He played against Wolves in the 1980 League Cup Final and, in his second season with the club, took part in another Super Cup Final, although this time the honours went to opponents Valencia.

Frank was also a member of the team that unjustly lost 1–0 in the World Club Championship match to Nacional of Montevideo, in Tokyo.

Apart from his defensive reliability, Frank was an asset going forwards with the ability to whip in a pinpoint cross or fire powerfully towards goal. His link-up play with John Robertson on the left-hand side became almost telepathic and helped create a mass of openings for the strikers. He also became something of a free-kick expert and produced several stunning goals for the Reds, notably a League Cup strike against Blackburn Rovers shortly after he had arrived at the club.

After a mere two seasons in Nottingham, the defender responded to a calling from his former club and went back to Leeds. Forest received only £300,000 in the transfer, but they had enjoyed a rare level of consistency from Frank. Over two full campaigns he had started 117 of the 121 first-team games that the club played.

Back at Leeds under former teammate Allan Clarke, Frank experienced relegation and then found himself playing under another manager for four years – his brother Eddie. A transfer to Sunderland followed in 1985 and four years later Frank stayed in the North East by switching to Darlington, a club who later handed him his first taste of management by offering him the chance to succeed Brian Little, initially in a player–manager position.

He later worked as an academy coach at Southampton and had a spell as an agent before becoming boss at Farnborough Town for the 2005–06 season. A year later he moved to Grays Athletic but only remained at the Conference club for around four months.

Frank also enjoyed a lengthy connection with the Scottish international side, winning 32 caps altogether – seven of which were gained during his time at Forest. His debut had come against Switzerland in 1976. Although he was not able to nail down a place in the squad for the World Cup Finals two years later, he did play in all of his country's matches in Spain in 1982.

Frank's son Andy also appeared for Forest, making 75 first-team appearances between 1998 and 2002.

Peter Grummitt

Date of birth: 19 August 1942, Bourne, Lincolnshire

Nottingham Forest record:
Appearances: League 313, FA Cup 26, League Cup 7, Others 6
Debut: 12 November 1960 v Bolton Wanderers (h) drew 2-2

Also played for: Bourne Town, Sheffield Wednesday, Brighton & Hove Albion

For English fans, the 1960s will forever be remembered as the decade when football rose head and shoulders above other sports to become the nation's favourite. The full impact of the World Cup Final success was immeasurable, except in terms of live attendances with crowds flocking to First Division matches. Clubs began to appreciate there was also a business side to the game and Nottingham Forest's gates increased significantly as a new crop of footballers were elevated to stardom.

Among them was Peter Grummitt, a goalkeeper of such outstanding promise who had been snapped up from Bourne Town, his local club, to prove his worth in the Forest reserves. Such was Peter's initial impact at the club that manager Johnny Carey had no qualms about thrusting him into the first team to replace the ageing Chick Thomson. His first match was to be at the City Ground against Bolton Wanderers.

The expectations of most young goalies would be to keep a clean sheet on debut or pull off a wonder save. For Peter it was a slightly more down-to-earth arrival in the big time. Even before he had touched the ball he was fishing around in the back of his own net for it, after a howler of an own goal by teammate Jim Iley.

The youngster impressed, nevertheless, and made the jersey his own – not missing a single League game for the next two years. He was able to participate in Forest's introduction to both the League Cup and European competitions and was an experienced pro by the time of the club's centenary year in 1965.

By that stage of his career Peter was being talked about as a potential England goalkeeper, but a certain Gordon Banks, plus one or two other outstanding candidates, ensured that this particular dream would go unfulfilled. Peter resigned himself instead to winning just three caps at Under-23 level, as well as an appearance for the Football League XI.

His consistency, allied to outstanding ball-handling and agile shot-stopping, ensured he would be an ever present throughout the 1966–67 season – a campaign which would thrust Forest into the headlines as serious Championship pretenders. Behind a reliable back four, the 'keeper was at the peak of his powers and helped preserve many valuable points with a succession of wonder saves.

Although Forest finished as runners-up in the title race they did manage to record the best defensive record in the League, conceding four fewer goals than Manchester United, the eventual champions. In his 42 appearances Peter was only beaten 41 times, keeping 13 clean sheets along the way. Three further clean sheets were recorded in the FA Cup competition but he was unable to prevent Spurs netting twice to knock Forest out at the semi-final stage.

It was another FA Cup tie, against Leeds United at Elland Road in February 1968, which saw Peter sustain the first serious injury of his career. His broken arm turned into a major setback for both club and player.

Although he did later return to the side, Forest had invested in another young 'keeper, Alan Hill, and it was clear that he would be given the opportunity to stake a claim for the jersey on a permanent basis.

In January 1970, after more than 350 first-team matches for the Reds, Peter was allowed to leave the City Ground to join Sheffield Wednesday. He left behind a considerable tally of appearances – as well as a host of memorable saves for the fans to remember him by.

To date, no goalkeeper has played in more League matches for Forest than Peter, although his overall appearance tally for the club was later overtaken by Mark Crossley. He spent three years at Hillsborough, compiling 121 League appearances before journeying south to join Brighton.

In four years on the south coast he helped clock up his career appearance tally to 570 League matches before finally hanging up his boots. Peter later ran a newsagents back in his home town of Bourne.

Bryn Gunn

Date of birth: 21 August 1958, Kettering, Northamptonshire

Nottingham Forest record:
Appearances: League 131, FA Cup 9, League Cup 17, Others 9
Goals: League 1, League Cup 1
Debut: 27 August 1975 v Rotherham United (h) won 5–1

Also played for: Shrewsbury Town (loan), Walsall (loan), Mansfield Town (loan),
                Peterborough United, Chesterfield, Corby Town, Oakham United
Managed: Corby Town

Despite his considerable loyalty to players, Brian Clough would not have kept a player on his club's pay roll for more than a decade unless they were of the highest calibre.

As an able deputy at either right-back or left-back, Bryn Gunn provided Forest with dependable cover for almost 13 years. Without ever being given an extended run in either position, it says much about his worth to the squad and the player's own loyalty to the club that he remained on the staff for so long. With his place never certain, Bryn had additional pressure on him every time he donned the Garibaldi Red shirt, yet his service to the club was amply rewarded with a substitute appearance and subsequent winners' medal in the second of the club's two European Cup wins.

Bryn was still a few days short of his 17th birthday when he first strode out to play for Brian Clough's first team in a pre-season friendly in Northern Ireland. In a match against Coleraine, otherwise memorable for an Ian Bowyer hat-trick, a handful of Forest supporters were present to see the young defender enjoy an accomplished debut in the number-two jersey. After a year as an apprentice he then signed professional forms and made his debut just a few days later, in a home League Cup tie against Rotherham United.

In that 1975–76 season, 'Gunny' appeared in 13 first-team matches, 10 of them in the League, with outings at a couple of the country's bigger grounds – Chelsea in the League and Manchester City in the League Cup.

The form and fitness of Viv Anderson on the right and Frank Clark and Colin Barrett on the left relegated Bryn to a couple of seasons in the reserves, during which time his game developed rapidly. At 6ft 2in tall he was rarely beaten in the air and robust in the challenge.

In 1978–79 he was an unused squad member for the first European Cup victory but played his part in the following season with appearances against Arges Pitesti and Dynamo Berlin in the early rounds.

His most memorable outing in the Forest colours came in Madrid on 28 May 1980 but was all too brief. In the tense, closing minutes of the European Cup Final against SV Hamburg Cloughie replaced Frank Gray, who had gone into the match carrying a slight niggle, with the fresh legs of Bryn. He also played in another high-profile match the following season, away in Valencia in the European Super Cup – a match that Forest lost by a single goal, to lose the tie on the away goals rule.

With the focus very much on his defensive duties, Bryn rarely got forward into goalscoring situations but he did register a League goal for the Reds in October 1982, in a 2–0 victory away at Luton Town.

It was very much in-vogue for Forest to take short mid-season breaks to warmer climes and Bryn scored another goal in a 5–0 win over Oman in January 1984; he also played for the club on similar trips to Qatar, Kuwait, Saudi Arabia and Iraq.

UEFA Cup appearances against FC Vorwaerts and Sturm Graz in the 1983–84 season and against FC Bruges a couple of years later enabled Bryn to accumulate even more European experience. In October 1984 he scored his only City Ground first-team goal – the final strike in a 3–1 League Cup victory over Portsmouth.

After loan spells at a number of lower League clubs Bryn was eventually allowed to leave Forest in August 1986, when he joined Peterborough United on a free transfer. He made 131 League appearances for the Posh and a further 91 for Chesterfield, whom he joined three years later.

Joining the non-League circuit in 1992 Bryn played for Corby Town, where he was also joint-manager for a while, and then continued his playing career at Oakham United. He then spent nine seasons on the coaching staff at Arnold Town before joining Desborough as assistant manager. 'Gunny' ended the 2006–07 season as reserve-team and Under-19s manager of Alfreton Town.

Daughter Jenny followed Bryn's other passion, cricket, and was a member of the England women's team that won the Ashes series against Australia in 2005 – a success to rank alongside the night her dad returned from Madrid with a European Cup-winners' medal hung around his neck.

Marlon Harewood

Date of birth: 25 August 1979, Hampstead, London

Nottingham Forest record:
Appearances: League 181, FA Cup 5, League Cup 16, Others 2
Goals: League 51, FA Cup 1, League Cup 3
Debut: 3 May 1998 v West Bromwich Albion (a) drew 1–1

Also played for: FC Haka (Finland, loan), Ipswich Town (loan), West Ham United,
Aston Villa

Among the generation of talented youngsters to pass through the Nottingham Forest academy in the late 1990s was the powerfully built Marlon Harewood. 'Marvellous Marlon', as the fans would dub him, forged a magnificent partnership with David Johnson, which took the Reds into the Play-offs in the spring of 2003.

His Forest debut came in the final match of the 1997–98 season, at the Hawthorns against West Brom on the day that the club celebrated their return to the Premiership. To gain more experience he was then allowed to go on a summer loan to play with FC Haka in Finland, where he scored three times in 12 outings for a side that went on to complete a League and Cup double.

The trip had served Marlon well and he was included in most of Forest's matches in the early part of the 1998–99 campaign, though mostly from the bench. His first senior goal for the club came at Orient in a League Cup tie and he followed that up with a priceless late equaliser at the Riverside to rescue a point against Middlesbrough, his first in the top flight.

Marlon's willingness to chase down lost causes and spirited determination won over the doubters who were initially concerned at his rawness and poor first touch. Observers could not help but be impressed by his strength and pace though – qualities which opposing defenders could clearly identify with.

Naturally, Marlon's confidence grew with experience and the striker matured quickly once Paul Hart had taken over as manager and conveyed his faith in him. In the 2002–03 season Marlon netted 20 League goals, five fewer than strike partner 'Johnno', to fire the Reds into the Play-offs.

His tally of goals was curiously compiled. In the first 16 matches of the season he scored only three times – all on the same afternoon – against Gillingham. His hat-trick, in a 4–0 home victory, was his first in professional football.

However satisfactory that may have been, there was better to come. On 22 February 2003 Marlon scored four goals in a match – the first Forest player to do so in a League game since Peter Withe in the 1977–78 Championship season. His contribution came against Stoke City in a 6–0 City Ground demolition – with all of his goals scored before the

break. An extract from the *Guardian's* match report describes the events:

'His first was the softest of the lot, as he mishit his shot on the turn to help the ball into the net from close range after a corner had been headed on. But his second, after 24 minutes, was a cracker. He played a neat one-two with Johnson and hammered the ball into the roof of the net at the near post, with goalkeeper Steve Banks beaten by the sheer ferocity of the shot.

'Harewood completed his hat-trick four minutes later with a simple finish, sidefooting the ball home from close range after a superb run and cross from Andrew Reid, who galloped three-quarters of the length of the pitch before setting up the chance.

'The striker did miss a simple chance by smashing a shot over the goal but almost scored again a minute before half-time when he headed another Reid cross against the base of the far post. But when Peter Marteinsson handled Matthieu Louis-Jean's follow-up shot, referee Uriah Rennie sent off the Stoke man and awarded Forest a penalty, which Harewood rolled into the net for his fourth.'

Forest's defeat to Sheffield United in those end-of-season Play-off matches signified the break-up of that Forest team and it was not long before Marlon was an item on the shopping list of several other sides.

In November 2003, after scoring in his final game against Wigan, Marlon signed for West Ham United. Most Forest supporters were somewhat bemused by the fact that he had gone to another Championship side for a seemingly inadequate fee of only £500,000. That feeling was enhanced when the striker returned with his new club four weeks later and scored for them after only seven minutes!

Over the course of the next three seasons, Marlon played his part to help the Hammers back into the top flight and then played in the 2006 FA Cup Final defeat of Liverpool, having scored the winner in the semi-final.

Now a top-class striker, Forest fans still wish 'Marvellous Marlon' well but regret the fact that he had to leave the City Ground to enhance his career.

Paul Hart

Date of birth: 4 May 1953, Golborne, Greater Manchester

Nottingham Forest record:
Appearances: League 70, FA Cup 3, League Cup 3, Others 11
Goals: League 1, FA Cup 1, Others 1
Debut: 27 August 1983 v Southampton (a) lost 0–1
Manager: July 2001–February 2004

Also played for: Stockport County, Blackpool, Leeds United, Sheffield Wednesday, Birmingham City, Notts County
Also managed: Chesterfield, Barnsley, Rushden & Diamonds

It was very much a case of semi-final frustration as far as Paul Hart's association with Nottingham Forest went. As a City Ground player he was a member of the team that reached the last four of the UEFA Cup in the 1983–84 season. As manager, 19 years later, his hopes of taking the club back into the Premiership were thwarted in the Play-offs.

Paul had served his footballing apprenticeship at Stockport County and played for both Blackpool and Leeds United before getting his chance to join the Reds. 'Leeds were in the Second Division at the time and I was coming up to 30 and keen to be playing in the top flight,' recalls Paul. 'I got a phone call from Eddie Gray, the Leeds boss, saying that Forest were interested and that their manager would like to meet me. I went down to the club and said, "Pleased to meet you, Mr Clough." He said, "You can call me Brian" – of course, I never did!'

Then followed the briefest of transfer negotiations. 'Cloughie just said, "If you think you are getting the money you are on here you are mistaken, but I'm not leaving this office until you sign for me." Of course, even though it meant a drop in wages, I was more than happy to sign!'

Paul settled in well at his new club and performed consistently as Forest continued to challenge both domestically and abroad. By March the Reds had progressed through to the quarter-finals of the UEFA Cup and were drawn against Sturm Graz, with the first leg due to be played at home. Paul remembers a huge disappointment for the club in the build-up to the game. 'On the Saturday before, we played at Wolves and would have gone top of the table if we'd won but we were terrible and I played my part, challenging Andy Gray and deflecting the ball in for the own-goal which decided the match.'

Redressing the balance would not have been a consideration for Paul, but he does recall the satisfaction of scoring against the Austrians. 'It was a header from an Ian Bowyer free-kick and it flew powerfully in from about 16 yards out.'

Overturning Graz put Forest through to a semi-final against Anderlecht and a 2–0 advantage from the home tie meant that the Reds travelled to Brussels in an optimistic mood ahead of the return. In subsequent years it later transpired that the match referee and various officials from the Belgian club had struck up a deal to ensure that the result was fixed.

'I think our manager had a suspicion on the night that something wasn't right, but as players we just got on with it. There were two decisions, though, that we knew the referee got wrong. Kenny Swain is alleged to have conceded a penalty but he wasn't within two yards of the guy when he went down and didn't touch him.'

Late in the match came a moment when Paul believed he had put his side into a European Final. 'My goal at the death was totally legitimate. There was no challenge on me, in fact there was no physical contact at all, but the ref disallowed it – presumably for pushing but nobody was sure because he wouldn't speak to us about it.' With a crooked official in charge, Forest were always going to be unsuccessful, but the disappointment of missing out on a place in the Final still rankles with Paul.

At the end of the following campaign, Paul left Forest to move to Hillsborough. 'The gaffer said at 32 I would only be used for around 18 games in the season that followed. I felt that I could contribute more and Wednesday were prepared to offer me that.'

Paul had already dipped his toes into the world of management (at Chesterfield) before being brought back to the City Ground in 1991. 'The phone rang at about 10.30 one night and it was Cloughie. He said, "If you're as good as I keep hearing and as I keep telling people then you'd better come and work for me," so I went back to Forest to help on the coaching side.'

After a successful period back at Leeds in charge of their academy, Paul returned to Forest for the third time as director of youth coaching. He did such a good job that he was promoted to manage the first team when David Platt left to take charge of the England Under-21 side in the summer of 2001.

'Harty' kept faith with many of the youngsters that he had helped to nurture through the junior ranks and was rewarded when his inexperienced side exceeded expectations with a place in the Play-offs. Unfortunately, they bowed out to Sheffield United at the semi-final stage. For cash-strapped Forest to be even in that position was almost entirely down to Paul. 'We did amazingly well to get to the Play-offs considering the financial limitations we were working under.'

Sadly, the same level of achievement deserted the club the following year and, after a spell of 14 games without victory, Paul was replaced as Forest boss in February 2004.

Terry Hennessey

Date of birth: 1 September 1942, Llay, Wrexham, Wales

Nottingham Forest record:
Appearances: League 159, FA Cup 12, League Cup 8, Others 4
Goals: League 5, FA Cup 1
Debut: 20 November 1965 v Blackpool (H) won 2–1

Also played for: Birmingham City, Derby County, Wales (39 caps)
Managed: Tamworth, Shepshed Charterhouse

Forest's captain in their 'oh-so-close' season was one of the most recognisable footballer's in the land, the prematurely-balding Terry Hennessey. A commanding presence, usually at centre-back although he ventured into midfield on rare occasions during his career, 'Tel' was an ever present during the 1966–67 campaign when the Reds fell just short of both the League title and an appearance in the Cup Final.

Terry had begun his career with Birmingham City and chalked up more than 200 first-team appearances for the St Andrews club between 1959 and 1965. He had collected a runners'-up medal as the Blues reached the Inter Cities Fairs Cup Final in 1961 and had shared in their League Cup triumph two years later. By the time he had joined Forest in November 1965 Terry had already won 16 Welsh caps, having made his debut against Northern Ireland three years earlier. He went on to skipper his country on many occasions and twice toured Brazil where he faced Pele, for what he later admitted was 'the high spot of my career'.

Playing alongside Bobby McKinlay, with whom he would enjoy a successful partnership over the next three and a half seasons, he made his debut at home to Blackpool in November 1965. Terry had cost the Reds a fee of £45,000 when Johnny Carey had signed him and it proved to be an astute piece of business by the Forest boss as Terry quickly settled into his new surroundings.

Goals would be something of a rarity during his career but Terry notched his first for the club in the return match against Blackpool in April 1966. That summer he was appointed club captain and his inspirational leadership qualities almost took Forest to their first-ever League title, finishing just behind champions Manchester United.

The FA Cup was seen as a more realistic opportunity to gain some silverware but the Garibaldis fell at the semi-final stage. Opponents Tottenham Hotspur had moved into a seemingly invincible two-goal advantage before Terry reignited fading Reds hopes by heading home a late corner, but time ran out before an equaliser could be salvaged.

Throughout the season Terry maintained an ever-present record in the number-four jersey and even accepted the responsibility of stepping forward to convert a couple of penalties in League matches against West Brom and Tottenham.

He was a commanding figure, well respected throughout the club and a good man to have at the helm when Forest endured one of the darkest days in their history. On 24 August 1968, during a home League match against Leeds United, the main stand caught fire. Thankfully, no one was badly injured but the entire structure was destroyed, along with the club's offices. Most of the memorabilia and records, collected over the years, also went up in smoke.

Notts County offered their facilities to their neighbours and Forest, led by Terry, played their next six home matches across the Trent. The fire had far-reaching effects, with the club's finances being stretched to the limit.

Under new manager Matt Gillies the club was struggling to stay afloat and many players were sold. Terry remained at the City Ground for another year as the restructuring continued around him, but his talents were not being ignored.

In February 1970 the then Derby County boss, Brian Clough, stepped in with an offer of £100,000 to take the Welsh international down the road to the Baseball Ground – the first time the Rams had paid that sum for anyone.

The following season Terry was restricted through injury to just 18 appearances as the First Division title was won and a combination of knee and Achilles tendon troubles eventually forced him to retire in 1973, aged just 31.

Terry later managed Tamworth and coached at Kimberley Town before moving to the States to coach Tulsa Roughnecks. A return to the East Midlands ensued with a two-year stint in charge of Shepshed Charterhouse before he went back to Tulsa and later on to Vancouver Whitecaps, where he worked as assistant manager to former Forest winger Alan Hinton.

His globetrotting spirit then took Terry and his family to Australia, where he settled and set up a soccer school in the Melbourne area, combined with duties as manager of a cling-film company.

Alex Higgins

Date of birth:	7 November 1863, Kilmarnock, East Ayrshire, Scotland
Died:	17 April 1920

Nottingham Forest record:

Appearances:	League 47, FA Cup 17
Goals:	League 18, FA Cup 10
Debut:	6 September 1890 v Bootle (a) won 5–1
Also played for:	Kilwinning, Irvine, Kilmarnock (all Scotland), Derby County, Scotland (1 cap)

The honour of scoring Nottingham Forest's first-ever goal in the Football League belongs to a Scotsman, Alexander 'Sandy' Higgins.

In an age when massive margins of victory were more commonplace than they are today, Sandy was a predator on the football field who loved to score his goals in multiples. On three occasions he netted four times in a match and he is still the only player to score five goals in a first-team fixture for Forest.

He joined the Reds from Derby County in the summer of 1890. A couple of years earlier he had played in the Rams' first-ever match in the Football League and he had been the club's top scorer in both of the two seasons he had played for them. His move to Forest meant joining a side still awaiting its entry into the Football League, but he certainly made his mark in the Football Alliance. In each of his first two games he scored goals on his way to hitting 19 in his debut season at the Town Ground club, as Forest were known then. Twice he netted four in a game – his rich harvests coming away against Darwen when he scored all of Forest's contributions in a 4–4 draw and, at Crewe, in a 7–0 mauling.

His best endeavours were saved for the FA Cup, though. On 17 January 1891, in a first-round match at Clapton Orient, Alex claimed five in a 14–0 victory, a scoreline which is likely to remain forever as the club's record win in the competition. Although his feat tends to be overlooked, teammate Tinsley Lindley scored four goals in the same match!

It was clear that Sandy had taken a liking to the FA Cup and that was emphasised when he scored five more in the next round – although the goals were spread between three in the drawn replay with Sunderland Albion and two more in the second replay which Forest won.

So prolific was Sandy that his goals played a major role as Forest won the Alliance in the 1891–92 season – his second with the club – the first major piece of silverware they had won. His two-season tally for the Reds was an amazing 46 goals from 38 Alliance matches and for the third time he scored four in a match during the 4–1 win at Lincoln City in February 1892.

As champions of the Alliance, Forest's bid to join the Football League was accepted and on 3 September 1892 they played their first match away at Everton and gained a creditable 2–2 draw, with Sandy scoring the club's opening goal at this level. He was to finish with a dozen League goals as the Garibaldis finished 10th out of the 16-club First Division.

Goals were much harder to come by at this level and Sandy only hit a total of five in the following season, including another in the FA Cup. In the four seasons he had played in the competition, the striker netted 18 FA Cup goals from just 17 appearances – only Sam Widdowson, who scored 19 in 23 matches between 1869 and 1887, has scored more for Forest.

Sandy was approaching his mid-30s when he decided to retire from football at the end of the 1893–94 season and return to Scotland.

Prior to venturing south of the border Sandy had played his football for Kilmarnock, one of the leading Scottish clubs of the age. His prowess in font of goal drew admiration from his national selectors, but he must be acknowledged as one of the unluckiest international players of all time. He only appeared once for Scotland – against Ireland in 1885 in Glasgow – and netted four goals in an 8–2 thrashing. Somewhat bizarrely, he was never selected again!

Higgins's son, also christened Alexander and known as Sandy, made 35 appearances for Forest after World War One. Prior to his arrival in Nottingham he had also played for Kilmarnock and was given a Scottish Cup-winners' medal by them despite having to pull out of the match due to the death of his father.

Peter Hindley

Date of birth: 19 May 1944, Worksop, Nottinghamshire

Nottingham Forest record:
Appearances: League 366, FA Cup 30, League Cup 14, Others 6
Goals: League 10, FA Cup 1
Debut: 6 March 1963 v West Bromwich Albion (a) drew 0–0

Also played for: Coventry City, Peterborough United

Peter Hindley was a solid, no-nonsense right-back and played over 400 times for the Nottingham Forest first team. He was also an ever present in the 1966–67 side who, under manager Johnny Carey, came so close to the League and Cup double.

As a young centre-forward, Peter had played for the Reds junior sides since 1959 and turned professional a couple of years later, just after his 17th birthday. He made his first couple of Forest appearances in the number-nine jersey, beginning with a fourth-round FA Cup tie at West Bromwich Albion. Manager Andy Beattie then tried him out at half-back before he eventually ended up in the number-two berth, sharing a full-back partnership with John Winfield that lasted more than a decade.

In representing the City Ground club Peter was emulating the achievements of his father, Frank – a centre-forward who made eight appearances for Forest in the 1938–39 season.

The 1964–65 season was an important one for Peter, now playing his football under new boss Carey: not only did he begin to make an impression with 29 First Division appearances but he also scored his first two goals for the club, his initial strike coming in a 3–2 home win over West Ham United on 19 December.

The year 1965 was an exciting time to be a young Forest player, with the club's centenary celebrations centred on an end-of-season tour and a special match to mark the occasion. In early May, Peter picked up a County Cup-winners' medal after Mansfield Town had been defeated 5–0 in the Final, and then he departed, along with the rest of the playing staff and officials, on a tiring but enjoyable five-week tour of the US and Canada. Eleven matches were played – nine of them won. The visit of Valencia, to help celebrate the centenary, provided a welcome distraction for a Forest side who spent the whole of the 1965–66 campaign hovering above the drop zone.

Tall and broad shouldered, Peter was affectionately nicknamed 'Tank' by the fans – a fitting reference to his near indestructibility as well as his powerful appearance. Having developed into a strong-tackling First Division defender, he received acknowledgement that his career was heading on the right tracks with a call-up to the England Under-23 side.

Forest's team-building had stabilised, particularly in defence, where Peter was part of a seldom-changed first-choice back four of himself, Terry Hennessey, Bobby McKinlay and John Winfield – all playing in front of 'keeper Peter Grummitt. If fans sought to wonder why the Reds' fortunes suddenly turned round, they only need absorb the fact that four of that unit played in every single match during the 1966–67 season – with Winfield missing only two through a slight injury.

Forest chased Manchester United to the wire in the League before having to settle for a runners'-up position, and in the FA Cup it was Spurs at the semi-final stage who halted their progress.

During the Cup run Peter scored the only FA Cup goal of his Forest career, getting up from the back to score a vital goal in the fifth-round replay at Swindon Town. The following year he played in all four of Forest's UEFA Cup matches and in 1970–71 he participated in the club's only two matches in the short-lived Texaco Cup competition. Playing against Scotland's Airdrieonians, the Reds drew both games 2–2, eventually bowing out, away from home, on a penalty shoot-out.

Again, that season Tank featured in every League match as his appearance tally approached the 300 mark. It was surpassed during the following campaign but, for the first time in his career, the right-back had to get used to life outside the top flight as Forest dropped into the old Second Division. Liam O'Kane's emergence into the first-team ranks began to limit Peter's opportunities and he played his final game for the Reds on 12 January 1974 against West Brom, the side he had debuted against 11 years earlier. Shortly afterwards he moved to Coventry City and later to Peterborough United.

Recognising his magnificent service to the club, Peter was given a testimonial match by the Forest board on 29 October 1974, with his Coventry City side providing the opposition.

Reds supporters who watched him play over the years would bear testimony that Tank gave his all for the club and only nine other players have made more than his 366 League appearances for Forest.

Steve Hodge

Date of birth: 25 October 1962, Nottingham

Nottingham Forest record:
Appearances: League 209, FA Cup 19, League Cup 32, Others 19
Goals: League 50, FA Cup 2, League Cup 8, Others 6
Debut: 15 May 1982 v Ipswich Town (a) won 3–1

Also played for: Aston Villa, Tottenham Hotspur, Leeds United, Derby County, Queen's Park Rangers, Watford, Leyton Orient, England (24 caps)

In two spells with Nottingham Forest, hard-working midfielder Steve Hodge became one of the most popular players at the City Ground. The local lad had graduated through the club's junior ranks to make a first-team debut on the final day of the 1981–82 season. When he left the City Ground for the second time nine years later, he was able to proudly reflect on the part he had played in a successful period in the Reds' history.

The energetic youngster staked his claim for a permanent berth at the start of the 1982–83 campaign and did not have to wait long to get his name on the score sheet. 'My first two goals for the club came at Anfield,' he reveals. 'It was only my fourth League start and I scored twice past Bruce Grobbelaar at the Kop End. It was a sort of "wonderland" situation as we led 3–2 at the break but typical Liverpool – they came back to win with an Ian Rush goal in the last minute!'

Forest finished fifth that season, earning them a spot in the UEFA Cup competition the year after. In what was dubbed the 'Battle Of Britain', the Reds were paired with Glasgow Celtic in the third round and could only manage a goalless draw beside the Trent. The build-up to the return leg was typical 'Cloughie'. 'We didn't train for three days before the match and then on the eve of the game the manager insisted that we had a couple of drinks to help us relax. Our away form was good and I was pretty confident about getting a good result, although a bit wary about their partisan crowd of around 70,000 people!'

Steve's confidence was justified, and it was his goal that set Forest on the way to victory. 'The goal came after about 65 minutes and once it went in things were a lot easier for us. Steve Wigley played the ball in, Dav [Peter Davenport] touched it back and I hit it past Paddy Bonner in the Celtic goal. I remember a feeling of both ecstasy and relief.'

Forest's progression in the competition was eventually halted in farcical circumstances against Anderlecht at the semi-final stage, spoiling a situation set up by 'Harry', as the fans liked to call him. 'The first leg at home was the biggest match most of us had played in and we were desperate to take a lead to Belgium for the return,' he recalls. 'I scored with about six minutes to go and then right at the end I got another, a diving header at the Trent End. It still remains one of my favourite goals and I thought it would have been enough to take us through.'

Following disappointment at the match-fixing events which cheated Forest out of a Final place, Steve went off to join the England Under-21 side and helped them to European Championship success, further pressing his own claims for higher recognition. That eventually came after Steve had left Forest to join Aston Villa in August 1985 and just over a year later he was transferred to Spurs, with whom he made a Cup Final appearance in 1987.

His return to Forest coincided with the start of the 1988–89 season, one of the most dramatic in the club's history. Steve played in the League Cup Final win over Luton Town and the Simod Cup success against Everton. He was also a member of the Forest side that stepped out at Hillsborough in the FA Cup semi-final against Liverpool. Steve admits that the Forest players did not actually see too much of what was going on. 'I knew things weren't right and thought there'd been a pitch invasion or something but then they quickly got us off and made us stay in the dressing room.'

The following season his bursts from the centre of the park culminated in him being the club's top scorer, with 14 goals. In addition, there was another League Cup triumph after Oldham Athletic had been beaten at Wembley.

There was yet another trip to the national stadium in May 1991 when the Reds progressed to the FA Cup Final, where they were beaten by Tottenham. Steve had to be content with a place on the bench. 'It was frustrating not to start and I had plenty of emotions that day with a Cup Final against my old team. I managed to get on after about an hour and it turned out to be my last appearance for Forest.'

He moved to Leeds and was part of the squad to lift the League title in 1992. During his successful playing career he mustered a significant number of trophies, medals and other artefacts to enjoy in his own privacy, but one item of memorabilia is now on view for the general public.

At the end of the 1986 World Cup quarter-final between England and Argentina – the infamous 'Hand of God' game – it was Steve who had the good fortune to exchange shirts with Diego Maradona and he has now donated it to the National Football Museum on a long-term lease. 'Who knows – one day I might get it back and sell it!'

Pierre van Hooijdonk

Date of birth: 29 November 1969, Steenbergen, Netherlands

Nottingham Forest record:
Appearances: League 71, FA Cup 1, League Cup 5
Goals: League 36, FA Cup 1, League Cup 4
Debut: 11 March 1997 v Blackburn Rovers (a) drew 1–1

Also played for: RBC Roosendaal (Netherlands), NAC Breda (Netherlands), Glasgow Celtic (Scotland), Vitesse Arnhem (Netherlands), Benfica (Portugal), Feyenoord (Netherlands), Fenerbahce (Turkey), Netherlands (40 caps)

The inclusion of Pierre van Hooijdonk among a tribute to Nottingham Forest legends will cause as much debate and fury as the actions of the Dutch striker at the start of the 1998–99 season. Then, unthinkably, Pierre committed a cardinal sin among professional sportsmen – he went on strike! Not angry at a breach of contract or his working conditions, Pierre had taken umbrage at the apparent lack of ambition by the Forest board. After playing a leading role in getting them promoted to the Premiership, he believed they had reneged on a promise to him to strengthen the squad sufficiently to be a force within the English game.

Petrus 'Pierre' Ferdinandus Johannes van Hooijdonk – to give him his full name – made his Forest debut towards the end of the 1996–97 season. The club, in turmoil and spiralling towards the First Division, had signed him from Celtic for £4.5 million. They hoped their latest acquisition would do what he had done throughout his career, score goals – and enough of them to keep the club in the top flight. As it happened, Pierre played in the final eight matches of the season but only scored once – at home to Leeds United – and the Reds humbly finished bottom of the table.

If history were to allow Pierre to emerge with any credit from his Forest days it would have to be for his attitude in stating that he wanted to remain at Nottingham and help the club to achieve promotion at the first time of asking. Justifying his reputation as an international class striker, the Dutchman netted 34 goals for Forest that season – 29 of them in the League. Under Dave Bassett's stewardship, the Reds won the title by three points to make the immediate return that Pierre had promised.

Among his goal collection were hat-tricks against Queens Park Rangers and Charlton Athletic, both at the City Ground. The power of his shooting was Pierre's most valuable commodity; he could hit the ball with such venom from either open play or from free-kicks that it did not usually matter whether he had put any swerve on it or not. Unsurprisingly for such a big man – he was 6ft 5in tall – he was an almighty handful in the air as well and few defenders were capable of keeping him quiet in the English First Division.

'Huggy', as he was nicknamed by the fans, spent the 1998 close season in Japan and South Korea as a member of the Netherlands' World Cup squad, content that Forest were constructing a squad capable of challenging with the best. Reality was very different, however – Forest had sold Kevin Campbell, who had scored 23 times playing alongside the Dutchman, and done little in the way of recruiting.

Pierre was furious and demanded a transfer. When he was told he had to stay and fulfil his contract he sulkily flew back to the Netherlands to train at NAC Breda, one of his former clubs. The impasse continued for several weeks and clearly had an unsettling effect on the side. Forest refused to listen to offers for their man and so, eventually, with a great deal of abuse being hurled upon him from every quarter, Pierre returned to Nottingham.

Any doubts as to what the dressing-room harmony might be like was removed when Pierre scored against Derby County in his third match back and none of his teammates went across to celebrate with him. Under such circumstances another relegation was inevitable, and Huggy got his wish and was allowed to move.

Since leaving the Reds he has continued to earn himself a reputation as a quality goalscorer, with frequent moves around the continent, although it was back home in Rotterdam where he enjoyed most success. So enamoured were they with their goal machine, a group of Feyenoord supporters released a single in tribute to the man they called 'Pi-Air'. Entitled *Put Your Hands Up For Pi-Air*, it made the Dutch charts in 2002.

You could understand their delight at his performances. That year he was named Dutch Footballer of the Year after topping the national scoring charts and hitting two goals in the club's 3–2 win over Borussia Dortmund in the UEFA Cup Final.

Lethal anywhere within shooting range, Pierre scored 52 goals from just 61 outings in his first stint with the club but then left to spend two years with Fenerbahce in Turkey, which brought more goals and two League Championships. He returned to Feyenoord in January 2006 and has vowed to wind down his playing career at the end of the 2006–07 season.

Fans all over Europe will be divisive on how good a striker Pierre was. At his best he could score from anywhere. He maintained a healthy strike ratio throughout his career and continued to get goals in every country he played in.

Sadly, though, it will not be his goals that are uppermost in the minds of most Forest fans when they remember Pierre van Hooijdonk!

Stewart Imlach

Date of birth:	6 January 1932, Lossiemouth, Moray, Scotland
Died:	October 2001

Nottingham Forest record:

Appearances:	League 184, FA Cup 19, Others 1
Goals:	League 43, FA Cup 5
Debut:	20 August 1955 v Liverpool (h) lost 1–3
Also played for:	Lossiemouth, Bury, Derby County, Luton Town, Coventry City, Crystal Palace, Chelmsford City, Scotland (4 caps)

On the day following the 1959 FA Cup Final, most newspaper reports concluded that the undoubted Man of the Match was Forest's left-winger Stewart Imlach. The Scottish international put in a tireless performance, raising the standards of energy and commitment on Wembley's biggest day of the year.

Stewart had arrived at the City Ground after signing from Derby County. Earlier, he had been introduced into English football by Bury, who had paid Lossiemouth, his local Highland League side, the princely sum of £150 for his signature.

Forest were in the old Second Division by the time Stewart had joined them in 1955 and any semblance of success was long overdue for the club. Short in stature – various accounts list him as being no more than 5ft 6in tall at most – Stewart was nevertheless blessed with astonishing pace and a relaxed, natural dribbling style. He had limitless levels of energy and quickly endeared himself to the City Ground faithful.

He scored five times during his opening campaign with the Reds but increased his output to a dozen in the 1956–57 season, one which ended in promotion via a runners'-up place in the League. Apart from his outstanding wing-play, Stewart became almost prolific in front of goal and even had a burst of eight in eight in games played between December 1956 and February 1957.

Back in the top division Forest were keen to make an impression and became a delight to watch, with their crisp passing game and entertaining brand of football. A 7–1 thrashing of Burnley took Forest top of the table by mid-September. Stewart scored two of the goals and was on target again in a 4–3 win at Tottenham, the club's 1,000th Division One goal.

Over 47,000 saw the home match against champions Manchester United on 12 October 1957, a City Ground record, with Stewart scoring the Reds' consolation in a narrow 2–1 defeat against the reigning champions. His performance that day so impressed the visiting manager, Matt Busby, that he was taken to recommend the winger to the Scottish selectors. Unfortunately, Busby was absent – recovering in hospital – when the two sides next met on 22 February 1958. Forest were the first side to visit Old Trafford after the Munich disaster and

'Stewie' again scored against them – the first League goal against United since the crash.

His international debut duly followed against Hungary at Hampden Park, meaning that Stewart had become the first Forest player to represent Scotland. He impressed, played against Poland in another friendly and was taken to Sweden for the World Cup Finals, where he played twice more, against Yugoslavia and France.

The 1958–59 season culminated in success for Forest in front of 100,000 fans at Wembley Stadium. Stew had a hand in both of Forest's goals, cutting the ball back for Roy Dwight to open the scoring and then feeding Billy Gray to supply the cross for Tommy Wilson's header. Important as his assists were, it was his unprecedented display of stamina that took the eye. At a numerical disadvantage, Forest were chasing shadows for most of the second half and none chased harder than Stewart. He was everywhere – seven years later Alan Ball received similar acclaim for his role in the World Cup Final.

As he pocketed his winners' medal Stewie could not have envisaged how quickly the winning line up would be disbanded. Just 12 months after helping defeat Luton at Wembley he was on his way south to sign for the Hatters. He then played for both Coventry City and Crystal Palace, as well as for non-League Chelmsford City, before curtailing his playing career having turned out 423 times for his six League clubs.

Later Stewart returned to Nottingham to serve as assistant manager at Notts County before moving to the North West, where he joined Everton's coaching staff under Harry Catterick. He had left the game and was enjoying his retirement on the golf courses when he was taken ill and sadly died in October 2001, aged just 69.

His son Gary, a television sports presenter, told the story of his father's life in his excellent book *My Father and Other Working-Class Football Heroes*. Winner of the Sports Book of the Year Award in 2005, this heart-warming dedication is recommended reading for all football supporters but will particularly appeal to fans of the Forest Cup-winning side.

Nigel Jemson

Date of birth: 10 August 1969, Hutton, Lancashire

Nottingham Forest record:
Appearances: League 47, FA Cup 4, League Cup 9, Others 1
Goals: League 13, FA Cup 3, League Cup 4
Debut: 26 December 1989 v Luton Town (a) drew 1–1

Also played for: Preston North End, Bolton Wanderers, Sheffield Wednesday, Grimsby Town, Notts County, Watford, Coventry City, Rotherham United, Oxford United, Bury, Ayr United, Shrewsbury Town, Ilkeston Town
Managed: Ilkeston Town

Whatever the team, whatever the occasion, to score a winning goal in a Wembley Cup Final is a special moment for any player and Nigel Jemson did the business for Forest in 1990. The League Cup competition has proved to be particularly kind to the Reds and when they lined up to face Oldham Athletic they were bidding to win it for the fourth time as well as retain the Cup, having won it 12 months earlier.

Brian Clough's side were the overwhelming favourites as the opposition were from the old Second Division. Nevertheless, it was not until the early stages of the second half that Forest made the breakthrough, with 'Jemmo' getting the all-important winner.

'The goal was unusual for Forest as it was pretty much route one stuff,' he recalls. 'Steve Sutton took a goal-kick downfield and I flicked it on to Nigel [Clough]. He controlled it and chested it down. I'd continued to follow the movement of the ball and he reverse-passed it back to me. I took it on with only the 'keeper [Andy Rhodes] to beat. I tried to bend it around him and, although he saved the initial effort, I was able to tuck home the rebound.' It proved to be a decisive moment in the contest and sweet reward for Nigel, who had joined the club from his home-town team Preston in March 1988 and shown himself to be a hard-working forward with a decent eye for goal.

In December 1990 Nigel was selected for the England Under-21 side, for the only time, lining up against Wales at Tranmere's Prenton Park.

Apart from his Wembley winner, the other big standout day in Nigel's Forest career was in a home FA Cup match against Southampton, when he registered a hat-trick. 'Everything just went right that day,' he remembers. 'I think Nigel [Clough] was on penalties but when we won one after about 10 minutes I just got the ball and said "I'll have it." There were a few surprised faces and I quickly realised the consequences if I missed, but fortunately I didn't and scored twice more. I think Stuart Pearce set me up for the third which I hit left-footed into the top corner.'

That result took Forest a step closer to another Wembley Final but, ultimately, it was to bring disappointment for Nigel.

'I was given a few days off after a first-team match and told to come back on the Wednesday and to have a run-out for an hour in a reserve-team game. I did – and got injured, ruling me out of the semi-final. I'd recovered by the time of the Final and was expecting to be involved but it was left to Stuart Pearce [the captain] to tell me I wasn't. No one can argue with Brian Clough's success – he had his ways and you had to stand by his decisions, but that was probably the worst moment of my career. The club signed Teddy Sheringham in the summer and I thought it was time to leave but for a while I played alongside him and Nigel, but then Sheffield Wednesday came in with a bid for me and I was allowed to leave.'

Nigel shares a philosophy with plenty of other good strikers when it comes to goalscoring. 'Every goal is a good goal – it doesn't matter where they go in from!' When pressed, though, he does recall one particular favourite from his Forest days. 'I scored a good goal at White Hart Lane against Tottenham when I practically ran half the length of the pitch before firing it into the roof of the net – that was definitely one of my better ones!'

The much-travelled striker continued to ply his trade for many years after leaving the City Ground and even has another Wembley experience to reminisce over. 'I scored for Rotherham in the Auto Windscreens Shield Final in 1996 – so I've got two in two there!'

Nigel's appetite for the game has taken him into management, where he continues to learn the trade at non-League Ilkeston Town. He still follows the fortunes of his former club, though. 'The best part of my career was spent at the City Ground,' he admits. 'Apart from the joy of scoring at Wembley that day, it was at the end where all the Forest fans were and that made it even more special!'

David Johnson

Date of birth: 15 August 1976, Kingston, Jamaica

Nottingham Forest record:
Appearances: League 148, FA Cup 5, League Cup 10, Others 2
Goals: League 46, League Cup 2, Others 2
Debut: 14 January 2001 v Crystal Palace (h) lost 0–3

Also played for: Manchester United, Bury, Ipswich Town, Sheffield Wednesday (loan), Burnley (loan), Sheffield United (loan), Hucknall Town, Jamaica (4 caps)

David Johnson cost Nottingham Forest £3 million when David Platt signed him from Ipswich Town in January 2001. A prolific striker throughout his career, he was seen as the man to fire the Reds back into the big time and he nearly succeeded – albeit a couple of years later!

'My first six months at Forest were something of a nightmare,' admits David. 'The team weren't functioning and I don't think the fans rated the manager too much but they were brilliant towards me. They kept saying, "Give him time – he'll get goals." It was a fairly tough time for me personally but once my family and I began to settle in Nottingham I really enjoyed being there.'

Forest's problems were not confined to the playing side and in an attempt to get 'Johnno' off the wage bill he was sent out on a couple of loan spells during the 2001–02 season. 'I'd had a bit of a fall-out with Paul Hart before I'd gone on loan. I always wanted to come back and he said he'd give everyone a fresh start so I got my head down, scored goals and hoped the fans would accept me back – again they were fantastic towards me! There comes a point when you fall in love with a club and realise this is the place where you want to be. It happened to me at Forest around that time.'

Johnno's return coincided with Marlon Harewood finding some decent form in front of goal. 'People talk about my friendship with Marlon. The truth is we just wanted to out-score each other. I played my game, he played his and if we could move defenders around it would usually create space for the other one.'

David has pleasant memories of 21 September 2002 – the day he scored all the goals in a 3–0 win at Grimsby. 'Marlon had scored a hat-trick against Gillingham in the previous match and he was absolutely buzzing – really full of it! I then did the same against Grimsby and everybody made a big point of congratulating me – to wind him up I think. My only concern was the matchball – I had to grab it and shove it quickly in my kitbag!'

The hat-trick was the start of a goalscoring sequence that brought David 10 goals in just six matches. His tally by the end of the campaign was 29 – comfortably the highest in the country –

although two of the goals came in a losing cause in the Play-offs against Sheffield United.

'In the Play-offs I don't think enough of our big players put in a big enough performance. I was so disappointed because we should have beaten them – we were a better team than they were. At half-time at Bramall Lane our dressing room was really buzzing – we thought we were through. "Get our suits ready for the Final" and all that stuff. Paul Hart really had to calm some players down and then it all went wrong inside 15 minutes of the second half.'

David suffered more misery against Sheffield United four months later, breaking his left leg and missing six months of the season. Some critics felt that he never really recovered the blistering pace he possessed before the injury. 'Looking back they were probably right,' he reflects. There was time, though, for a little personal touch that meant so much to Johnno.

'I think it was the proudest moment of my career when Joe Kinnear arrived and appointed me club captain. I'd been the club's Player of the Year and been top goalscorer, but to captain Forest topped everything.'

A succession of injuries finally forced David to call time on his League career, but he still fondly recalls a couple of his Forest goals. 'Playing against Ipswich at home I managed to beat Paul Gerrard from about 25 yards – I wouldn't normally shoot from that distance in training.'

His other favourite conjures up an amusing image. 'We were playing Wimbledon at Selhurst and were 2–0 up. I missed a couple of sitters and they got back to 2–2. Four minutes into stoppage time I scored with an overhead kick to win it. Some fans came on to celebrate – in my exuberance I rugby tackled one of them. He had a brand new cream jacket on which was practically ruined after I'd dumped him in the mud!'

David reveals that he would have liked to have created a little bit of history at Forest. 'I was quite prepared to stay there for the rest of my career and would have loved to have ended up as the club's all-time top goalscorer. To have been remembered as one of the club's real legends was something I often thought about.'

Roy Keane

Date of birth: 10 August 1971, Cork, Republic of Ireland

Nottingham Forest record:
Appearances: League 114, FA Cup 18, League Cup 17, Others 5
Goals: League 22, FA Cup 3, League Cup 6, Others 2
Debut: 28 August 1990 v Liverpool (a) lost 0–2

Also played for: Cobh Ramblers, Manchester United, Glasgow Celtic (Scotland),
Republic of Ireland (67 caps)
Managed: Sunderland

Roy Keane learned his trade well at Nottingham Forest and went on to become one of the all-time great midfielders. Signed by Brian Clough from Irish League side Cobh Ramblers in the summer of 1990, he ended his first season in English football by appearing in the FA Cup Final. In an all-too-brief three-year stay at the City Ground, the Irishman demonstrated a commitment and will to win which would become his trademark in future years. To become a driving force in the centre of the park, you need to be a battler – and Roy showed that he had few equals in the professional game.

In his book *Keane: The Autobiography*, Roy recalls how he had travelled up to Anfield early in his Forest career, believing he had gone solely to help the kit man before a League match against Liverpool. When his manager observed him and asked him what he was doing, Roy explained that he was helping to put the kit out. Cloughie then told him to 'Get hold of a number-seven shirt. You're playing!'

From that impressive day onwards, it was clear that Forest had captured a raw diamond, a player who would give his all for the cause – a quality that impresses supporters better than any other. With energy to burn – and the vision to spot a half chance – it became a common occurrence to see Roy arrive late into the box to finish off a typical Forest build up.

His first goal for the club came in a 4–1 League Cup win over Burnley at the City Ground in September 1990, and he registered eight in the League – a total that would have been impressive enough for a young striker in his first season, let alone a midfield player. With an FA Cup run advancing nicely, Roy became even more vital to the side's cause. He scored the sixth-round winner away at Norwich City and added another in the semi-final win over West Ham United.

Defeat to Spurs in the Final provided a crushing anti-climax to Roy's first season in the game, but he did not have too long to dwell on the setback as he was called up for his Republic of Ireland debut shortly afterwards.

There were two further occasions when Roy had the opportunity to sample the Wembley atmosphere as a Forest player, both of which came in 1992. Although the Reds beat Southampton by three goals to two in the Zenith Data Systems Cup Final, they succumbed to a solitary Manchester United goal in the League Cup Final – by far the more prestigious of the two competitions.

The 1992–93 season turned out to be the bleakest in recent history for Forest supporters. Not only did Clough decide to draw the curtains on his illustrious managerial career, but also the club lost the top-flight status they had cherished for 16 years. Despite languishing towards the bottom of the table all season, no one could question Roy's commitment to the cause. He never gave anything less than 100 percent and worked tirelessly to try and revive the club's fortunes.

Forest picked up £3.75 million from Manchester United when Roy signed for them in the summer of 1993. It was decent business for both clubs as Forest were never going to be able to hang on to one of their prize assets in the lower League, and United gained a player who would help them to dominate the domestic game for more than a decade.

Suspension cruelly robbed Roy of a place in the Champions League Final in 1999, but his five-star performance in the semi-final win over Juventus fully entitled him to his medal – adding to the raft of League and Cup successes he won at Old Trafford.

Roy became an outstanding captain of both club and country – he embodied the very definition of the word 'winner'. He amassed 67 Republic of Ireland caps in all, although it would certainly have been more but for injury and for the controversial manner of his departure from the 2002 World Cup Finals in Japan and South Korea after a very public fall-out with coach Mick McCarthy.

His triumphant playing career wound down in 2006 with a brief but successful stint playing in the green and white hoops of Celtic, whom he helped to secure the League title and win the Scottish League Cup.

During the early part of the 2006–07 season Roy embarked on his first steps in management when he took over the reins at Sunderland. Serving under two of the game's most successful and unpredictable man-managers will have given him the greatest possible insight to what may lie ahead. Many onlookers believe that, one day, Roy will become the manager at one of his former clubs – is it too inconceivable to believe that he might return to Forest?

Brian Laws

Date of birth: 14 October 1961, Wallsend, Tyne and Wear

Nottingham Forest record:
Appearances: League 147, FA Cup 18, League Cup 32, Others 12
Goals: League 4, FA Cup 1
Debut: 8 October 1988 v Queen's Park Rangers (a) won 2–1

Also played for: Burnley, Huddersfield Town, Middlesbrough, Grimsby Town
Managed: Grimsby Town, Scunthorpe United, Sheffield Wednesday

Forest have been blessed with some decent right-backs over the years and picked up one of their most consistent performers when Brian Clough raided his old side, Middlesbrough, in the summer of 1988. Brian Laws had gained valuable League experience at Burnley, as well as on Teesside, before agreeing to move to Nottingham, but his transfer was not totally straightforward. 'I wasn't offered the terms I'd been hoping for at Middlesbrough and decided it was time to move on. I was told of Forest's interest and went down to meet the manager.'

Brian recalls that first interview with his soon-to-be boss. 'He asked me if I was a good player or a bad player! I replied that he must have formed his own opinion when he'd watched me. Cloughie said he'd never seen me but was acting on the say-so of Ron Fenton, his assistant. I said, "In that case, I'm a good player!" It was rare of anyone to get the last word over Mr Clough and the reply was typical. "Time will tell," said Clough. "If you do turn out to be a good 'un then I signed you, if you don't then Ron Fenton's to blame!"'

Brian had to wait three months before his debut but then grasped the number-two jersey and hung on to it for most of the remaining matches of a never-to-be-forgotten season. Forest finished third in the League that season but the achievement pales into insignificance compared to two matches inside six days in April 1989. First came the excitement of a League Cup win over Luton Town. 'For several years Wembley became our second home,' recalls Brian. 'But the best experience for me will always be the first time I played there, in the win over Luton.'

With Cup success still very fresh in the memory, Forest headed off to Hillsborough for the ill-fated FA Cup semi-final against Liverpool. 'I remember it as though it were yesterday,' says the defender. 'Things happen in football but they don't matter – this was such a tragedy, a real disaster. I remember it so clearly and I guess I'll never forget

the dreadful scenes of that day.' Although Forest eventually lost the semi-final when it was replayed, Brian did end the season back at Wembley when the Reds saw off Everton to win the Simod Cup Final.

Strong in the tackle and with enough pace and purpose to get forward in support, he became a hugely popular and influential member of the side. His second season at the club brought another League Cup-winners' medal, with Oldham Athletic beaten under the Twin Towers. The campaign was also memorable for the pick of Brian's handful of goals for the club. 'It was at home against Coventry City and I blasted a 25-yarder past Steve Ogrizovic at the Bridgford Road End.'

Towards the end of the 1990–91 season Forest progressed to their first FA Cup Final since 1959. Hopes were high that Cloughie could claim the one trophy that had eluded him throughout his career, but if the defeat was disappointing for the manager it was also a bitter pill for Brian, who was omitted from the starting line up in favour of Gary Charles. 'I was upset to be left out and also by the way I was told. The manager had written the team on a scrumpled piece of paper and given it to Stuart Pearce [the captain] to read out.'

Although Brian did get on later, replacing Lee Glover, the manner of his non-selection meant that the highlight of the day occurred before kick-off. 'The teams were introduced to Princess Diana before the start and I have a photograph on my office wall of the moment we shook hands.'

Brian left Forest in December 1994 to take up a player-manager position at Grimsby Town. His six years at the City Ground had been highly eventful, culminating in relegation from the top flight and the swift turnaround under new boss Frank Clark. 'I thoroughly enjoyed my time at Nottingham,' he admits. 'In many ways they were the best years of my life. The fans were great with me and I'd love to see the club become successful again soon.'

Harry Linacre

Date of birth: 1881, Aston-upon-Trent, Derbyshire
Died: 11 May 1957

Nottingham Forest record:
Appearances: League 308, FA Cup 27
Debut: 4 November 1899 v Bury (a) drew 2–2

Also played for: Aston-upon-Trent, Draycott Mills, Derby County, England
(2 caps)

Harry Linacre was the custodian of the Forest goal for the first nine years of the 20th century – playing in more than 300 League matches for the club as well as being selected to represent England. The young Harry played his early football for Loughborough Grammar School before turning out for local non-League sides Aston-upon-Trent and Draycott Mills. In 1898 he made a couple of League appearances for Derby County, standing in as cover, but the following summer he signed for Nottingham Forest on the recommendation of two of his uncles who played for the club, Frank and Fred Forman.

His association with the Garibaldis was to span the next decade, beginning with a League debut against Bury in November 1899. For much of that season Harry had to play second fiddle behind the ageing first choice Dennis Allsop, but then he took over the 'keepers jersey on a permanent basis at the start of the following campaign. Forest achieved a fourth-place finish at the end of the 1900–01 season, their highest position to that point, and Harry was an ever present, conceding just 36 goals in his 34 appearances.

At 6ft tall, he was an imposing presence in the Reds' goal and was one of the most agile 'keepers of his era. Rarely seen without his flat cap, he became a firm favourite with the Forest supporters. He saved a vital penalty-kick in an FA Cup quarter-final win over Stoke City in 1902 but illness forced him to miss the semi-final, which the Reds lost to Southampton.

Maintaining form and fitness over the next three seasons brought Harry into the international reckoning, and he was finally rewarded with two England appearances and selection for a Football League XI. His international caps came in a 3–1 victory over the Welsh at Anfield Road, Liverpool, on 27 March 1905 and a 1–0 win against Scotland, five days later, at Crystal Palace. Shortly afterwards Harry joined up with his Forest teammates for a voyage to South America. An invitation from the Argentinian FA had met with a positive response from the forward-thinking Forest board and the players and officials set sail aboard the *Danube* for a three-week journey.

One match was played against Penarol in Montevideo, Uruguay, seven more were played on Argentinian soil and all were won, with Forest outscoring their opponents by 57 goals to four. However successful the trip might have been as far as a public relations exercise, it was draining for the players and their tiredness was a contributory factor in a poor start to the League campaign. They never really recovered but went into their final fixture still hoping for the win that would keep them up.

A 4–1 defeat at Everton meant they finished below Middlesbrough on goal average and had to accept their first relegation as a consequence. Life in Division Two was much easier, though, particularly at home. After drawing their opening fixture, they won their next nine at the City Ground, a feat that would remain unequalled until the 1953–54 season.

In the autumn, the Garibaldi Reds put together a run of seven consecutive wins to go top and they closed out the campaign by going 17 matches unbeaten to win the title by three points from Chelsea, with Leicester City 12 points adrift.

Harry's medal was well deserved – he played in 32 of the matches and kept 12 clean sheets. Back in the top flight, he kept another clean sheet on 21 September 1907 as the Reds defeated Chelsea 6–0 at the City Ground – the first occasion that the London club had conceded six goals in League football.

On 10 April 1909 Harry had a benefit match in his honour, with 10,000 people attending a 1–1 draw against Bristol City. A couple of days later he played his final League game versus Bury – the side he had made his Forest debut against. This time the Lancashire club spoiled the occasion with a 2–0 victory.

Harry's importance to the side was highlighted when the Reds were relegated yet again, a year after his retirement. Almost 100 years after his final game for Forest, Harry Linacre's tally of 308 is still sufficient for him to be listed among the club's top 20 League appearance makers.

Tinsley Lindley

Date of birth: 27 October 1865, Nottingham
Died: 31 March 1940

Nottingham Forest record:
Appearances: FA Cup 25
Goals: FA Cup 15
Debut: 17 February 1883 v Wolverhampton (h) won 6–1

Also played for: Cambridge University, Corinthians, Casuals, London Swifts, Crusaders, Notts County, Preston North End, England (13 caps)

Tinsley Lindley could be described as a true all-rounder – he excelled at every sport he turned his hand to and led a successful life away from the sporting fields. Like the annoying school swot, everything seemed to come easily and naturally to Tinsley – he was a learned man, had a wide circle of friends and was undoubtedly extremely popular with the ladies!

The son of Leonard Lindley, a lace dresser, he was brought up in Clipstone Street, Nottingham, and attended Nottingham High School before being accepted at Cambridge University. His debut for Forest had created plenty of attention, with the newcomer hitting a hat-trick in a 6–1 win over Wolverhampton.

The club's fixture list at the time was mainly filled with friendlies against highly rated opposition. A paying crowd would watch the games – and even then Forest had a decent following. In another friendly against Sheffield in October 1883, Tinsley scored seven times in a 9–1 demolition. Hat-tricks and four goals in a game were becoming commonplace for the young centre-forward, but his eccentricity was as noticeable as his goalscoring.

He refused to wear the type of football boot that was prevalent at the time, claiming they diminished his sprinting ability. Instead he would wear his normal everyday footwear – comfier, no doubt, but inappropriate for the unsophisticated tackling of the day, as well as the glue-pot pitches.

In the 1884–85 season Tinsley was a member of the Forest side that reached the semi-finals of the FA Cup, where they were beaten by Queens Park in a replay at Edinburgh. His abilities were displayed to an even wider audience after he moved to Cambridge. He not only became a 'blue' at football (in five consecutive seasons), but he also played first-class cricket as a right-handed batsman and slow bowler, was an accomplished sprinter and represented Old Leysians (and later Notts RUFC) at rugby union. As an amateur player, Tinsley would switch clubs with great regularity and make himself available for whichever important fixture suited his needs. He would notify Forest whenever he intended to return to Nottingham and would invariably be 'accommodated' in the starting XI!

Apart from his phenomenal prowess in front of goal, he mixed in the right circles and joined the Corinthians, a team that 'embraced the ethos of sportsmanship and fair play'. The driving force behind the Corinths was N.L. Jackson, the assistant secretary of the Football Association.

Although his talents warranted it, Lindley was quickly brought to the attention of the national selectors and made his full England debut against Ireland in Belfast, scoring one of the goals in a 6–1 victory. Over the next five years he won 13 caps, four of them as captain, and he scored 14 goals. Tinsley hit a hat-trick against the Irish in 1887 – part of a run that brought him goals in six consecutive internationals.

He represented Notts in first-class cricket in 1888 and a year later, while still playing, he was called to the Bar and later lectured on law at Nottingham University before becoming a county court judge. His propensity to play wherever and whenever it suited cost Notts County dearly, when he turned out twice for them in Football League matches in 1889. Aston Villa, one of the opposing sides, protested to the Football League, who imposed a £5 fine and a one-point deduction to County. Tinsley took it upon himself to personally organise an appeal, but the original verdict was then increased to a £30 fine and two-point deduction! Later, Tinsley turned out once for Preston North End but would always fit in games for the Garibaldis whenever he could.

On 17 January 1891 Forest were due to play an FA Cup tie at Clapton and there were fitness doubts surrounding the availability of Sandy Higgins, the club's leading scorer at the time. Tinsley was asked to step in and arrived to find that Higgins had passed himself fit to play.

Both men played, Higgins hitting five goals and Tinsley four as the Reds ran up a 14–0 victory – a scoreline which still remains as their record Cup victory and largest-ever away win.

In January 1918 Tinsley was awarded the OBE for the sterling work he had performed during World War One in connection with the special constable movement. Seventeen years later he was again honoured, becoming the recipient of the King's Jubilee Medal.

Dr Tinsley Lindley, one of the county's great sporting characters, was still a resident of Nottingham when he died in 1940, aged 74.

Larry Lloyd

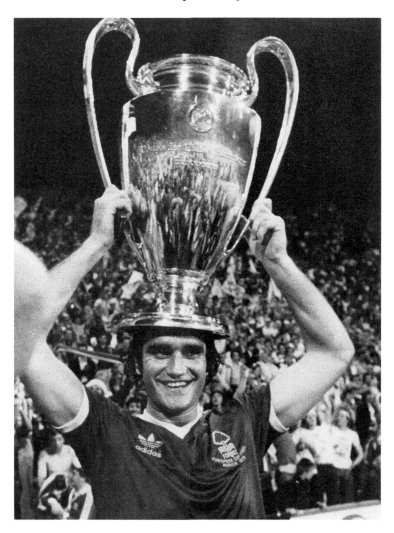

Date of birth: 6 October 1948, Bristol

Nottingham Forest record:
Appearances: League 148, FA Cup 14, League Cup 23, Others 30
Goals: League 6, FA Cup 1, League Cup 3, Others 3
Debut: 2 October 1976 v Hull City (a) lost 0–1

Also played for: Bristol Rovers, Liverpool, Coventry City, Wigan Athletic, England (4 caps)
Managed: Wigan Athletic, Notts County

Any footballer would be extremely proud to be associated with two of the game's most successful clubs, and Larry Lloyd can rightly claim to have a place among the hearts of the fans on both Merseyside and in Nottingham.

A physically imposing presence, Larry proved to be a real giant of a man during both of Forest's European Cup triumphs and was an inspirational figure as the club rose rapidly from Second Division also-rans into proven champions. His League career had begun at Bristol Rovers but started to take shape when the great Liverpool manager Bill Shankly identified him as the long-term successor to Ron Yeats, the club's veteran Scottish international skipper, and signed him for £50,000.

Standing well over 6ft tall, Larry was more than capable in the air but the Merseysiders were able to successfully develop his skill on the ground and improve his passing ability tenfold. After a season in the reserves he blossomed into a top-flight defender and was fast-tracked into the England set-up, winning the first of his four caps in May 1971 when he played in a goalless draw against Wales at Wembley.

During his time at Anfield, Larry scored just five times in his 217 first-team appearances, although he could pick his moments – scoring the winner in the 1972–73 UEFA Cup Final against Borussia Mönchengladbach. That same year he also collected a League Championship medal and would have won an FA Cup-winners' medal in 1974 but for a thigh injury which ruled him out of the Final.

The emergence of Phil Thompson in the Liverpool backline was beginning to restrict Larry's first-team opportunities and he elected to move to Coventry City for £240,000 that summer. A couple of years later he was allowed out on loan to Nottingham Forest – with Brian Clough desperate to add some solidity to his defence. The move was quickly made permanent for a fee of around £60,000 and Larry was able to add an Anglo-Scottish Cup-winners' medal to his trophy cabinet, as well as helping the Reds clinch promotion back to the First Division.

Throughout their time together at the club, Larry's central-defensive partnership with Kenny Burns was pivotal in denying opposition forwards even the slightest glimpse of Peter Shilton's goal and was the foundation for all that followed. The difficulty in overcoming Forest was never better illustrated than by the unbeaten run which had stretched from November 1977 until the following December – 42 matches, an English League record which stood until broken by Arsenal a quarter of a century later.

Over a three-year stretch the Reds enjoyed success after success and Larry was involved throughout, winning another League Championship medal (to add to the one he had won at Liverpool), two European Cups, two League Cups and a European Super Cup-winners' medal. He even bagged one of his rare goals at Wembley Stadium in the Charity Shield win over Ipswich Town.

Many Forest fans still feel that the 1980 League Cup Final would have been won had Larry played – making it a hat-trick of victories in the competition. That season the big centre-half played in every one of the club's 63 other matches, but a number of bookings meant he was ruled out of the showpiece against Wolves due to a one-match ban. As all Reds fans now recall, a defensive misunderstanding enabled Andy Gray – the man Lloyd would have marked – to snare the winner for the Molineux side. There was even a recall to the national side for the first time in eight years, although it was not the fairy-tale comeback that Larry would have hoped for, as an out-of-sorts England were emphatically beaten 4–1 by the Welsh in Wrexham.

In 1981, after playing in the Super Cup defeat to Valencia and the World Club Championship loss in Tokyo to Nacional of Uruguay, Larry was tempted by the offer of a player–manager's job at Wigan Athletic. He led them to promotion before returning to Nottingham to succeed Howard Wilkinson as Notts County's manager.

Larry later enjoyed a spell back at the City Ground entertaining corporate hospitality guests. He also proved himself to be a very popular and forthright media pundit, commenting on Forest's fortunes before leaving these shores to settle in Spain.

A larger-than-life character, off the field as well as on it, the signing of Larry Lloyd was undoubtedly one of the best decisions Brian Clough ever made.

Des Lyttle

Date of birth: 24 September 1971, Wolverhampton, West Midlands

Nottingham Forest record:
Appearances: League 193, FA Cup 16, League Cup 21, Others 8
Goals: League 3
Debut: 15 August 1993 v Southend United (a) drew 1–1

Also played for: Worcester City, Swansea City, West Bromwich Albion, Forest Green Rovers

Des Lyttle was Forest's right-back for two successful promotion campaigns during the 1990s. He joined the Reds in the wake of their relegation from the top flight at the end of the 1992–93 season – Brian Clough's last at the club.

'Frank Clark signed me from Swansea,' says Des. 'I'd played against his Leyton Orient side three or four times the previous season so I guess his interest in me must have stemmed from that. I had no inkling really and was due to sign a new contract when Frank Burrows called me and said Forest were interested.'

Although Forest were facing up to life outside the top flight, the opportunity was too good for Des to refuse. 'At the time it was no contest – little Swansea or massive Forest. I jumped at the chance to join!' Clark immediately pitched the young defender into his first team. 'I have to admit to being a bit in awe at the start,' confesses Des. 'There was the likes of Pearcey, the England captain, Stan Collymore had just signed and people like Mark Crossley and Steve Chettle had plenty of Premiership experience.'

Initial nerves were not apparent as Des made the number-two jersey his own, making 44 appearances as his first season at the club ended in immediate promotion back to the top flight. He even managed to get his name on the score sheet, against Charlton Athletic on New Year's Day, but he admits to not remembering the goal at all. 'I can remember my next one, though – away against Aston Villa on my 24th birthday. All my family and friends were there watching. We were trailing 1–0 in the last minute but I got forward to convert a diving header from an Ian Woan cross to give us a point!'

The speedy defender says he will never forget playing in the UEFA Cup for Forest. 'They were probably the biggest set of matches in my career. I really enjoyed it all, flying to different countries and pitting your wits against different challenges.'

Having advanced to the quarter-finals at the expense of Auxerre, Malmo and Lyon, the Reds were finally eliminated at the hands of those European veterans, Bayern Munich. 'We did well over there, only losing by one goal, but they beat us 5–1 at home. They were a good side, lots of class, but shouldn't have beaten us by that many!'

The opportunity of facing better players always appealed to Des, especially in the Premiership. 'I would always look to see who was on the left wing and really enjoyed facing the likes of Ryan Giggs, David Ginola and Steve McManaman and don't think I was ever really given the run around by any of them. Giggs came off a few times against us so I always thought that was a bit of a feather in my cap!'

During his six-year association with the City Ground club Des experienced some turbulent times, as Forest went up and down on two occasions and he played under four different managers: Frank Clark, Stuart Pearce, Dave Bassett and Ron Atkinson. It was almost a fifth after David Platt assumed the reins but in the summer of 1999 Des was allowed to leave on a free transfer without too much of a fight. 'I was out of contract but still came back for pre-season a week early and trained for a few days under the new manager, but he said he couldn't be sure about me. I had an offer to go and play for Watford in the Premiership so felt I had to take it.'

Well into his mid-30s, Des still plays at Conference North level for Worcester City but with an eye to the future he has already taken steps for the next stage of his career. 'I've done my coaching badges and currently help out at the Wolves Academy. Football is what I know best and I believe I've got something to offer as a coach.'

He also reveals that he still has a soft spot for his former club. 'I had the best time of my life at Forest – it really is a great club and Nottingham is a fabulous city with some really lovely people. For me, the promotions and good times far outweighed the relegation years.'

Joe McDonald

Date of birth: 10 February 1929, Blantyre, South Lanarkshire, Scotland
Died: 7 September 2003

Nottingham Forest record:
Appearances: League 109, FA Cup 12, League Cup 2, Others 1
Debut: 3 September 1958 v Manchester United (a) drew 1–1

Also played for: Bellshill Athletic, Falkirk, Sunderland, Wisbech Town, Ramsgate, Scotland (2 caps)
Managed: Ramsgate, Yeovil Town

Scottish international Joe McDonald arrived at the City Ground in July 1958 and quickly asserted himself as Forest's first-choice left full-back in time to collect an FA Cup-winners' medal at the end of his initial season with the club. Joe had accumulated a vast amount of experience since leaving Scottish junior football to join Falkirk in December 1951 and, just over two years later, he was transferred to Sunderland for a fee of around £5,500.

His development on Wearside was rapid and a sign that his progress was being monitored came when he was selected to play for Great Britain against the Rest of Europe in a special match to mark the 75th anniversary of the Irish FA. He was then capped twice at senior level by Scotland, with appearances against both Wales and Northern Ireland in 1956. Also that year he played in a losing FA Cup semi-final – his Sunderland side going down to Manchester City on a Villa Park glue pot.

Joe was respected by teammates and opponents alike, and he was given the rather resplendent nickname 'the gentleman of soccer'. This was more in reference to his polite off-field demeanour rather than his 'they shall not pass' approach to defending.

At the end of the 1957–58 season Sunderland were relegated from the First Division. Having played 137 times for the club, Joe was forced to consider his options and with great reluctance he decided to leave. Billy Walker came in with a bid of around £5,000 and the defender was happy to secure his top-flight status with a move to Nottingham. Geoff Thomas, Forest's long-serving left-back, began the campaign in the number-three jersey but Joe came into the side for a difficult away match at Old Trafford. From then on he made the position his own, making 44 appearances in the first team that season – including all nine ties in the FA Cup competition.

Having missed out on a Final place three years earlier, Joe was doubly keen not to lose at the semi-final stage again so was overjoyed at his side's gritty win over Aston Villa.

Forest had to wait for confirmation of their opponents, as the Luton Town and Norwich City semi-final had gone to a replay. Eventually the Hatters squeezed through and Joe could look forward to a tussle against a former Sunderland teammate at Wembley. Billy Bingham, one of the most feared and respected wingers in the land, had left Roker Park at the same time as Joe and had been instrumental in helping Luton to the Final.

The Garibaldis could not claim to be suffering from over-confidence going into the match – they had won only three of 13 matches since beating Villa. Among those defeats had been a 5–1 mauling at Luton – a match Joe missed through injury. Nevertheless, on the big day Forest did not disappoint their loyal followers. Despite having to leave the action for a few minutes when he blocked a shot with his face, Joe returned and was able to keep the dangerous Bingham quiet – an important contribution in ensuring the Cup was won!

Joe played for two more seasons at the City Ground, appearing in the Charity Shield defeat by Wolves and the first League Cup campaign in the 1960–61 season. In over 120 first-team games for the Reds, he confirmed that defending was his priority by not getting himself on the score sheet once, thus failing to add to the only goal of his career – for Sunderland against Portsmouth in 1954.

After leaving Forest Joe joined the non-League circuit with a stint at Wisbech Town, where he frightened opposition wingers into submission for a couple of years before accepting a player-manager position at Ramsgate.

He served them from 1963 to 1965 before being appointed to take over the managerial reigns at Yeovil Town where he remained until his dismissal in May 1967, effectively bringing an end to his full-time involvement in the game.

Joe and his family emigrated to Australia in the 1980s and settled near to Adelaide, where he lived in retirement until his death in 2003.

John McGovern

Date of birth: 28 October 1949, Montrose, Angus, Scotland

Nottingham Forest record:
Appearances: League 253, FA Cup 18, League Cup 33, Others 31
Goals: League 6, FA Cup 1, League Cup 3, Others 1
Debut: 22 February 1975 v Cardiff City (h) drew 0–0

Also played for: Hartlepools United, Derby County, Leeds United, Bolton Wanderers
Managed: Bolton Wanderers, Horwich RMI, Chorley, Rotherham United, Woking

Forest's European Cup-winning captain on both occasions was midfielder John McGovern, who had reached the City Ground via a similar path to the club's most colourful manager. 'I was still at school, aged 15, and about to sit my O levels, when Brian Clough first wanted me to sign for him at Hartlepool,' recalls John. 'My dad had died when I was 11, so there was only my mam who had any say in it really. With Brian's persuasive manner and my total dedication to become a footballer it became a big decision for the family to take. My gran came to stay with us at Christmas and Cloughie began charming her into letting me sign and eventually I became Hartlepool's first-ever apprentice, signing professional forms as soon as I was 17.'

The Scot followed his manager to Derby County – where he won promotion and a League Championship – and to Leeds United before eventually reuniting with his mentor at the City Ground in 1975. 'When Brian tried to sign me again, Ann, my good lady, said that she knew what Brian was like and I wasn't to let him talk me into taking a drop in wages. Of course, when I went to negotiate the contract I took a 30-pound drop – so got a right rollicking when I got home!'

Forest more than got their money's worth. John became skipper as the rebuilding process began to gain momentum. In 1976–77 the Reds lifted the Anglo-Scottish Cup, beating Orient in the Final. That was only the first part of a double, as promotion back to the top flight was also secured on the last day of the season. 'We played Millwall and their full-back headed an own-goal to give us a 1–0 win. We had to wait for other results to see if we'd done enough and just scraped through in third place.'

Clough strengthened his squad for an assault on the title but also had the unexpected bonus of taking his side to League Cup success, although it was not John who went up to lift the silverware. 'We'd played Liverpool at Wembley and after an hour I'd had to come off with a pretty bad groin injury which ruled me out of the Old Trafford replay. I was watching from the stands as Kenny Burns lifted the Cup after our victory.'

John's disappointment at missing that match was quickly forgotten as the Reds won the Championship by seven points from Liverpool. Although the successful European campaigns followed and there were further domestic honours, 'Mac' rates the League title as the stand-out moment of his career. 'You can have a bit of luck in Cup competitions but to be the best over 42 League matches is quite an achievement and to go up and lift the trophy made me so proud.'

He remembers the moment when the title dream moved a little closer. 'I was sitting in the bath at Newcastle around Christmas time and we'd just won to go top. David Needham asked me about our chances and I just said that "Nobody will catch us now." The manager's focus had remained constant and I genuinely believed we'd do it from that moment.'

The hard-working midfielder remained one of the unsung heroes as the Reds enjoyed the most successful period in their history. 'When Brian Clough signed me for Forest he paid me the greatest of compliments. I knew what he wanted from me, and it was nothing less than I expected from myself – to give 100 percent in every game I played.'

John's attitude and commitment was never called into question and it frustrates him that he was constantly overlooked by the Scottish selectors. His days at Forest drew to an end in the summer of 1982 when he moved to Bolton as player-manager. Over the course of the next two decades he worked at a number of clubs as either manager or assistant before getting the opportunity to become a regular again at the City Ground, as a member of the media. 'I've really enjoyed covering Forest matches for BBC Radio Nottingham over the past few years. For an ex-player to watch his old side every week, from the best seat in the house, is a real privilege.'

In 2005 John was again sent on European Cup duty for Forest – as the club's representative in Geneva for the 50th anniversary celebrations. 'It made me so very proud to think of the contribution we'd made in the history of that competition.'

Duncan McKenzie

Date of birth: 10 June 1950, Ipswich, Suffolk

Nottingham Forest record:
Appearances: League 117, FA Cup 6, League Cup 8
Goals: League 41, FA Cup 2, League Cup 3
Debut: 20 September 1969 v Sunderland (a) lost 1–2

Also played for: Mansfield Town (loan), Leeds United, Anderlecht (Belgium), Everton, Chelsea, Blackburn Rovers

Duncan McKenzie was one of Forest's greatest-ever talents. Yet, sadly, the club did not appreciate what they had until he had left. There are many Reds supporters today who believe he turned in the most outstanding individual performance ever by anyone in a Garibaldi shirt. 'I'm still great friends with John Robertson,' says Duncan. 'He still says, "I won two European Cups yet all they talk about at Forest is you against Manchester City!"'

The match in question was an FA Cup fourth-round tie at the City Ground. With an air of depression around due to a national power strike, Forest had played the previous round on a Sunday and decided to repeat the experiment against a City side riding top of the First Division.

With Duncan at the very peak of his game Forest ripped their opponents to shreds, winning by four goals to one. Bearing in mind the day of the match, he remembers one of the funnier asides made. 'As City were about to kick-off for the fourth time Francis Lee turned to Mike Summerbee and said, "We'll never make a Sunday League team!"'

The Forest number seven turned in a five-star performance that day, yet it had taken several years of frustration before he was allowed the chance to prove his worth. 'Matt Gillies was a manager who believed in experience,' says Duncan. 'Basically, you had to be over 30 in his book. I'd played one game early in my career when Barry Lyons took ill and Colin Hall, the reserve winger, was out injured, but then I had to wait – and wait – for another chance.' Others were aware of his blossoming talent. 'I later found out that two of our first teamers, Ronnie Rees and John Barnwell, had gone to Gillies asking him to select me but he'd said, "No – you can't rely on kids." It was the way of the world – few people played teenagers.'

Duncan gained some invaluable experience with a couple of loan spells at Mansfield Town and endured even more frustration after getting his first senior goals for Forest in April 1971. 'It was Easter weekend and the club had two games in two days. We were at Manchester City on the Good Friday and the manager put myself and Tommy Jackson in, so that he could rest Ian Storey-Moore and Peter Cormack for the Saturday match against West Ham. He thought we'd get stuffed but I scored twice and Jacko got the other as we won 3–1. The next day he said he was resting us, as "We looked tired!"'

By the 1973–74 season Duncan's apprenticeship was well and truly over, as he teased and tormented countless Second Division defences. The FA Cup tie against Manchester City gave him the chance to show what he could do against some of the best players in the land. 'It was just one of those days,' he modestly confides. 'If I'd played with my eyes shut I'm sure everything would still have come off.'

Duncan scored one of Forest's four but had a hand in the rest as he tortured the beleaguered City backline. Was it his greatest-ever performance? 'I think the Everton fans rave about a couple and there were one or two at Leeds but it was certainly my best for Forest and it didn't do my career prospects any harm, coming when it did. The match was a sell-out and all of the national press were there, so if anybody had any doubts about my ability that performance perhaps helped dispel them.'

Goals in each of his final five matches for Forest enabled Duncan to end the season with a total of 28 goals – the highest in the country. He agreed to a new contract with the club but when manager Allan Brown did not even turn up for their agreed meeting, he decided to take his cards (literally!) and move on.

'My wife was eight months pregnant and I was out of a job but I needn't have worried. Freddie Goodwin called, wanting me to go to Birmingham, and then Bill Nicholson enquired if I'd sign for Spurs, then Cloughie rang me: "Come and sign for Leeds." Half an hour later I was sat in a hotel in Sheffield and signed for him.'

During his time with Forest, Duncan learned the party trick with which he would be associated for the rest of his career. 'Down by the Trent, on the way to training, there was a five-bar gate – about 4ft 6in high. I used to jump over it. One day Brian Williamson, our reserve goalie, pointed to Tommy Cavanagh's [the trainer] mini, said it was about the same height as the gate and offered me a fiver to jump over it. I was only on about 12 quid a week at the time so I did it!'

The stunt won Duncan many more bets over the years and he even performed it in front of a much larger audience. 'I did it at Elland Road on the night of Paul Reaney's testimonial – there were about 30,000 there!'

Since hanging up his boots Duncan has become a well-respected member of the football media as well as an entertaining after-dinner speaker. Whenever he is among Forest fans, though, the topic will eventually turn back to the day he destroyed Manchester City.

Bobby McKinlay

Date of birth: 10 October 1932, Lochgelly, Fife, Scotland
Died: August 2002

Nottingham Forest record:
Appearances: League 614, FA Cup 53, League Cup 11, Others 7
Goals: League 9, FA Cup 1
Debut: 27 October 1951 v Coventry City (a) drew 3–3

Also played for: Bowhill Rovers (Scotland)

Any footballer who has played in more matches for his club than anyone else deserves to be afforded the accolade of 'legend'. No one deserves this label more than Forest's 'Mr Dependable', Bobby McKinlay.

At 6ft tall, Bobby (or, less frequently, just Bob) stood head and shoulders above most other players on the pitch. Appropriate then that he should also stand well clear of his rivals when it comes to appearances for Nottingham Forest.

The central defender played in a staggering 614 League games for the Reds, a feat that will almost certainly never be equalled. As sturdy as a seasoned oak, the elegant, upright Scot established a permanency that can only be respected by anyone who understands the game. Niggling hamstrings, calves or ankle ailments seemed to bypass Bobby. Either that, or his pain threshold knew no boundaries.

Equally admirable for a top-flight defender, Bobby had no disciplinary record to speak of. Never dismissed, he was booked only twice in 20 years. It says something about the strength of the Scottish national side, or the restricted vision of their selectors, that Bobby was not allowed to fulfil his ambition of pulling on the dark-blue jersey and participating in international competition.

He had joined the City Ground staff as a youngster having played junior football in Scotland, mainly at outside-right. His father Rab had played for Cowdenbeath but it was his uncle Billy that was to play a more decisive role in shaping Bobby's future. Billy McKinlay had played in over 350 matches for Forest and was now their Scottish scout. He had no hesitation in recommending his nephew to the club.

Bobby learnt his trade in the early 1950s, while helping the reserves to a succession of Midland League titles. First-team outings were at a premium until the 1954–55 season when he began to get a regular foothold in the side. The following year he scored his first goal for the club, at home to Lincoln City, and the year after he played a pivotal role as the side won promotion to the top flight.

Forest's opening First Division fixture was against Preston North End and Bobby earned spectacular reviews for the way he completely shut out the threat of the great England international Tom Finney.

Bobby's career high was undoubtedly the FA Cup win of 1959, a match with more twists and turns than Snake Pass. Forest's supposed edge was nullified somewhat when they were reduced to 10 men after Roy Dwight's horrific injury. Leaders are required at such crucial moments and the Reds' number five was magnificent in his desperation to keep Luton out.

Just prior to the Cup Final, on 22 April 1959, Bobby had missed a game against Leeds United through injury. The next time he was absent from the team sheet was on 23 October 1965, for a home match against Aston Villa – the run of consecutive appearances had reached 265, another record that is also unlikely ever to be repeated. During that period he had assumed the club captaincy, but after four years in charge he relinquished the role to Terry Hennessey.

In 1965 Bobby chalked up his 500th appearance for the club and was also awarded a testimonial, with more than 18,000 fans paying their respect by attending a fixture against Celtic.

Eight years after winning his Cup medal Bobby was still going strong and was part of the Forest side that came so close to snatching both major domestic honours. They finished second in the League behind Manchester United, the club's best-ever finish to that point, and reached the semi-final of the FA Cup again, losing to Spurs at Hillsborough.

Typically, Bobby had been an ever present that season and was again the following year. In eight out of nine campaigns he had missed just one match, a level of consistency that defies modern-day logic.

All good things eventually come to an end and the years finally caught up with the defensive stalwart. He donned the Garibaldi shirt for the last time in a loss at Newcastle on 15 November 1969. The Scot continued to serve Forest well, joining the backroom staff. He had become increasingly involved in the coaching side while still playing under Johnny Carey, and he continued when Matt Gillies took over.

Later Bobby changed professions altogether, working as a prison officer at Lowdham Grange Detention Centre.

Football lost one of its great ambassadors when Bobby died in 2002, aged just 69.

John MacPherson

Date of birth: 28 February 1867, Motherwell, North Lanarkshire, Scotland
Died: 1935

Nottingham Forest record:
Appearances: League 225, FA Cup 34, Others 13
Goals: League 25, FA Cup 1, Others 4
Debut: 3 September 1891 v Burton Swifts (h) won 7–0

Also played for: Cambuslang, Heart of Midlothian, Motherwell, Scotland (1 cap)

John MacPherson is a member of a very select group of Nottingham Forest players – one of only five who have scored for the club in an FA Cup Final. The former Scottish international netted in the 3–1 win over Derby County in 1898. Forest were already closing in on the victory, leading by two Arthur Capes goals to a single reply from Derby's Steve Bloomer. With less than four minutes remaining, John, the Foresters captain and centre-half, received the ball 10 yards out, side-stepped a couple of challenges and drove the ball home to seal the win for his side and set up massive celebrations both within the ground and back in Nottingham.

Before journeying south to join the Reds, John had played for Heart of Midlothian, whom he had joined from the non-League side Cambuslang. During the 1890–91 season he had helped the Edinburgh club to victory in the Scottish Cup Final, as well as winning an international cap against England.

During the summer of 1891 he joined Forest as a professional and made his debut in the Football Alliance Championship on the opening afternoon of the season. A thumping 7–0 victory over Burton Swifts was an emphatic way for the club to signal their intentions. This was to be the Reds' most successful campaign thus far, as they finished top of the League to win their first tangible piece of silverware. John had played his part, appearing in 19 of the 22 League matches. The season could have been even more memorable but West Brom dashed FA Cup hopes at the semi-final stage – the fourth time that Forest had fallen at the penultimate hurdle.

On the back of this success, and with several professionals now on the staff, Forest made the decision to join the Football League and kicked off the new season as a member of a 16-team First Division. John had returned to Scotland after the Alliance success and intended to rejoin Hearts on a permanent basis, but he saw greater opportunities now that Forest had become a League club and came back to Nottingham, although having missed the opening seven matches of the season.

Of the remaining 23 games in the programme, John figured in 21 of them, proving to be a model of consistency, and he scored his first League goal in a home win over Sheffield Wednesday on Christmas Eve 1892.

Over the next nine seasons he was rarely absent from the Foresters' starting line up and was appointed club captain in 1894, as the Reds continued to establish themselves.

The year 1898 was to be Forest's breakthrough year. Eighth in the League was respectable, if undistinguished, but good progress was made in the early rounds of the FA Cup at the expense of Grimsby Town, Gainsborough Trinity and West Bromwich Albion. Yet another semi-final to contest and this time Forest were victorious after a controversial replay, which saw opponents Southampton claim the snowy conditions should have forced an abandonment. Nevertheless, it was the Reds who went through to their first Final to face Derby County.

In a quirk of the fixture list, Forest had to visit their Cup Final opponents just five days before the big showpiece. Not wanting to show their hand, wholesale changes were made to the Garibaldis line up, with John one of several first-choice stars to be omitted.

Not surprisingly, the match was lost 5–0, making Derby firm favourites to emulate the win in the next meeting. The Final was to be played at Crystal Palace, so Forest travelled to London on the day before the game and stayed at the Salisbury Hotel on Fleet Street.

On a warm, sunny day, 62,000 spectators crammed into the ground. The majority of them expected a Derby win, but the Reds overcame the odds and ran out worthy winners. After the final whistle had been sounded John led his players to receive the FA Cup from Lord Rosebery. The jubilation of those present at the ground gave only a taste of what was to come when the side returned home. The railway station was crammed with fans, several deep, anxious to catch sight of their heroes and the Cup itself. John was lifted shoulder-high as a band welcomed their return.

Although nothing else would come close to the Cup win, John continued to play for Forest for three more years and appeared in yet another semi-final defeat in 1900 – this time to Bury.

Returning to Scotland to see out his career, the veteran centre-half played for Motherwell for a year and then another short spell at his first club, Cambuslang.

In his later life John emigrated to Saskatchewan in Canada and it is believed he died there around 1935 – 24 years before Jack Burkitt would emulate him as the only other Nottingham Forest captain to lift the FA Cup.

David Martin

Date of birth: 1 February 1914, Belfast, Northern Ireland
Died: 9 January 1991

Nottingham Forest record:
Appearances: League 81, FA Cup 3
Goals: League 41, FA Cup 5
Debut: 29 August 1936 v Burnley (a) lost 0–3

Also played for: Cliftonville, Royal Ulster Rifles, Wolverhampton Wanderers, Notts County, Glentoran, Derry City, Ballymoney United, Ballymena United, Northern Ireland (10 caps)

There have been many fictional movie heroes who did not lead anywhere near as hectic a life as David Kirker Martin. As Forest's centre-forward he scored 46 goals from 84 appearances immediately before World War Two.

Throughout his career David Martin was known simply as 'Boy' or 'Davy Boy', nicknames acquired after serving as a drummer boy in the Royal Ulster Rifles. An orphan, he had also earned himself a reputation as a bit of a prizefighter during his teenage years in Belfast and the Rifles were seen as an appropriate outlet for his youthful aggression.

Apart from being handy with his fists, Davy was a splendid footballer. At just 5ft 8in tall, he relied on speed and instinct rather than power or aerial ability, and he impressed the Belfast Celtic scouts so much that they paid the princely sum of £5 to buy him out of the army.

In 1933 the young striker won the first of 10 international caps for Northern Ireland and a year later moved to Wolves for a fee of £5,000. After recording 18 goals in 27 appearances for the Molineux club, Forest manager Harry Wightman forked out a club-record fee of £7,000 to bring the Ulsterman to Nottingham.

He joined Forest for the start of the 1936–37 season and had to wait a couple of matches before getting his first goals for the club – a brace against Fulham in a 5–3 home victory. Whether he gleaned any extra confidence from opening his account, or whether it was just coincidence, he then went on a scoring spree which resulted in him netting in eight consecutive games, bagging 10 goals in the process. From his 37 League appearances Davy bagged a phenomenal return of 29 goals. With no one else reaching double figures, it was no surprise that the Reds struggled all year before ending the campaign in 18th position.

Without Davy's contribution it would have taken a near-miracle to prevent the club from being relegated – in fact, something akin to what happened 12 months later!

The Reds had underachieved all season and went into the final game needing at least a point to stay up. As fate would have it, Forest had to play at Barnsley, the other side desperately striving to stay up. With less than five minutes remaining things looked bleak – although Davy had scored early on to put the visitors ahead, the Tykes had stormed back to lead 2–1.

One foot already in the Third Division, Forest poured forwards desperate for the goal that would save their souls. Right-back Reg Trim fired optimistically towards goal but straight into the arms of Binns, Barnsley's 6ft-tall goalkeeper. Ball firmly in his grasp, he was startled to suddenly be on the receiving end of a shoulder charge from the diminutive Davy Boy, which forced man and ball over the goalline. The home supporters were in uproar as the referee awarded the goal.

Forest had been spared from the drop only on a goal average of 0.002, with the Yorkshire side understandably unhappy about proceedings. Boy was feted as the hero who had saved Forest from the drop, but his temperament had always remained a little suspect and a succession of fall-outs with his manager and a number of referees hastened his departure from the club. Forty-one goals from 81 League appearances during a difficult couple of seasons had been a good return on their investment for Forest.

Curiously, Boy only played in three FA Cup matches for the Reds and he scored in all of them as well. He hit two against Sheffield United in his first season at the City Ground, another pair a year later in a win over Southampton and the consolation in Forest's next round exit at the hands of Middlesbrough.

In November 1938 Davy crossed the Trent to join Notts County and continued to convert a fair proportion of chances that came his way, netting 16 goals from 29 outings.

During World War Two Davy was wounded during active service but made a full recovery and was able to resume his football career back in Northern Ireland.

One of life's real characters, Davy Boy Martin died in Belfast in 1991, aged 76.

Johnny Metgod

Date of birth: 27 February 1958, Amsterdam, Netherlands

Nottingham Forest record:
Appearances: League 116, FA Cup 7, League Cup 14, Others 2
Goals: League 15, League Cup 2
Debut: 25 August 1984 v Sheffield Wednesday (a) lost 1–3

Also played for: DWS Amsterdam, Haarlem, AZ67 Alkmaar (all Netherlands), Real Madrid (Spain), Tottenham Hotspur, Feyenoord (Netherlands), Netherlands (21 caps)
Managed: Excelsior (Netherlands)

Purely and simply – Johnny Metgod oozed class. The tall, elegant midfielder joined Forest from Real Madrid in August 1984 and gained a cult following on Trentside that is likely to remain forever.

At 6ft 4in tall Johnny filled in as a more than capable central defender at various times in his career, but it was in the middle of the park where he appeared to be at his best. His languid running style, precise distribution and ferocious shooting had persuaded the Bernabeu giants to sign him from Dutch football in 1982.

Despite the earlier successes of Johan Cryuff and Johan Neeskens in Barcelona, Johnny admits to being something of a trailblazer. 'It was still very unusual for anyone from my country to play abroad at that time – especially in Spain – and I felt it was a challenge I had to accept.'

Having first played for his country in November 1978 Johnny was a seasoned international, although he admits he played for the Netherlands during their 'in between' years. 'When I got into the Dutch team they were rebuilding after the 1978 World Cup Finals,' he says. 'The major disappointment from my time in the side is that we didn't qualify for a major championship, although we should have reached the 1982 World Cup but went to France only needing a draw and lost 2-0!'

A Spanish Cup runners'-up medal was the only tangible reward for Johnny during his time at Madrid after two seasons and 49 League appearances, he decided to try his luck in England and accepted the call to sign for Forest for a fee of around £300,000. His Reds debut ended in defeat in an away match against Sheffield Wednesday, but he bounced back by scoring on his home debut in a 2-0 win over Arsenal.

The prospect of joining a club so successful in European competition would have been an attractive lure for Johnny, but Forest slipped quietly out of the UEFA Cup at the first hurdle, beaten by Belgian side Club Brugge. When Forest exited the FA Cup as well, beaten by Wimbledon, Johnny sampled the unpredictability of his manager for the first time. Rather than spend a free week training beside the Trent, Brian Clough flew his side to war-torn Iraq to play a couple of matches in Baghdad!

Despite his own influential presence, Forest were unable to add to their impressive honours list during Johnny's three years at the club. Nevertheless, he did leave the fans with some golden moments, particularly from deadball situations.

His stunning free-kick against Manchester United, early in his Forest days, gave the fans an insight into his ability to produce a goal from nothing. Superb though it was, it was out-matched by an even better goal on 2 April 1986.

It is unlikely that anyone has struck a more venomous shot than the free-kick which ripped past West Ham goalie Phil Parkes and into the net during a First Division match at the City Ground. In 2007 the *Nottingham Evening Post* readers voted this goal as Forest's best ever from a free-kick.

In the summer of 1987, after three seasons at the City Ground, Johnny joined Spurs for £250,000. Many saw him as the ideal replacement for the recently-departed Glenn Hoddle, but a hernia operation restricted him to just a dozen appearances for the North London side and after one season he was allowed to return home, with a move to Feyenoord.

He remained at De Kuip until ending his playing days in January 1994. Johnny then joined the club's backroom staff, initially working on youth development but then later as the assistant first-team coach where he has remained ever since, apart from a brief spell managing Excelsior, another Rotterdam-based side.

Johnny has made several infrequent trips back to the City Ground in recent years and has competed for Forest in the indoor masters tournaments. On each occasion he admits to being 'staggered' at the esteem in which he is still held by Reds supporters.

'I love going back to Nottingham,' he says. 'I made many friends during my time at Forest and have always been made to feel very welcome there. I wish the club all the very best for the future.'

Gary Mills

Date of birth: 11 November 1961, Northampton

Appearances: League 136, FA Cup 5, League Cup 21, Others 10
Goals: League 12, League Cup 2
Debut: 9 September 1978 v Arsenal (h) won 2–1

Also played for: Seattle Sounders (US), Derby County, Notts County, Leicester
City, Grantham Town, Gresley Rovers, Boston United
Managed: Grantham Town, Kings Lynn, Notts County, Tamworth, Alfreton
Town

Gary Mills was a successful member of Nottingham Forest's European Cup campaigns and he more than played his part in the 1980 victory over SV Hamburg in Madrid, when at 18 years 198 days he became the youngest recipient of a winners' medal.

Trevor Francis's ankle injury in the build-up to that Final was one of a number of selection conundrums that manager Brian Clough faced. He opted to replace the million-pound man with the youthful exuberance of Gary – an energetic replacement who could be relied upon to run and run all day.

The selection – as with most of the manager's decisions – proved to be wise. Gary did not let any of the German players enjoy the luxury of time on the ball before he was at them, harassing, tackling and putting them under pressure.

The additional bonus – and one that few could have foreseen – was his role in the game-winning decider, helping move the ball on from Frank Gray to goalscorer John Robertson.

It was perhaps fitting that 'Millsy' should emerge centre stage to collect his medal because he had made a significant contribution at the start of Forest's defence of their crown.

The First Round draw had pitted the Reds against Oesters Vaxjo of Sweden. A routine 2–0 victory in the home leg seemed comfortable enough at the time but when their opponents scored in the return and then Martin O'Neill had limped off injured, it seemed as if the tide might be turning.

Gary's introduction was spectacular and significant. In a tight, nervy affair, the youngster produced a man of the match performance and put over a pinpoint cross from which Tony Woodcock scored to make the game safe.

Uncharacteristically, Cloughie appeared very relieved at the final whistle. 'We didn't play all that well but there was a lot of pleasure in watching Gary Mills. No one, with the possible exception of Peter Shilton, did more to see us through to the next round.'

The son of former Northampton Town player Roly Mills, who clocked up 305 League appearances between 1951 and 1964, Gary entered the Forest record books on his first appearance.

He was just 16 years 302 days old when he made his debut, wearing the number-seven jersey, against Arsenal on 9 September 1978. Forest won the match 2–1 with Gary becoming the youngest ever player to appear in the Reds' first team. The record stood until October 2001 when Craig Westcarr, who was 45 days younger, played against Burnley.

Gary's first goal for Forest came on 15 May 1979 in a 2–1 victory at Leeds United. Although mainly used in midfield during his time at the City Ground, the youngster proved to be a valuable asset, equally capable of slotting in at either full-back or up front.

Apart from the Hamburg game, Gary also played for Forest in one other major European fixture – the home leg of the Super Cup against Valencia in November 1980.

Never a consistently high goalscorer, mainly due to the number of differing roles and positions he was asked to perform, Gary's best season was 1980–81 when he scored seven times. In addition that term, in a first-team friendly against touring US side Tampa Bay Rowdies, he hit a hat-trick in a 7–1 win in front of 18,500 City Ground fans.

A former Schoolboy, Youth and Under-21 international, Gary had also played international rugby as a youngster. He left the City Ground to play in the North American Soccer League in March 1982 but returned to spend four more years at his first club and take his first-team appearances to 178.

The rest of Gary's playing career was spent mainly in the East Midlands, enjoying success at Leicester City and Notts County, with whom he won the Anglo-Italian Cup in 1996.

A holder of the UEFA 'A' Coaching badge, 'Millsy' returned to manage the Magpies between January and November 2004 and has since been in charge at both Alfreton Town and Tamworth.

Gary's knowledge and insight into the game has also been put to good use with stints as a popular and forthright match summariser on local radio.

Grenville Morris

Date of birth:	13 April 1877, Builth, Powys, Wales
Died:	27 November 1959

Nottingham Forest record:

Appearances:	League 423, FA Cup 37
Goals:	League 199, FA Cup 18
Debut:	3 December 1898 v Bury (a) lost 0–2

Also played for: Builth Town, Aberystwyth Town, Bury, Swindon Town, Wales (21 caps)

Nottingham Forest's all-time record scorer is Grenville Morris. During a 15-year stay at the City Ground the Welsh international scored a staggering 217 goals for the Reds, with 199 of them coming in League matches!

Whatever £200 meant to the club in 1898, it was surely recouped many times over after Forest paid that sum to sign 'Gren' from Swindon Town. By that stage of his career he had already represented his country on five occasions, having first played for Wales at 18 when he scored in a 6–1 win over Ireland at Wrexham.

He had first been capped while playing at centre-forward for Aberystwyth Town, but following a move to Swindon a year later he was switched to an inside-forward position. The transfer had not been solely for footballing reasons, with the Wiltshire club offering Gren employment as a draughtsman with a local railway company.

Forest offered no such frills when they eventually got their man, partway through the 1898–99 season. In the wake of the FA Cup success, some eight months earlier, the Reds had moved to their new home, the City Ground, and were determined to establish themselves as one of the major forces in the land.

Grenville's acquisition was seen as a shrewd bit of business for the club, considering he arrived in League football with a scoring record of a century of goals from just 75 matches. That form had continued at Swindon, where he became nicknamed 'The Prince of Inside-Lefts', or, occasionally, 'The Prince of Inside-Forwards'!

'The Prince' made his Forest debut in a 2–0 defeat away at Bury, a club that Gren had briefly played for before joining Swindon. His home debut had a happier outcome, though, as he figured on the score sheet in a thrilling 3–3 draw against local rivals Derby County.

Elegant and sophisticated off the field, Grenville was also fairly phlegmatic on it – rarely getting upset with teammates or opposition and never booked during his career. Welsh international teammate Billy Meredith was so impressed with his moustachioed colleague that he described him at the time as 'a great player, a great schemer, a tricky dribbler and with a fine shot'. Praise indeed!

Gren had gone to Forest hoping to win some silverware, so his disappointment was acute after Forest blew the 1900 FA Cup semi-final replay against Bury, despite leading 2–0 with only 10 minutes left to play. The frustration became even more intense when they fell at the same stage two years later. During the 1902–03 season he scored in eight consecutive matches, notching a total of 11 goals in the process. With 26 goals, 24 of them in the League, this was Grenville's most productive time in the game.

For seven out of 10 seasons he finished as the club's leading scorer, including the 1905–06 campaign when the club were relegated and the year after when they bounced straight back after winning the Second Division title. In 1909 he scored two of the goals in Forest's highest-ever win, a 12–0 success over Leicester Fosse. That year he was awarded a benefit match against Bradford City.

By this stage of his career Gren had taken over as skipper of the Foresters, an appointment he proudly cherished for the next five seasons. The first match to be played at Notts County's new ground on Meadow Lane was the League derby between the city rivals in September 1910, and it was Gren who scored Forest's equaliser in a 1–1 draw. Among his haul for Forest were five League hat-tricks, scored against West Brom in 1900, Bury in 1904, Manchester City in 1908 and in 1909 he repeated the feat against both Manchester United and Sheffield Wednesday. Gren's 199th and final League goal for the Reds came against Grimsby Town in April 1913. He played twice more but was unable to take his total to a double century.

During his days as a Forester he won a further 16 Welsh caps, but an injury on international duty in 1911 crucially ruled him out of the League run-in and was a contributory factor in the Reds being relegated yet again.

A keen love of tennis ensured that Gren remained extremely fit throughout his career and he began to pursue the game with even more intensity after retiring from football. He did attempt to qualify for Wimbledon but the authorities would not grant him the necessary amateur status in order to do so.

He joined the Nottinghamshire LTA and coached youngsters for many years, as well as continuing to run his own coal merchants business in the city. 'The Immortal Gren' passed away in 1959, aged 82.

Henry Newton

Date of birth: 18 February 1944, Nottingham

Nottingham Forest record:
Appearances: League 282, FA Cup 18, League Cup 10, Others 5
Goals: League 17, FA Cup 0, League Cup 1, Others 1
Debut: 8 October 1963 v Leicester City (h) won 2–0

Also played for: Everton, Derby County, Walsall

Among the crop of highly talented youngsters to break into Forest's side of the 1960s was local product Henry Newton. Henry had played for Nottingham Schoolboys as a left-winger but his natural position was in midfield. He joined the groundstaff under Billy Walker but had to learn his trade in the juniors and the reserve team before graduating through into first-team contention. For a young Forest supporter it was a dream come true. 'I'd always followed the team,' he recalls. 'My heroes were Jack Burkitt and Jeff Whitefoot and suddenly I found myself playing and training with them.'

Although his primary role was to win the ball and break up opposition attacks, the youngster possessed a priceless commodity for a midfielder – the ability to score vital goals. 'My first goal for Forest was at Molyneux against Wolves and I always seemed to do well against them. One year there I scored a couple of goals but in between I had to go off for stitches after clashing heads with our own Bobby McKinlay. For a long time afterwards he would jokingly threaten to "do" me again!

'I always seemed to score a lot of goals in practice matches and reserve games so I was sometimes pushed further forward. My primary role was the defensive-covering part of the game, though.'

Henry's development coincided with the club firmly establishing themselves in the domestic game. In the 1966–67 season Forest were so close to picking up major silverware with a League runners'-up berth and a place in the last four of the FA Cup. 'The supporters were magnificent all that season. They were very vocal and really played a major part in the Cup run. Everyone still talks about the Everton match but I still remember the third-round tie at home to Plymouth. The noise from the stands was just amazing.'

Forest's first European adventure ended in something of an anticlimax in the 1967–68 season. After beating Eintracht Frankfurt the Reds gained a 2–1 first-leg advantage over FC Zurich in the second round, with Henry scoring one of the goals. A 1–0 defeat in the return in Switzerland ended matters on the away goal rule but the English side showed their naivety. 'We didn't even know the rules,' recalls Henry. 'We thought it was all square and going to extra-time!'

It is difficult to think of anyone who has come as close to playing for England without actually doing so. Henry played for the England Under-23 side on four occasions but endured plenty of frustration when it came to full international recognition. 'I was called up for plenty of squads,' he admits. 'But it was an age when substitutes were rarely used, except for injury.' Nevertheless, the big moment appeared to be imminent. 'We were playing Holland at Wembley – it was the match in which Ian [Storey-Moore] made his debut. Colin Bell picked up an injury and I was told to get my tracksuit off and get ready. As I did so the manager suddenly decided to send Alan Mullery on instead!'

Henry later learned that the manager was thinking of his welfare when he did not put him on. 'The Wembley pitch was in a pretty poor state at the time and Sir Alf Ramsey didn't think it fair to expect me to perform under those conditions. I really don't bear Alf any grudges but I'd have loved to have got on – even if it was just for a few minutes.' With the Mexico World Cup of 1970 drawing ever closer, there were some who felt that Henry would make the squad. 'Esso brought out a coin collection and I was one of the 28 players featured in it. Sadly, although I was in the provisional squad of 40, I didn't make the 22 who travelled.'

In October 1970 Henry's stay at the City Ground was over. 'I clearly wasn't in Matt Gillies's plans and the club accepted a bid from Everton. I didn't want to leave Forest but so much had changed and Gillies wanted to bring his own players in.' Henry made just 77 League appearances for the Toffees before returning to the East Midlands with Derby County. He was Brian Clough's last signing for the club and part of Dave Mackay's team that won the First Division Championship in 1974–75.

After making 149 appearances for the Rams and a handful of games for Walsall, arthritis forced an early end to Henry's career and heralded a new life running a sub-post office. However busy, he always found time to improve his golf game and keep up with the fortunes of his home-town club. 'I loved my time at Forest and get down to see them as often as I can. I really hope it's not too long before they're back up where they belong.'

John O'Hare

Date of birth: 24 September 1946, Dumbarton, Scotland

Nottingham Forest record:
Appearances: League 101, FA Cup 8, League Cup 16, Others 8
Goals: League 14, FA Cup 1, League Cup 8, Others 2
Debut: 28 February 1975 v Oxford United (a) drew 1–1

Also played for: Sunderland, Derby County, Leeds United, Belper Town, Scotland
(13 caps)

For seasoned Forest fans there have been very few experiences to rival the euphoria of the 1978 League Cup Final replay win over Liverpool. Starved of success for so long, that was the evening when they started to believe that the good times had finally arrived.

If anything could make the celebratory tipple slide down even easier it was the fact that the victory was slightly contentious – at least as far as the opposition supporters were concerned. John Robertson's winning penalty-kick was amazing but to this day a debate rages over whether the award was correct after Liverpool's Phil Thompson had chopped down John O'Hare.

'There's no doubting it was a foul,' recalls the former Scottish international striker. 'We broke from a corner and I'd made a run forward. Woody [Tony Woodcock] had the ball on the left and played it in to me as Phil put in his challenge and brought me down. At the time I thought it was a clear penalty and didn't think any more about the decision until a bloke shoved a microphone under my nose at the final whistle and asked if it had been inside or out. I just felt that it was a penalty and told him that the TV replays would clear it up!'

In many ways it was fitting that John (known as 'Solly' to all his mates) should have played a key role in the Cup win. He was the archetypal Brian Clough player – having been with his 'gaffer' at Sunderland, Derby County and Leeds United before arriving at the City Ground. The respect is still clear to see, as John reflects on his relationship with the great man. 'From the time he started taking training at Sunderland I knew he was something special. His sessions were so different from anything I'd ever done before. I went to Derby because of him – and then Leeds. When I followed him to Forest it meant a massive drop in wages, which I did regret a bit – but it's not all about money, is it?'

Despite Cloughie's aura, John did not expect things to develop as they did at the City Ground. 'No one could have expected the transformation to happen as it did. I do feel that things might not have happened as well had Peter Taylor not come when he did because he seemed to re-energise the place.'

John's first winners' medal with Forest was from the Anglo-Scottish Cup competition. 'I really can't remember too much about it all,' he admits. 'I know I enjoyed the nights we went back to Scotland though!' He was not even in the UK when the next piece of the Forest jigsaw fell into place. 'Cloughie

allowed me to go off and play for Dallas in the summer and I was over there when I heard that Bolton hadn't won their last match and we were promoted to the First Division.'

Never an automatic selection, John did play enough games the following season to collect a Championship medal but his impact on the League Cup win was crucial. Apart from his involvement in the Final, he scored a critical goal in the semi-final against Leeds.

'I wasn't even sure I'd be playing,' he reflects. 'But we stopped off at Sheffield on the way up and Cloughie read the team out then. I was a bit surprised to be playing but scored the best goal of my Forest career after a one-two with Ian Bowyer. I hit a drive from the edge of the area which was as sweet as any other goal I'd scored.'

That goal helped Forest into the Final and John was named on the bench for the Wembley showpiece. 'It was a pretty awful game really. Chris Woods [Forest's goalkeeper] made a few decent stops – nothing too special. When John McGovern got injured I replaced him and kept the shirt for the replay.'

Although Solly had played most of his career as a striker, he was versatile enough to slot into his captain's vacant midfield role but admitted there were few instructions. 'I was just told to go out there, get the ball and give it!' His attacking instincts did bear fruit, though, as his burst forward resulted in Phil Thompson's reckless challenge – a moment that Forest fans will enjoy forever.

John remained a Forest player until May 1980, bowing out after coming on as a substitute in the European Cup Final win over Hamburg in Madrid. He later lifted the mystery surrounding the Solly nickname.

'Some people thought it was because of the famous Real Madrid midfielder Luis Del Sol but it's not quite as glamorous as that. There's a kids' nursery rhyme Solomon Grundy – you know, born on a Monday, christened on Tuesday etc. Well I could say that faster than anyone at school so they started calling me Solomon, then it got shortened. School nicknames usually don't last long but Bobby Kerr came from the same village and he brought it up when we played at Sunderland together. Colin Todd was there and called me it at Derby, so it's always followed me around!'

Liam O'Kane

Date of birth: 17 June 1948, Londonderry, Northern Ireland

Nottingham Forest record:
Appearances: League 189, FA Cup 20, League Cup 13, Others 2
Goals: FA Cup 1
Debut: 30 April 1969 v Leeds United (a) lost 0–1

Also played for: Derry City, Northern Ireland (20 caps)

In many ways, Liam O'Kane can be considered one of the unluckiest players ever to represent Forest, yet the club stalwart does not see it that way. 'I came over for a trial and ended up staying at the City Ground for 36 years!' he explains. A succession of injuries interrupted and finally ended what should have been a glittering career, yet his misfortune would have been much worse but for an invitation to join Forest's backroom staff.

As with so many other youngsters, fate played a hand in giving Liam a break. 'I'd only appeared in about eight games for Derry City when a Forest scout came and invited me for a trial. I lined up at centre-half in a practice match and found myself up against Joe Baker. I had a bit of pace then and did reasonably well and was invited to sign for the club.'

The first signs of an injury curse for Liam came as soon as he pulled on a first-team jersey. As he recalls, 'I made my debut on the final day of the season away at Leeds and went for a ball with Norman Hunter, which was 60:40 in my favour. He didn't hold back and caught me. At the time I think a few people thought it was a broken leg but it turned out to be just a trapped nerve.'

Happily recovered, Liam began to establish himself at the highest level and to forge a solid partnership alongside Bob Chapman at the heart of the Reds' defence. In the 1970–71 season he was part of an extraordinarily consistent back-line of Barron, Hindley, Chapman, O'Kane and Winfield – a quintet that featured in every single match.

During the following campaign Liam demonstrated his versatility by proving capable of slotting in at right-back. It was in this position that his injury curse struck again in a First Division match against Everton on 11 December 1971. 'One of their players caught me and I ended up with a double fracture of the leg.'

Out of first-team contention for more than 15 months, Liam could only look on helplessly as Forest slid into the Second Division. Back to his best, he was again an ever present during the 1973–74 season, when he also appeared among the list of Forest's scorers for the only time.

Everyone who was present at St James' Park that day will never forget his only goal in the Garibaldi red shirt. 'I scored in the FA Cup game against Newcastle United that was halted by a pitch invasion. We had a corner on our left and I waited just outside the box. When it came through to me I just swung my right leg at it and watched it fly into the top corner!' Later, an angry mob invaded the pitch, clearly unhappy at the home side's display. 'I was all right because I went and stood with two of my Northern Ireland teammates, Liam McFaul and David Craig, but I know several of our players got knocked about a bit and were unsettled by it all.'

Like the rest of the Forest contingent, Liam has always maintained that his side were well on the way to victory before the disturbance and that it was wrong not to play either the rearranged match or the replay back in Nottingham. That incident came shortly after he had made a piece of unwanted history playing in a match at Middlesbrough, by becoming the first Reds player to be sent off in an away League fixture in over 50 years.

'I was dismissed for a second offence but couldn't do anything about it. Their left-winger just pushed the ball past me and ran straight into me and the referee sent me off for obstruction. We appealed and fortunately the tribunal overturned the decision.'

Although Liam's career was ruthlessly cut short, he did have the honour of winning 20 international caps for Northern Ireland and has one standout memory. 'The biggest moment for me was when I managed to get our goal in a 1–1 draw against Portugal in a World Cup qualifier in Lisbon.'

On 21 February 1976 at Bristol City's Ashton Gate came the final chapter in Liam's catalogue of setbacks. 'I chased an opponent into a corner – he checked and as I did so my knees gave way. I'd done the ligaments in both. I recovered sufficiently to play about 20 reserve matches but I knew it wasn't right and had to accept the inevitable. I was finished at 26 – an age when footballers should be coming into their prime.'

Pondering on his future, Liam got a boost when Brian Clough invited him to take charge of the club's youngsters. 'I'll always be thankful to Jimmy Gordon, the first-team coach, for asking Brian to give me a chance on the coaching staff. I did my badges and over the years moved up to first-team coach – though under Cloughie not many players needed coaching!'

Through good times and bad, Liam served the club with great distinction, but the association ended during the stewardship of Joe Kinnear in December 2004. He remains a popular visitor to the City Ground, though, and is quite rightly revered for the loyalty and outstanding service he has devoted to Nottingham Forest.

Martin O'Neill

Date of birth: 1 March 1952, Kilrea, County Londonderry, Northern Ireland

Nottingham Forest record:
Appearances: League 285, FA Cup 28, League Cup 35, Others 23
Goals: League 48, FA Cup 3, League Cup 8, Others 3
Debut: 13 November 1971 v West Bromwich Albion (h) won 4–1

Also played for: Distillery, Norwich City, Manchester City, Notts County, Northern Ireland (64 caps)
Managed: Grantham Town, Shepshed Charterhouse, Wycombe Wanderers, Norwich City, Leicester City, Glasgow Celtic (Scotland), Aston Villa

There are not too many of the really great managers who can also lay claim to having been a truly outstanding player as well but Martin O'Neill would comfortably sit in that category.

A hard-working midfielder, his best years were undoubtedly given to Forest, whom he joined in October 1971 as a 19-year-old. He was far from being a raw novice, having scored twice in Distillery's Irish Cup Final win the previous season and also having scored a goal against Barcelona in the European Cup.

Martin had been taking a degree in Law at the Queen's University of Belfast but left his studies behind when he moved to Nottingham. Just prior to joining Forest he had also made his international debut, appearing as a substitute against the USSR in a European Championship qualifier. It was also from the bench that Martin made his Forest debut – coming on to score in a 4-1 home win over West Brom. Curiously, he replaced John Robertson that day – the two were to remain close friends over the years and would work side by side when Martin went into management.

His first year at Forest ended with the disappointment of relegation. Playing his football in the old Second Division did not bring about the expected development: he had flitted in and out of the first team on a regular basis and was on the transfer list prior to Brian Clough arriving at the City Ground.

The 1976–77 season saw Martin pick up his first medal from the English game – a winners' medal from the Anglo-Scottish Cup competition. More importantly, the Reds had achieved promotion and the Irishman had played his part with nine goals in 40 League appearances.

Over the next four seasons, Martin was at the forefront of all the club's success. Apart from the League Championship win in 1978, he played in the three consecutive League Cup Finals, one European Cup triumph, two Super Cups and the World Club Championship. Injury ahead of the 1979 Malmo match was his only enforced absence.

Apart from his clever link-up play and canny distribution, Martin could always be relied upon to chip in with a few vital goals and he netted twice at Wembley in the 5-0 Charity Shield demolition of Ipswich Town. His first goal came after the ball broke kindly to him on the edge of the box and a well-placed side foot found the bottom corner. His second was a beauty – chesting down a 'Robbo' cross before cracking home a half volley. He also registered a hat-trick for the club – getting three of the goals in a 6-0 home win over Chelsea.

Martin departed from the Forest ranks in the same manner in which he had started by going out as a goalscorer – getting two in a 3-1 win over Arsenal in February 1981.

After playing 371 times for the Reds, he began the first of two short spells at Norwich City. He ended up back in Nottingham in August 1983 but retired 18 months later due to a persistent knee injury.

At the time of his retirement, Martin had represented his country on 64 occasions with the highlight being the 1982 World Cup Finals in Spain, where he captained Northern Ireland to a famous win over the host nation in Valencia. His first steps in management were in non-League circles with Grantham Town and Shepshed Charterhouse, but he began to gain deserved recognition for pioneering Wycombe Wanderers' journey into the Football League.

A brief spell back at Norwich precluded a successful time at Leicester City, where he twice won the League Cup. Martin was suddenly being touted as the hottest young boss around and furthered his reputation in Scotland, where he picked up a succession of domestic honours with Celtic, as well as leading them to the 2003 UEFA Cup Final.

Awarded the OBE in 2004 for his services to sport, the softly spoken Irishman then took 15 months out of the game for personal reasons. Just prior to the 2006–07 season he returned to top-flight management once more by assuming the mantle at Aston Villa, again assisted by his former Forest teammate John Robertson.

Whenever the City Ground hot seat has been vacated over the past decade, Martin's name has always figured highly on the wish list of every fan. It's clear the immensely likeable former Red would be welcome back any day.

Garry Parker

Date of birth:　7 September 1965, Oxford

Nottingham Forest record:
Appearances:　League 103, FA Cup 16, League Cup 23, Others 9
Goals:　League 17, FA Cup 5, League Cup 4, Others 3
Debut:　30 April 1988 v Wimbledon (h) drew 0-0

Also played for:　Luton Town, Hull City, Aston Villa, Leicester City

Whenever a DVD of the greatest-ever Wembley goals is compiled, you can be sure that Garry Parker's 1989 effort for Forest will be rated among the best. With the Reds trailing 2-1 in the Simod Cup Final, opponents Everton forced a corner.

'When the kick was taken I was inside my own six-yard box,' recalls Garry. 'Des Walker headed the ball away as far as Nigel Clough, who passed it on to me in space. As I broke forward, only Paul Bracewell tried to chase me but I left him behind, ran all the way to the edge of their box and drove it in, past Neville Southall's right hand.'

The wonder goal was the highlight of an astonishing match, which the Reds went on to win 4-3 after extra-time. It was also Garry's second of the contest, as he had earlier cancelled out Everton's opener. 'That came after one of our corners found me at the back post. I hit it down and a fortunate bounce took it over the 'keeper. If I'd hit it properly I'm sure he'd have saved it!'

Garry had joined Forest in 1988 from Hull City for a fee of around £260,000. Over the course of the next three and a half years he played in most of the club's bigger matches – although not always in his favoured central-midfield role. 'I took over on the left from Brian Rice and built up a decent rapport with Stuart Pearce and Steve Hodge on that side of the pitch, but when Neil Webb was sold I went to the manager and told him that I could do the job in the middle – and he moved me.'

A close-range goal from Garry helped the Reds defeat Manchester United on their own pitch in the FA Cup sixth round in 1989. 'Franz Carr played it in from the right and I was almost on the goalline – it was nothing more than a tap-in but it was nice to beat them!'

The win took Forest into a last four meeting with Liverpool – at Hillsborough. 'Going into that game we really fancied our chances. We really thought we were going to do them.' The tragic events that unfolded that afternoon rendered football as an irrelevance and the Forest players were quickly ushered into their dressing room and away from the devastating scenes unfolding outside. 'They'd just hit the bar – then we were suddenly waved off the pitch and kept inside until Cloughie briefed us as to what was going on. It was clearly a horrific incident.'

Despite Forest's confidence ahead of the first match, they were outgunned when the sides met again, this time at Old Trafford. 'We just weren't involved that night,' says Garry. 'They were much the better team and played us off the park.'

Garry played in successive League Cup Finals for Forest, earning winners' medals against Luton Town in 1989 and Oldham Athletic 12 months later. 'The Luton game meant a lot to me as it was my first winners' medal, but I actually enjoyed the Oldham Final more because I played much better in that one!'

Trips to Wembley were commonplace during Garry's days with the Reds, although a series of wins were watered down a little by the disappointment of the 1991 FA Cup Final loss to Tottenham.

'That was the most disappointing match of my life. We all knew it was the one thing that Cloughie hadn't won and we knew how much he wanted to win it. We fancied it big time – we'd hit seven against Chelsea and five against Norwich leading up to the Final but we didn't play as well as we could have and paid the consequences.'

The game was only a couple of minutes old when Garry felt the impact of a rash challenge by Paul Gascoigne.

'He caught me in the chest with his studs. I tried to stand up but I was badly winded and the pain was unbelievable. I still believe that some sort of action should have been taken against Gazza then – he was running about like a loose cannon and did Gary Charles soon after with another bad challenge.'

While Gazza deservedly has his own place among the rich history of our national stadium, no one can deny that so too does Garry Parker.

Tom Peacock

Date of birth: 14 September 1912, Morton, Derbyshire

Nottingham Forest record:
Appearances: League 109, FA Cup 11
Goals: League 57, FA Cup 5
Debut: 9 September 1933 v Oldham Athletic (h) lost 1–3

Also played for: Chesterfield, Bath City, Melton Mowbray, Chelsea

Tom Peacock achieved a feat for Nottingham Forest that will surely never be bettered. During the space of a seven-week period, between November and December 1935, the striker scored four goals in a League match – on three separate occasions!

A schoolteacher by profession, Tom signed full time for Forest after graduating from Nottingham University. Manager Noel Watson had wanted to sign him much earlier after watching him play for the varsity side, but the striker had opted to fulfil a teaching obligation in Somerset first and to play his football as an amateur for Bath City.

Tall and rangy, he had good pace and an opportunist's eye, which enabled him to benchmark his Forest career with a debut goal in a home defeat against Oldham Athletic. Despite this early promise he was unable to claim a first-team jersey again until mid-December, three months later. After a blank in an away match at Bradford City, the folly of leaving Tom on the sidelines for so long was made very evident. In his next game, just his third League match and second at home, he struck four times in a 6–1 thrashing of Port Vale, a side that would soon come to fear the sight of Tom Peacock's name on the opposition team sheet!

Curiously, Tom went four matches without scoring after his feast against the Valiants but then proved that his ability to score goals in clusters was not a one-off by hitting a hat-trick against Queen's Park Rangers in his first FA Cup tie for Forest.

By the end of the season Tom had appeared in 18 League and Cup matches and registered a total of 11 goals, a foretaste of what he would provide over the next couple of years when his strike partnership with Johnny Dent would blossom. In each of the 1934–35 and 1935–36 seasons Tom would emerge as the Reds' top scorer, bagging 21 goals each time – although the collective efforts of the players could propel the side no higher than ninth in the Second Division.

Tom's sequence of 'fours' began on 9 November 1935, with Barnsley defeated 6–0 at the City Ground. A fortnight later, Forest's next home match, saw Port Vale again being put to the sword.

In one of the more astonishing scorelines that the Reds have ever recorded they ran riot, winning by a margin of nine goals to two. Around a month later, on Boxing Day, Tom was at it again, netting four of the goals in a 6–0 win over Doncaster Rovers and helping the side to a fifth straight home win.

In the prime form of his life, Tom's playing career was then seriously disrupted with a succession of injuries, culminating in the removal of a couple of cartilages. Over the course of the next three seasons he was only fit and available to start in a total of 28 League matches, which produced nine goals – but, significantly, yet another hat-trick! Against Fulham on 5 September 1936 he scored three in a 5–3 win. As on the previous five occasions, it was recorded in a home match – talk about saving your best for your own fans!

Tom's last League goal for the Garibaldis came in a 2–2 draw against Tranmere Rovers in February 1939, although he made another 17 guest appearances during the war years, contributing six goals. He also played a few matches for Chelsea under a similar arrangement.

Upon the outbreak of war Tom joined the Royal Air Force, rising to the rank of flight sergeant. He would regularly turn out for the full RAF football side, where his partner in attack would be Ted Drake, the former Arsenal and England player.

League football resumed at the start of the 1945–46 season and Tom remained on the Forest books. He was to add only one further appearance to his tally, though, playing away against Derby County on 13 October 1945. He then resurrected his teaching career and later became headmaster of St Edmund's Primary School at Mansfield Woodhouse.

It is clear from his scoring record that Tom was undoubtedly one of the top marksmen of his day. But for his injuries – and the conflict – he may well have gone on to take his place among the all-time greats. Nevertheless, those Forest supporters who did witness his goal-scoring achievements will never forget the man they called 'Four-goal Peacock'.

Stuart Pearce

Date of birth: 24 April 1962, Hammersmith, London

Nottingham Forest record:
Appearances: League 401, FA Cup 37, League Cup 60, Others 24
Goals: League 63, FA Cup 9, League Cup 10, Others 6
Debut: 17 August 1985 v Luton Town (a) drew 1–1
Caretaker manager: December 1996–February 1997

Also played for: Wealdstone, Coventry City, Newcastle United, West Ham United, Manchester City, England (78 caps)
Also managed: Manchester City, England Under-21s

Stuart Pearce is, quite simply, one of the finest left full-backs ever to play the game. Demonstrably proud to represent club and country, he never shirked a single challenge throughout his entire career and will be remembered as one of Forest's all-time greats. His clenched fist salute to the Trent End before every home match showed that he meant business and in over 500 first-team games for the Reds he never gave anything less than his all.

When Brian Clough signed Stuart from Coventry City he was buying more than a good defender – he was buying a 'first lieutenant': a player who would become the manager's eyes, ears and mouthpiece out on the pitch – as true a leader as there has ever been.

Curiously for a player who scored goals at a healthy rate throughout his career, Stuart only chipped in with one during his first season at the City Ground – at a home victory over Ipswich Town. Plenty more would follow, though! Venomous left-footed strikes – particularly from free-kicks and penalties – became commonplace, and the anticipation of the supporters was only matched by the anxiety of the opposing goalkeeper.

At the end of his second full season at the City Ground, Stuart won his first international cap, playing against Brazil at Wembley. His selection made him the 999th player to appear for England (Forest teammate Neil Webb became the 1000th!).

With 76 of his 78 appearances coming while he was a Forester, Stuart is the club's most-capped international of all time. Few football fans will ever forget the extreme emotions he went through during penalty shoot-outs at the 1990 World Cup quarter-finals and then the European Championships in England six years later.

Stuart's fair but uncompromising style of play earned him the nickname of 'Psycho' from the Forest faithful, with whom he developed a special bond, more so after he took over as captain in 1987.

In almost a decade of outstanding and devoted loyalty he led the side to two League Cup successes and other Wembley victories in both the Simod Cup and the Zenith Data Systems Cup Finals. In the latter, in 1992, Stuart was injured, forcing him to miss out on another League Cup Final – which ended with defeat against Manchester United.

Possibly the biggest disappointment of his career came in the FA Cup Final of 1991. After scoring one of the semi-final goals against West Ham United, Psycho put Forest ahead at Wembley with one of his trademark free-kicks, but an afternoon of misfortune and lost opportunity eventually went the way of Tottenham Hotspur.

Stuart's commitment to the Forest cause strengthened when he stayed with them after relegation at the end of the 1992–93 campaign and he led them straight back up in Frank Clark's first season as manager.

In December 1996 Stuart stepped into the breach and became caretaker manager after Clark's departure. With the side struggling at the wrong end of the table, he helped spark something of a revival and collected a Manager of the Month award – giving early notice of the wisdom he had accumulated under his mentor, Cloughie. Nevertheless, despite the arrival and help of Dave Bassett, initially as general manager, the odds were stacked against safety and the club had to undergo another drop into the lower tier.

Still with plenty to offer as a player, the fans and club accepted that Stuart's decision to stay in the Premiership and sign for Newcastle United could not be criticised – and a City Ground full house turned out for his testimonial match between the two clubs.

David Gibson of Newark has followed the Reds for over 40 years and rates Stuart as his all-time Forest favourite. 'He always gave total commitment to club and country,' says David. 'He was the perfect captain because his enthusiasm would inspire those around him. It was said that some players would run through a brick wall for Cloughie – and if it was true of anyone, then it certainly would have been Stuart!'

With 522 first-team appearances, only Bobby McKinlay and Ian Bowyer have appeared more times for Forest. Of the other incredible career statistics of which the player can be immensely proud, he has represented the Reds in more League Cup ties than anyone else and scored more goals than any other defender for the club.

The man who made the left-back position fashionable also did the same for his football club and the fans will always be grateful.

Johnny Quigley

Date of birth: 28 June 1935, Glasgow, Scotland
Died: 30 November 2004

Nottingham Forest record:
Appearances: League 236, FA Cup 26, League Cup 5, Others 3
Goals: League 51, FA Cup 4, League Cup 3
Debut: 5 October 1957 v Tottenham Hotspur (a) won 4–3

Also played for: Ashfield Juniors (Scotland), Huddersfield Town, Bristol City, Mansfield Town

Johnny Quigley was a tough-tackling inside-forward who will be best remembered by Forest fans as much for scoring the winning goal in the 1959 FA Cup semi-final as for his tireless performance in the Final itself.

The Scot had been brought to Nottingham from Scottish amateur football by manager Billy Walker in July 1957 and scored the winning goal on his debut in a 4–3 thriller at Spurs.

Adapting quickly to life in the First Division, Johnny began to forge a reputation as a fine distributor of the ball who was also capable of getting forward into goal-scoring positions. He was immensely popular with the other players, who soon realised that he was more than capable of handling himself in the no-nonsense midfield battlegrounds. His prowess in front of goal was never emphasised better than on 8 November 1958, when he became the first Forest player to score a First Division hat-trick since the war, hitting three in a 4–0 home win over Manchester City.

By this stage of his career Johnny was beginning to attract the attention of the international selectors and he was invited to join up with the Scottish squad for a couple of training sessions and trial matches. Sadly, the opportunity to represent his country in a full international was never fulfilled.

Whatever disappointment Johnny experienced at his continued omission from the national team was partially compensated for by the winning of an FA Cup medal in 1959. Forest progressed to their first Wembley Final at the expense of Aston Villa, with the semi-final clash at Hillsborough being best described as 'anything but a classic'. Although the opposition were fighting a relegation battle, they had a proud history in the FA Cup and had been winners just two years earlier. They were not going to roll over and submit easily.

With so much at stake the first goal was always going to be crucial and it arrived shortly after half-time. Quigley, on another of his bursts from the centre of the park, got past Johnny Dixon, the Villa captain, to fire low past goalkeeper Nigel Sims and into the corner of the net. The Forest fans were jubilant and fulsome in their praise for the scorer.

There were no further goals so Forest could celebrate their passage through to a May appointment at the Twin Towers against Luton Town.

On a sun-drenched day, Johnny had an early opportunity to put Forest ahead, but that was soon forgotten as the side opened up a two-goal advantage. Roy Dwight's injury – in the days before substitutions – balanced things up, though. Forest had the lead but Luton had an extra player. Johnny's lung-busting runs and resolute tackling were never more vital and he performed heroically to break down a wave of attacks and give his defenders the protection they required.

If the Cup Final was the stand-out match of Johnny's career, he could also proudly claim to have played in a number of other significant firsts in Forest's history. Three months after the success over Luton, Johnny lined up in the Forest side beaten by Wolves, the League champions. This was the first occasion that the Reds had competed in the Charity Shield. One year later saw the introduction of the League Cup competition and, although Johnny did not play in the first-round win over Halifax Town, he netted twice in the round-two win over Bristol City.

In 1961 Forest were invited to participate in the Inter Cities Fairs Cup, their first European adventure. The draw paired them up against Valencia. Although the Reds had won a friendly against the same opposition in Spain a couple of years earlier, this time they were no match. Johnny and his teammates were beaten 2–0 away and then 5–1 in the return leg.

His days at the City Ground drew to a close when he moved to Huddersfield Town in February 1965. He had played over 250 times for the Reds, notching up more than 50 League goals. After 18-month spells at both Huddersfield and then Bristol City, Johnny returned to Nottinghamshire to skipper Mansfield Town and play his part in two memorable FA Cup runs with the Stags, including a 3–0 win over a star-studded West Ham United side.

He later coached Mansfield before moving to work in the Middle East for several years. Johnny died in Nottingham in 2004, aged 69.

Andy Reid

Date of birth: 29 July 1982, Dublin, Republic of Ireland

Nottingham Forest record:
Appearances: League 144, FA Cup 6, League Cup 8, Others 2
Goals: League 21, FA Cup 2, League Cup 1, Others 1
Debut: 29 November 2000 v Sheffield United (h) won 2–0

Also played for: Tottenham Hotspur, Charlton Athletic, Republic of Ireland (22 caps)

Not for the first time, the Nottingham Forest academy unearthed a sparkling gem when Andy Reid graduated into the first-team ranks. At just 18, the young Irishman made an instant impact, scoring on his debut and dazzling the supporters with some mazy dribbles and accurate crosses.

During his early months of first-team football some seasoned Forest watchers observed that the young Dubliner bore a passing resemblance to John Robertson, of Forest's European Cup-winning sides. Like Robbo, Andy had a preference for the left flank, as well as possessing other physical similarities.

Despite constant managerial upheaval, he became a pivotal figure as the Reds endeavoured to build a side capable of sustaining a promotion challenge. Once Paul Hart had succeeded David Platt as manager, Andy became the heartbeat of the side, being used not only from his wide position but also as a central playmaker capable of unlocking the tightest of defences.

Andy's deadball delivery and ferocious shooting made him a firm favourite with the Trentsiders and he scored a series of spectacular goals, including a wonderful solo effort at West Ham to enhance his reputation. He also netted what seemed to be a crucial goal against Sheffield United in the second-leg Play-off semi-final in May 2003 before Forest capsized under pressure from the home side.

With suitors beginning to notice his extraordinary talent, Andy earned a call up to the international ranks and made his Republic of Ireland bow against Canada in a 3–0 victory at Lansdowne Road. Popular opinion made him the Man of the Match and earned him an extended run in the side. Andy's introduction to the national ranks was timely and spectacular in terms of both performance and statistics.

He did not feature on the losing side in any of his opening 15 appearances while wearing the green of his country. These games included a drawn friendly against world champions Brazil and an impressive victory over the Dutch in the Amsterdam Arena. Reidy's first goal at the highest level came from a free-kick, from all of 40 yards against Cyprus, which eluded everyone and

dropped in. He followed that up with a superb 25-yard curling effort against Bulgaria.

During the 2003–04 season Andy was an ever present in the Forest ranks, scoring 13 goals in the League. His ability to grasp a match by the scruff of the neck became ever more vital for the Forest cause, but his best efforts were not enough to inspire his side to another Play-off challenge.

A managerial merry-go-round commenced at the City Ground with Joe Kinnear replacing Paul Hart, but there was little cause for optimism as the first nine League matches of the 2004–05 season passed without a victory.

It was clear that Andy – by now an automatic selection for his country – would soon be playing his football at a higher level than the lower echelons of the second tier. The midfielder's final game for Forest was an FA Cup fourth-round tie against Peterborough United on 29 January 2005. After months of speculation about his future he joined Tottenham Hotspur in a joint deal with teammate Michael Dawson, for a combined fee of around £8 million.

With a plethora of midfield talent available at White Hart Lane, Andy was not really given an extended run in the first team due in the main to a knee-ligament injury. Once recovered, he was deemed surplus to requirements and was allowed to join Charlton Athletic in August 2006. He was again unable to maintain a clean bill of health for long and his progress was hampered by a hamstring injury, which required surgery. Having made just 16 League appearances for the Addicks he was ruled out of a run-in, which ultimately saw his side plunge back into the Championship.

Andy will be hoping to remain fully fit throughout the 2007–08 campaign to enable the abundance of talent at his disposal to once again shine for club and country.

During the four or so years that Andy Reid pulled on a first-team jersey for Forest he could never be accused of giving anything but his best, however trying the circumstances.

A wonderfully gifted player, he brought a great amount of pleasure to those who watched him at the City Ground – a testimony that every footballer should strive to achieve.

John Robertson

Date of birth: 20 January 1953, Uddingston, South Lanarkshire, Scotland

Nottingham Forest record:
Appearances: League 398, FA Cup 36, League Cup 46, Others 34
Goals: League 61, FA Cup 10, League Cup 16, Others 8
Debut: 10 October 1970 v Blackpool (h) won 3–1

Also played for: Derby County, Corby Town, Scotland (28 caps)

In the history of the European Cup competition very few players can claim to have played in two Finals, created the winning goal in one and scored the only goal in the other. John Robertson had many fine days in the Garibaldi Red but his performances in Munich and Madrid will never be forgotten by Forest's exultant supporters.

Such heady days were unthinkable when the young winger began his career at the City Ground. In only his second year as a bit-part player the club tumbled unceremoniously out of the top flight. By the time of its return five years later, John had confounded his critics and missed just one match in the promotion-winning season of 1976–77.

Those who had wondered at his appearance and commitment were made to eat their words. 'Much is made of the fact that Clough and Taylor were supposed to have turned around my career but I'd had a good season playing under Dave Mackay and then did my cartilage in the summer of 1973,' recalls John. 'My knee was very sore for a long time afterwards and it's probably true that I was feeling sorry for myself for a while, but I'd already realised that I had to change my attitude if I was going to succeed.'

'Robbo' blossomed on the old Division One stage and helped the Reds to the title at the first time of asking, as well as converting the winning penalty in the League Cup Final against Liverpool. 'That was the biggest penalty I'd taken up to that point and there was a great deal of pressure on it. Ray Clemence did get a touch to that one but fortunately it went in!'

Over the next few years John found himself in the same situation on many occasions, both for club and country. 'It's always a bit of a guessing game between you and the 'keeper but I usually preferred to hit it to his right. I once remember playing for Scotland against England and Trevor Francis told Joe Corrigan where I'd hit it. I thought about changing my mind but knew if I hit it well enough it would go in and it did. I missed the odd one in my career but never a really important one!'

Watching John sweetly strike home his penalties right-footed emphasises just how good a job he did as Forest's left-winger. It was usually a case of beat the man and whip in the cross – and that is exactly what he did to win the European Cup against Malmo. 'People ask how I picked Trevor Francis out but I just hit it into space at the far post as I usually did and he did really well to get in that position to score.'

John's cunning ability to provide the perfect cross was often taken for granted. 'When I watched the television rerun of the Malmo game, the commentator was questioning why I didn't provide more crosses like that. Sometimes it's not that easy – defenders know what you are about and don't let you. Ian Bowyer helped create Trevor's goal because he was able to get the ball out to me so quickly!'

One year later in the Final against Hamburg, John found he had to come inside to find success. 'I laid the ball off to Gary Birtles and he fought like hell to get it back to me. I got my shot off first time and thought, straight away, "That's got a chance." It curved beautifully past the 'keeper and went in – what an unbelievable feeling that was.'

Robbo recalls, with pride, just how good Forest had become over a short space of time and remembers some very spectacular team performances. 'Some days we were just brilliant,' he says. 'A 4–0 win at Old Trafford against Manchester United when we were on our way to the League title was the top of them all for me. But there were some other outstanding games: a 3–1 win at Leeds in the League Cup, a 5–0 win over West Ham, a 4–0 win over Ipswich – there were a few.'

A brief, controversial move to Derby County in 1983 made John realise what he had been missing and he soon returned for a second stint at Forest. After his playing days were over the Scot briefly ran a pub before returning to the game to successfully work with Martin O'Neill at Wycombe, Leicester, Celtic and Aston Villa.

Bryan Roy

Date of birth: 12 February 1970, Amsterdam, Netherlands

Nottingham Forest record:
Appearances: League 85, FA Cup 11, League Cup 8, Others 6
Goals: League 24, FA Cup 1, League Cup 2, Others 1
Debut: 20 August 1994 v Ipswich Town (a) won 1–0

Also played for: Ajax (Netherlands), Foggia (Italy), Hertha Berlin (Germany), NAC Breda (Netherlands), Netherlands (32 caps)

By scoring the winning goal on his Premiership debut, Bryan Roy ensured himself of immediate favouritism among the Forest supporters. Already a seasoned Dutch international by the time he arrived on Trentside in the summer of 1994, Bryan had served a rigorous apprenticeship by progressing through the Ajax Academy. He had helped his home-town club achieve League and UEFA Cup success before moving to Italy, where he enhanced his reputation at Foggia in the tough-tackling Serie A. His move to Nottingham came about as manager Frank Clark stepped up his search for a proven left-sided player in readiness for the Reds' return to the top division. The criteria was more than matched with the capture of Roy, signed for a then club-record fee of £2.9 million.

Having just played a starring role in the Netherlands' march to the quarter-finals of the US '94 World Cup, the flying winger was at the peak of his powers and was seen as an astute addition to Clark's promotion-winning squad. With Stan Collymore capable of converting anything in front of goal, the supply line from the left helped create mayhem and havoc among the best backlines in the country, but the new acquisition proved to be much more than a touchline-hugging crosser of the ball. Bryan showed himself to be comfortable with either foot and also demonstrated a capacity to be a ferocious striker of the ball. So much so that he followed up his opening-day winner at Ipswich with a series of eye-catching performances, helping Forest to exceed all expectations as they won eight and drew three of their first 11 matches and remained in the top six throughout the campaign.

Their third-place finish was sufficient to qualify the club for European competition. Bryan's haul of 15 goals, all but two of which were scored in the League, was a significantly higher return than even the manager could have hoped for. During three successive matches towards the end of the season, the flying Dutchman netted twice in each game on the way to his most productive season ever.

In the middle of that three-game sequence, on 29 March 1995 Bryan appeared for the 32nd and final time for the Netherlands. His international career had lasted for five years and brought his country nine goals. Without the goal threat of Collymore, Forest – and Bryan – found life much more difficult the following season, although the Dutchman again reached double figures, including a goal against Malmo as the Reds progressed to round four of the UEFA Cup.

His third and final season with Forest was more turbulent. Bryan flitted in and out of a struggling side, through a combination of form and fitness. Ironically, though, despite relegation for the club, the enigmatic winger ended his days in the Garibaldi Red just as he had started – with a goal against Wimbledon on his final appearance.

After Forest's relegation at the end of the 1996–97 season they were in no position to deny Bryan his request for a transfer and were happy to accept a bid of £1.5 million from Hertha Berlin. Like fellow Dutchman Johnny Metgod, the Forest faithful had taken to the skilful Amsterdamer, but the player ensured he would quickly be forgotten around the City Ground with a few ill-chosen parting comments. 'Nottingham has nothing to recommend it except Robin Hood – and he's dead,' was the reported quote on his arrival in Germany. The *Nottingham Evening Post* was quick to respond. 'And now he's gone to Berlin – a city with nothing but a wall, and that's been knocked down!'

With just three goals from 50 appearances, Hertha did not get the best out of Bryan and he returned to his homeland with a move to NAC Breda. Injuries began to take their toll and he played his final match for them in May 2001.

Now back where he began, as an integral part of the Ajax Academy, there are many who feel that Bryan's playing career may eventually be eclipsed by an even more successful time as a coach. It is beyond question, however, that his most prolific spell as a player was during his time at the City Ground.

Peter Shilton

Date of birth: 18 September 1949, Leicester

Nottingham Forest record:
Appearances: League 202, FA Cup 18, League Cup 26, Others 26
Debut: 17 September 1977 v Aston Villa (h) won 2–1

Also played for: Leicester City, Stoke City, Southampton, Derby County, Plymouth Argyle, Bolton Wanderers, Leyton Orient, England (125 caps)
Managed: Plymouth Argyle

Forest's double European Cup-winning goalkeeper was one of the most dedicated performers the game has ever seen. A long-time Clough target, Peter Shilton was prised away from Stoke City in 1977 for just £270,000 and sold for profit five years later, having boosted his medal collection in spectacular fashion while at the City Ground.

The young 'Shilts' had graduated through the ranks at his home-town club Leicester City and succeeded the great Gordon Banks as first choice. He played for the Foxes in the 1969 FA Cup Final, aged just 19, and more than 20 years later he was still at the very top of his profession, keeping goal for his country at Italia '90 where he helped England reach the World Cup semi-finals.

Form as well as fitness were the contributory factors in Peter's longevity in the game, and he was at his finest during his stay in Nottingham. He joined the club during their first season back in the top flight, appearing in the remaining 37 matches he was available for and conceded only 18 goals as Forest wrapped up their first League title.

The Championship was secured in an away match at Coventry City on 22 April 1978. In his book, *Peter Shilton: The Autobiography*, the former international reveals that he made what he considers to have been one of his greatest-ever saves that afternoon, moving quickly across his goal to turn over a close-range header from Mick Ferguson.

Peter's arrival at the City Ground confirmed Forest's defence as the meanest in the country. After losing at Leeds United on 19 November 1977 they remained undefeated in the League until a loss at Liverpool on 9 December 1978 – a record-breaking run of 42 League matches, a sequence that included 25 clean sheets – all with Shilts in goal. In home matches the unbeaten run was even longer – 51 games without losing between April 1977 and November 1979. Apart from being immensely agile and an excellent shot-stopper, Peter was commanding inside his own penalty area and maintained an almost telepathic understanding with the central defenders employed in front of him – usually the reliable pairing of Kenny Burns and Larry Lloyd.

Although Peter was Cup tied for the League Cup competition in 1978 (Chris Woods kept goal in the Final), he did win a medal the following season against Southampton, as well as keeping his goal intact in the Charity Shield win over Ipswich Town. Bigger matches followed, though, as the Reds became champions of Europe in 1979 and defended their crown a year later. Against Malmo Peter was rarely tested but in the win over Hamburg he was frequently put under pressure, although more often than not the Germans were restricted to shots from outside the area.

Renowned for his thorough professionalism and taxing training regime, Peter was the model of consistency for Forest and he did not miss a League match from his debut until March 1981, when Lee Smelt deputised in a match at West Brom. He played in more than 200 League games for Forest before deciding that it was the right stage of his career to accept a new challenge and moved to Southampton in the 1982 close season for a fee of £300,000.

That same summer he kept goal for England in the World Cup Finals in Spain. Peter's fitness, form and dedication enabled him to take part in two other Finals – Mexico in 1986, where he was controversially out-leapt by Maradona's 'Hand of God' goal, and Italy in 1990, where he ended his international career after a record-breaking 125 caps.

Peter continued to play on at League level for a number of clubs and in December 1996 he became the first player in Football League history to appear in 1,000 League matches when he turned out for Leyton Orient against Brighton & Hove Albion.

Among the many accolades to come Peter's way was his award of PFA Player of the Year in 1978 and later both the MBE and CBE for his services to sport.

While there have been many outstanding goalkeepers in Nottingham Forest's rich history, purely in statistical terms there have been none to rival the achievements of Peter Leslie Shilton.

Alf Spouncer

Date of birth: 1 July 1877, Gainsborough, Lincolnshire
Died: 31 August 1962

Nottingham Forest record:
Appearances: League 300, FA Cup 36
Goals: League 47, FA Cup 5
Debut: 4 September 1897 v Notts County (h) drew 1–1

Also played for: Gainsborough Trinity, Sheffield United, England (1 cap)

William Alfred Spouncer was the first in a long line of skilful wingers who have served Nottingham Forest down the years. He joined the Reds in the summer of 1897, having already spent two spells with his home-town club Gainsborough Trinity as well as a couple of seasons at Sheffield United. Alf, as he preferred to be known, made his League debut for the Reds on the opening day of the season in the derby clash against Notts County – a match that finished 1–1. With his tricky wing play and precision crossing, Forest knew they had recruited well – Alf had cost them a transfer fee of £125, considerable money for a 20-year-old!

On the occasions when he was allowed to wander freely away from his flank, Alf demonstrated that he possessed a powerful shot in either foot. He netted four goals in his first League campaign, plus the decider in a 3–2 FA Cup quarter-final win over West Brom – a key moment in the march to the Final as a late recovery saw Forest emerge triumphant after trailing 0–2.

Forest's 3–1 success over Derby County saw them lift the Cup for the first time and Alf was instrumental in the win. His dribbling skills won the free-kick which enabled the Reds to take the lead and he later battled hard to earn the corner from which John McPherson forced home the all-important third goal. With Billy Wragg carrying an injury, sustained early in that Final, Alf's value to the side was never greater. The reorganisation forced him inside to play an unfamiliar role, in which he simply shone.

Despite it coming so early in his career, the Cup success was one of the major highlights of Alf's career, although he did briefly go on to earn international recognition. In 1900 he was selected for his only England appearance, a 1–1 draw against Wales at the Arms Park in Cardiff. For 13 seasons he tormented full-backs up and down the land and helped set up countless opportunities for Grenville Morris, Forest's leading scorer of the day.

During the 1905 close season Forest embarked on a lengthy and arduous trip to South America, where they played one match in Uruguay and seven in Argentina. All of the matches were won convincingly – the first time an English top-flight side had so ruthlessly beaten international opponents. Despite the Atlantic crossing being three weeks' duration each way, Alf loved every minute of the tour, relishing the sights and the way of life. Sadly, despite Forest making a few quid out of the journey and returning with an unblemished record, the players were shattered and it told throughout the subsequent League season when the club was relegated for the first time.

Tiredness and lack of proper preparation were undoubtedly key factors in the slide into Division Two. Forest were fortunate, though, in that they were able to hold on to most of their key players – Alf included – and they swept to the title, ending the season with a 17-match unbeaten run.

Forest finished ninth in Division One in 1907–08 but struggled again the following year. Towards the end of the season they had to beat Leicester Fosse to stay up. Leicester were already relegated but no one expected them to be swept aside in such convincing manner as Forest destroyed them 12–0 – a scoreline that remains today as the club's highest League victory. Three Forest players scored hat-tricks in the demolition: Enoch West, Bill Hooper and Alf himself, whose goals were not only his first treble for the club but also his last ever. He played five more times at the start of the next season to take his tally of League appearances for Forest to exactly 300.

After hanging up his boots he travelled around Europe, his thirst whetted by the South American adventure. He spent time coaching at Barcelona before returning home to work for a flour-making company in London. He remained there until the outbreak of the war in 1914, when he was called up to serve in the Black Watch.

Alf eventually retired to Essex and until his death in 1962, he was the last remaining survivor of Forest's 1898 FA Cup-winning side.

Steve Stone

Date of birth: 20 August 1971, Gateshead, Tyne and Wear

Nottingham Forest record:
Appearances: League 192, FA Cup 11, League Cup 14, Others 10
Goals: League 23, League Cup 2, Others 2
Debut: 2 May 1992 v West Ham United (a) lost 0–3

Also played for: Aston Villa, Portsmouth, Leeds United, England (9 caps)

If medals were awarded for sheer tenacity and determination then Steve Stone would have won the gold many times over. He overcame three broken legs to fulfil his dream of becoming a professional footballer and never gave anything less than 100 percent when wearing a Nottingham Forest shirt. 'There's no excuse for not putting in the effort,' he maintains. 'Even if you're having an absolute stinker you've still got to work hard and I've always believed the fans respect that.'

Steve's determination to do his best for Forest stretches back to when he was a 13-year-old schoolboy. 'I felt I was getting overlooked. Other kids were being watched and given trials so I wrote a letter to about 10 clubs asking for a chance.'

Several sent patronising responses but Forest did something better – they went and watched him. 'Bill Emery, Forest's scout in the North East, came and saw me play and then went and spoke to my dad. Within six weeks of that letter I travelled down and played in three trial matches. I was a bit overawed at first but Alan Hill, the youth development coach at the time, actually came onto the pitch to ask me my name, so I thought I must be doing OK!'

Forest signed Steve up as soon as they could but then had to wait while the player overcame a series of set-backs. 'Between the ages of 17 and 20 I broke my right leg three times – all playing football. Each time it was a bad tackle but I wasn't the best tackler in the world myself, so perhaps some of it was down to me!'

Most youngsters would have given up on their ambition and decided enough is enough – but not Steve. 'Playing football was all I knew and all I wanted to do. Every time it was a set-back but each time I knew I was getting closer and closer to the first team and that's what drove me on. The club were very supportive and kept renewing my contract while I recovered.' Eventually a fully fit Steve was given his chance, coming on as a substitute away at West Ham. 'It was Des Walker's final match for the club before he left to go to Italy.'

He then had to wait until the closing weeks of the following season before making his first start – and he celebrated it with a goal. 'It was away at Middlesbrough and I'd got about 40 of my family and friends there. Woany [Ian Woan] played a short corner to Nigel [Clough]. I made a run into the box and got on the end of his cross to score with a diving header, which gave us a 2–1 win!' Steve admits his selection for that match had been timely. 'I knew I was ready for first-team football and was thinking about moving on to find a club that would play me regularly. Cloughie later admitted that he'd probably held me back longer than he should have.'

Relegation at the end of that season was a bitter experience for everyone at the City Ground, but out of every cloud...'There was a bit of a clear-out at the club so I found myself starting virtually every match the following year under Frank Clark and playing in a central-midfield position, which I enjoyed.'

Yet it was wide on the right flank that 'Stoney' played for most of his career, helping Forest win promotion back to the top flight and then qualify for Europe, as well as getting an England call-up and then a place in the Euro '96 squad. 'We were on the crest of a wave and then it all turned around again – Stan Collymore left and myself, Stuart Pearce and Bryan Roy all got injured. You can't compete if you are suddenly without four of your key players.'

Steve snapped the tendon on his patella, ruling him out for almost the whole 1996–97 season. Fully recovered, he then returned to win a First Division Championship medal under Dave Bassett before leaving the City Ground to sign for Aston Villa in March 1999. 'I probably should have gone a bit earlier but I was naïve enough to think things would get better and that we'd make a load of new signings. The club's finances ensured it didn't work out that way.'

Curiously, Steve rates his final goal for Forest as his best. 'No one remembers it. It was against Manchester United in the League Cup away at Old Trafford and we lost – but I scored with a 30-yard screamer!'

The abiding memory of Steve in a Forest shirt will be of a player who gave his all every time he played – teasing and tormenting defenders before whipping in a dangerous cross. Typically, he credits his great mate Ian Woan for making him look good. 'Woany and me worked well together and he made my job a whole lot easier – he used to find me regularly with that glorious left foot of his and he never got as much praise as he should have.'

Ian Storey-Moore

Date of birth: 17 January 1945, Ipswich, Suffolk

Nottingham Forest record:
Appearances: League 236, FA Cup 19, League Cup 13, Others 4
Goals: League 105, FA Cup 6, League Cup 5, Others 2
Debut: 10 May 1963 v Ipswich Town (h) won 2-1

Also played for: Manchester United, Burton Albion, Chicago Sting (US), Shepshed Charterhouse, England (1 cap)
Managed: Burton Albion, Shepshed Charterhouse

Had he plied his trade in a different era then Ian Storey-Moore would have been a global superstar. Film-star looks and talent to match, it is sad that his career was cut short by injury and is best defined by one afternoon that even he does not regard as his finest. In five out of six seasons Ian finished as the club's top scorer, an achievement of which he is understandably proud. 'It's not bad for someone who wasn't an out-and-out striker. I've been quite fortunate that I've always been able to score goals at whatever level I've played at.'

His debut for Forest had come at the end of the 1962–63 season, at home to Ipswich Town. 'The manager just gave me a run-out because he wanted to have a look at me. I laid on a goal and I think I did reasonably well, but it was back to the reserves for the start of the next season.'

He did not have that long to wait for another opportunity and complemented his play with his first senior goal. 'We played Sheffield United at home on Boxing Day. The pitch was atrocious – I'm sure the match wouldn't have been played nowadays. I scored as we went 3–0 up – but they pulled it back to get a 3–3 draw. A couple of days later we had to play them again, at Bramall Lane, and I scored both of our goals as we won 2–1. I remember feeling "three goals for Christmas isn't a bad start!"'

Although it was Andy Beattie who pitched Ian in for his debut, he played most of his Forest career under Johnny Carey and was grateful that the manager was not regimented in his approach. 'I was a floating left-winger,' he explains. 'My starting position was out wide but I was always given a licence to roam. I didn't want to be tied down and liked to have a wander, where I felt I would be able to make more of a contribution.'

Perhaps unfairly, the Forest number 11 will forever be associated with just one match – the FA Cup sixth-round tie on 8 April 1967 at home to Everton, the holders of the trophy. In a see-saw contest, Ian's hat-trick clinched the match 3–2 for the Reds. Fans still talk to him about that day but, modestly, he instead praises the performance of a teammate. 'Frank Wignall was the inspiration behind our win. I got the goals and the plaudits that go with that but he was a real handful that day. Many people have said it was my finest performance for Forest but it wasn't by a long way. In fact, apart from the goals, I hardly contributed at all!'

Like many of his teammates, it was the atmosphere inside the City Ground that day that the player remembers so vividly. 'It really was incredible – my poor old mother had to leave because she felt she was going to faint because it got so tense!' Ian does have one slight regret as he recalls his most memorable day in a Forest shirt. 'I didn't get to keep the match ball. I'm not sure if we did that then, probably because they were too expensive to give away!'

If that was the stand-out match of Ian's career, there is one goal that he treasures above the rest – scored at home against Arsenal. 'I picked the ball up just outside our own box at the Trent End of the ground, ran the length of the pitch before sticking it in the net past Bob Wilson at the other end.'

In the 1970–71 season he scored another hat-trick for the Reds at home to Crystal Palace, and he remembers one of the goals in particular. 'My first goal that day was my 100th for the club – it was a header from a cross by Barry Lyons.'

The clamour for Ian's services intensified and in March 1972 he joined Manchester United – but not before being paraded at the Baseball Ground as a newly signed Derby County player. 'Forest didn't want me to leave but Brian Clough assured me that the deal had been done and the release paperwork had been signed – perhaps naively I believed him and allowed myself to be paraded on the pitch.'

The Forest board would not let Ian sign for their closest rivals but he was allowed to join Manchester United a few days later. At just 28, though, his top-flight career was prematurely halted by injuries. He was able to turn out at non-League level for a while, as well as playing in Major League Soccer in the US, but he will forever be linked to that one magical afternoon beside the Trent.

Pete Moorcroft from Mapperley, a Forest fan for more than half a century, still regards the match as a classic. 'Apart from being the most memorable game I've ever seen, the third goal was something special. Ian had three attempts to get the ball in the net: the first attempt hit the crossbar, then Andy Rankin, the goalkeeper, saved the second and, as it came back off the woodwork again, Ian put his third attempt into the Everton net. Not only was it the winning goal, it also meant we went into the semi-finals.'

Steve Sutton

Date of birth: 16 April 1961, Hartington, Derbyshire

Nottingham Forest record:
Appearances: League 199, FA Cup 14, League Cup 33, Other 11
Debut: 25 October 1980 v Norwich City (a) drew 1–1

Also played for: Mansfield Town (loan), Coventry City (loan), Luton Town (loan), Derby County, Reading (loan), Birmingham City, Grantham Town

Steve Sutton would say he was a 'steady goalkeeper, capable of pulling off a big save when it were needed'. In reality, he was much, much better than that and was rewarded by helping Forest to three Cup Final victories at Wembley. His apprenticeship enabled him to study a master at close quarters. 'There were four of us goalkeepers who pretty much worked together every day: Peter Shilton, Chris Woods, myself and another young apprentice. In truth, we really just tagged along to help Shilts with his routine as much as anything. It was revealing to see his work ethic and a great education just to see how he went about his job.'

Steve's first-team debut arrived in October 1980 but was missed by his own manager. 'Cloughie had been poorly and was at home convalescing, so Peter Taylor was in charge of team affairs. We travelled down to Norwich for an overnight stop but without Shilts, who apparently had flu. I was told he would travel separately so his flu didn't get passed around the rest of the lads. Around 10 o'clock the next morning I was told I had better prepare myself as he wasn't coming.'

The match ended all square and 'Sutty', as he was known, checked the national press for their reaction. 'I thought my debut had gone OK and I'd made a couple of decent stops but the report in the *Daily Telegraph* said that I "came out like a Moonstruck Parrot". I'm still not sure what they meant by that!'

Steve had a constant battle to claim the first-team jersey at Forest with Shilts, and later when the likes of Hans van Breukelen and Hans Segers were all competing for the place. 'I never really enjoyed having a rival for the shirt,' says Steve. 'I liked the confidence of knowing that I was the number one. It wasn't really until the 1985–86 season that I realised what I could achieve.'

The 1988–89 season was a memorable one for Steve, in terms of fulfilling a boyhood dream. 'Every young footballer dreams of playing in a Cup Final at Wembley.' Forest got there twice in the space of a few weeks – facing Luton Town in the League Cup Final and then Everton in the Simod Cup. 'The League Cup didn't have the hype surrounding it that's associated with the Final nowadays, but it was a dream come true to play in a Wembley Final in front of a sell-out crowd on a red-hot day.'

A second success was not far away, winning a topsy-turvy Simod tie 4–3. 'The Everton match was quite extraordinary. I don't really think anyone was too interested in that tournament until we got down to the last four but then it ended with another Wembley Final, a great day out and another trophy to take back home on the bus.'

Sandwiched between those two memorable victories was one of football's blackest days – the FA Cup semi-final at Hillsborough on 15 April 1989. 'Going into the match we felt that we'd closed the gap on Liverpool and could have beaten them. We felt that we could have sold 80,000 tickets to our fans who wanted to be there and at kick-off the Forest end was full, but the Liverpool end was only full in the middle not at the sides. They hit our crossbar early on and then I was aware of fans running on to the pitch at the far end. Obviously I didn't really know what was happening and we were quickly taken off the pitch. In many ways it's left more of a scar on my wife than me because she was in the stands watching it all.'

The following season Steve won another League Cup-winners' medal but was then left out of the next match against Manchester United. However, they brought him back for the last game of the season for what turned out to be his 199th and final League match for the club. 'I just wish I'd played against United and reached the 200 mark,' he reflects.

Looking back on his days at the City Ground, the former goalie has one big regret. 'The Heysal ban on English clubs was particularly disappointing. We qualified for five consecutive years but weren't allowed to play and those big European matches are where you want to be in your career. I'd played a few UEFA Cup games before the ban – against the likes of Celtic and Bruges – and wished I'd had the opportunity to do it more often.'

Many observers feel Steve was particularly unlucky not to get any sort of international recognition. 'I wasn't flash but I was reliable and performed consistently and we were doing well in the top flight all the time I played, so I sometimes wonder if I might have sneaked into a squad or two. At that time they began looking at the likes of David Seaman and Dave Beasant as third choice; I felt I was in the same category as them.' Few Forest fans would disagree.

Steve is still a City Ground regular and helps with the development of Forest's crop of outstanding young goalkeepers by coaching them at the club's academy; they are in good hands.

Peter Taylor

Date of birth: 2 July 1928, Nottingham
Died: 4 October 1990

Nottingham Forest record:
Assistant manager: 1976–1982

Played for: Coventry City, Middlesbrough, Port Vale
Also managed: Burton Albion, Brighton & Hove Albion, Derby County

Uniquely, Peter Taylor is the only one of the 100 Legends of Nottingham Forest not to have either played for or managed the club – although he was briefly associated with the Reds as a young amateur goalkeeper. As Brian Clough's right-hand man, though, Pete played a crucial role during Forest's 'glory years'. Indeed, for a time, the pair even rivalled Morecambe and Wise as the country's top double act!

Peter made 86 appearances for Coventry City between 1950 and 1955 before moving to Middlesbrough, where he made 140 more appearances and met up with Clough for the first time. He made a lasting impression by complimenting the striker on the quality of his finishing!

After hanging up his boots as a player in 1962, Peter was offered the manager's job at Burton Albion. He guided them to victory in the Southern League Cup two years later before accepting the invitation that was to change his footballing life – joining Hartlepools United (as they were then called) to become assistant to BC.

The pair developed a good working relationship, which was to serve them – and a succession of clubs – very well over the next 27 years. While his partner's strengths lay in motivating and inspiring his staff, Peter's contribution was often at the other end of the spectrum – spotting raw talent and having the vision to identify if it could be nurtured into something beneficial.

After Hartlepools' fortunes had been revived, the pair then moved to the Baseball Ground and transformed Derby County, taking the Rams from the second tier to the Football League Championship. They next went to Brighton together, hoping to achieve similar results. Clough left, though, leaving Peter to manage the Seagulls on his own for a couple of years before accepting the call to rejoin his great and trusted friend at the City Ground.

Forest players maintain that the transformation at the club began from the moment that Peter walked through the door. Clough himself was reinvigorated – there seemed to be a sense of purpose about the place that had not existed before. Within a year of Peter renewing his partnership with Brian, Forest had been promoted.

The rest of the success story has been documented countless times as the Reds began collecting silverware like an enthusiastic antique dealer: the League Championship, two European Cups, two League Cups, the Charity Shield and the European Super Cup – all secured in a three-season blitz.

Before the 1979 League Cup Final win over Southampton, Cloughie asked Peter to lead the side out. The previous season, before the Final against Liverpool, the Football League had refused Forest's request to allow both men to accompany the players out from the Wembley tunnel. 'The League refused both of us the privilege,' Peter said afterwards. 'So Brian said it was only right that I take the team out this time. It was a proud moment for me and my family.'

There's no doubt that his contribution to Forest's success is hard to define, yet it is no less important. He would provide a calm, reassuring word to those in need or give sound tactical advice to others. A hugely intelligent student of the game, he preferred to operate in shadow rather than the spotlight and to use two words instead of three. His judgement was usually impeccable and Brian trusted him implicitly.

Each tried to describe their contribution to the cause. Cloughie said, 'I'm not equipped to manage successfully without Peter. I am the shop window and he is the goods in the back.' His assistant countered, 'We just gelled together. My strength was buying and selecting the right player, then Brian's man-management would shape him.'

In May 1982 Peter announced his retirement but was lured back into the game six months later by the prospect of rejoining Derby County as their manager. Sadly, two events then materialised that ultimately ruined a great friendship. First, Forest were drawn away against Derby in the FA Cup – and Taylor's new side triumphed 2–0.

Then, allegedly while Clough was away on holiday – and totally unaware – John Robertson, the vastly experienced Forest winger, was persuaded to sign for Derby. Peter retired for the second time in 1984.

In October 1990, at just 62 years of age, Peter died while on holiday in Majorca. Although the pair had never reconciled their differences, Brian attended the funeral and later spoke of his sorrow at never having made up with his former partner.

Geoff Thomas

Date of birth: 21 February 1926, Derby

Nottingham Forest record:
Appearances: League 403, FA Cup 28
Goals: League 1
Debut: 31 August 1946 v Barnsley (a) lost 2–3

Also played for: Bourne Town
Managed: Bourne Town

Geoff Thomas is among the handful of players who have appeared in more than 400 Football League matches for Nottingham Forest. His association with the Reds lasted almost 19 years, and encompassed two successful promotions and the sympathy of all supporters when he became the unlucky 12th man and missed out on an FA Cup Final place.

Gerald Shannon Thomas was born in Derby and represented Derbyshire Schools before joining Forest to gain some valuable experience in the wartime friendlies. Capable of playing in either full-back position, he made his debut in 1944 while still only 17. By the time that League football had been given the green light to restart after the hostilities, Geoff had played in more than 40 'unofficial' matches and sealed the right-back position as his own.

The Reds were pitched into the new Second Division and kicked off their post-war League campaign away at Barnsley. Although the season began with defeat, the country rejoiced as things began to get back to normal.

The first in a series of injuries that Geoff would sustain throughout his long career curtailed his involvement in that opening season. Sadly, he was forced to miss out on a very special day in the Reds' season – an FA Cup win over a Manchester United side, already destined for greatness.

Forest's League form was far from spectacular in the late 1940s and Billy Walker's side were relegated from Division Two at the end of the 1948–49 season, in which Geoff had played in 39 of the matches. Towards the end of that season the manager gave a debut at left-half to Billy Whare, a player who would form half of one of Forest's most dependable full-back partnerships. Whare was more comfortable at right-back, so his inclusion in the line up meant that Geoff was switched to the left. Over the next decade the pair of them formed a solid and consistent full-back pairing, with Jack Hutchinson usually deputising should either of them be out injured.

The 1950–51 season brought promotion and a cheer for all Forest fans as the Third Division South title was won, with Geoff featuring in all but one of the matches. His presence in the side certainly had a calming effect on those around him as Forest clinched the title, finishing six points ahead of runners'-up Norwich City.

Forest consolidated at the higher level and came within a couple of points of achieving back-to-back promotions. Elevation to the top flight would have to wait for another five years, a period in which the full-back developed into one of the best around. He was an ever present during the 1954–55 season and had confirmation of his form when he was selected to play for an FA XI.

Nevertheless, as a goal scorer Geoff was on a par with Des Walker, another high-quality Forest defender who, several decades later, showed similar levels of loyalty to Forest and also managed just one goal to show for his efforts. Geoff's only strike came on 31 August 1955, exactly nine years since his League debut, helping his team to a 2–0 home win against Leicester City.

Forest finally freed themselves of the Second Division at the end of the 1956–57 campaign, returning to the top flight after an absence of 32 years. The Reds were back among the big boys and only had a couple more years to wait before landing a prestigious piece of silverware – the FA Cup itself.

Wearing the number-three jersey, Geoff had played in 41 of the League matches in Forest's return to the First Division but the arrival of Scottish international Joe McDonald from Sunderland put his place under serious threat for the first time the year after. Although he dipped in and out of the League team whenever either Joe or Billy Whare took a knock, both men remained fit throughout all nine of Forest's FA Cup ties.

Geoff was the perennial 12th man – always ready but never used – and he was again the unfortunate player to be omitted as Forest advanced to the big day at Wembley. As it transpired, his major task on the day was to comfort broken-leg victim Roy Dwight on his way to hospital. In later years, Dwight's injury would have enabled Geoff to come on, play his part and collect a medal. Alas, the use of substitutes was neither possible nor allowed in 1959.

He stayed on at Forest for one more season and compiled another handful of appearances, to take his League tally for the Reds beyond the 400 mark – a milestone completed against Luton Town on 6 February 1960.

Shortly afterwards, Geoff bade his farewells to all at the City Ground and moved into the non-League game for a spell as player-manager of Bourne Town.

Charlie 'Chick' Thomson

Date of birth: 2 March 1930, Perth, Scotland

Nottingham Forest record:
Appearances: League 121, FA Cup 13, League Cup 1, Others 1
Debut: 24 August 1957 v Preston North End (h) won 2–1

Also played for: Blairgowrie, Clyde, Chelsea, Valley Sports

Forest's FA Cup-winning goalkeeper in 1959 was the popular and utterly dependable Scot 'Chick' Thomson. Born Charles Richard Thomson, he was known to all and sundry as just Chick by the time he joined Forest – arriving with a First Division Championship medal from his days at Chelsea.

Goalkeeping was a Thomson family trait: his father had kept goal for both Alloa and Falkirk and young Chick followed the trend when he began his career with Blairgowrie, an amateur side from Perthshire. He was soon earning good reports and was taken on by Clyde, for whom he made an astonishing impact on his debut. He was thrust into the starting XI for the Scottish Cup Final against Rangers at Hampden Park and helped his side to a 2–2 draw (Clyde lost the replay!)

The legendary Ted Drake saw Chick playing for the army during his national service and signed him from Clyde when he took over at Chelsea. The goalie played in the final 16 matches of the run-in and was instrumental in the Blues winning their first Championship. He is credited with making a stunning last-minute save to preserve a 1–0 victory over Wolves, their main rivals for the title.

Within two years Chick had slipped behind Bill Robertson in the pecking order as first-choice 'keeper at Stamford Bridge and was happy to move to the City Ground in the quest for regular football. The Reds had just clinched promotion back to the old First Division and Billy Walker was looking to strengthen his squad for the new challenge.

At only 27 years of age, Chick was at the peak of his powers at the time of his Forest debut – a home win over Preston North End. Missing only three first-team matches all season, the new goalie proved himself to be a fine shot-stopper, as well as providing calmness and assurity to the defenders in front of him.

Chick played in both matches against Manchester United during that season – the home game attracting a then City Ground record attendance of 47,804 and the return at Old Trafford coming immediately after the Munich Air disaster had so cruelly decimated the United squad. Under difficult and trying circumstances, all of the Forest players were praised for the compassion and sportsmanship they showed that day. Satisfyingly, he also kept a clean sheet against Chelsea on his first return to Stamford Bridge since leaving the West London club.

A top-10 finish gave the Reds something to build on for the 1958–59 season but it was the FA Cup, rather than the League, which took the limelight. With three clean sheets en route to the Final, Chick had been an important figure as Forest sealed their first trip to the Twin Towers to face Luton Town. On the big day itself, he looked to be in for an easy ride as his teammates helped themselves to a two-goal lead, but after Roy Dwight's injury Luton capitalised on their one-man advantage and laid siege on the Forest goal.

Although they breached his goal once, Luton's forwards were continually frustrated as Chick repeatedly claimed crosses, gathered loose balls or saved goal-bound attempts. Allan Brown, later to manage Forest, was particularly frustrated to see his fierce drive parried away. Chick later recalled that he had to go and collect his false teeth before climbing the steps to collect his medal from the Queen. The Wembley win was the standout moment in his days as a Forester, although he continued to play for the club for another 18 months or so.

Before the start of the 1959–60 season Chick kept goal for the Cup holders in the traditional Charity Shield curtain-raiser and a year later he played in Forest's first-ever match in the League Cup competition, keeping a clean sheet at home to Halifax Town on 6 October 1960. His final match for the club came just a month later, away at Wolves. Although he was still only in his early 30s, Chick then found himself behind Peter Grummitt in the pecking order and opted to join Valley Sports, a non-League team from Rugby, where he wound down his playing days.

Living in retirement in Nottingham, Chick has continued to follow the Reds' fortunes for almost half a century – wondering who will be the next Forest goalkeeper to emulate him and collect an FA Cup-winners' medal!

Des Walker

Date of birth: 26 November 1965, Hackney, London

Nottingham Forest record:
Appearances: League 323, FA Cup 30, League Cup 41, Others 14
Goals: League 1
Debut: 13 March 1984 v Everton (h) won 1–0

Also played for: Sampdoria (Italy), Sheffield Wednesday, Burton Albion, England
(59 caps)

What an extraordinary footballer Des Walker was. Throughout his career there were some critics foolhardy enough to try and pick at the bare bones of his ability: some felt brave enough to question his tackling, there were those who felt he was not outstanding in the air. Others said he was too quiet on the pitch and his goalscoring record was virtually non-existent. Nevertheless, his speed of thought was matched by an ability to out-sprint even the quickest of opponents, a package which elevated him up among the finest defenders of his generation. 'You'll never beat Des Walker!' Rarely has a terrace chant been so accurate and so respectful, and the admiration between supporter and player was entirely mutual – Des loved playing for Forest!

He had been an apprentice at the City Ground before turning professional in December 1983 and his arrival in the first team followed just three months later. Over the course of the next eight years Des brought a solidity and purpose to the Nottingham Forest defence. Loose-limbed and athletic-looking, his ability to read and manipulate a situation long before it happened was almost psychic. He could sniff out danger long before the alarm bells had even thought about ringing.

As his career blossomed, his medal drawer swelled. He helped Forest to three League Cup Finals (two of which were won), the 1991 FA Cup Final, the Simod Cup success in 1989 and the Zenith Data Systems Cup win in 1992. Of those, the memory of the FA Cup defeat to Spurs will never be allowed to die. There, coldly, in black and white for all time the winning goal will be recorded as 'Walker – own-goal'.

Not that the Forest number four was remotely at fault: Nayim took a corner from the right, Paul Stewart glanced it on and Des, anticipating the back-post threat, got there before Gary Mabbutt but could only deflect it past 'keeper Mark Crossley. It was as if fate had decided to play the cruellest of tricks on a footballer that otherwise was seldom exposed.

By that stage of his career Des was a seasoned international. After winning seven caps at Under-21 level he made his full England debut against Denmark in 1989 and was firmly established in the side by the time of the World Cup Finals the following year. He also featured in the European Championships of 1992, a year that had begun with an extraordinary event: on New Year's Day Des had scored a goal at the right end – the only one of his career! Playing at home to Luton Town and trailing in the last minute, he had gone on an upfield foray and suddenly found himself in a situation that he had not encountered before. Nevertheless, he tucked away the chance amid near-hysteria from teammates and fans alike.

As one of the world's best defenders it was inevitable that the big clubs would keep testing Forest's resolve about hanging on to one of their prize assets and eventually the right money (and the player's own ambitions) saw Des leave for Sampdoria in the summer of 1992, but the Italians (managed by Sven-Göran Eriksson) often played him out of position and did not get the most out of him. After just one full season in Serie A he returned to the Premiership with Sheffield Wednesday.

In 2002, 10 years after leaving the City Ground, Des returned to Forest and displayed form and fitness that made it look as if he had never been away. Adding experience to a youthful side, he helped them come close to promotion with a place in the Play-offs at the end of the 2002–03 season. He played on for one more campaign, intending to retire at the end of the 2003–04 season, but he was called up to serve for one last time. Having joined the Forest coaching staff, and with the club desperately short of defensive cover, he found himself being used as a substitute for the opening match of the next campaign away at Wigan. It was his 398th outing for the Reds, placing him in 14th position on the club's all-time list of appearance makers.

After finally bowing out of the professional game, he was awarded a testimonial match by the Reds in May 2005. The evening was memorable for another goal by Des – and an uncharacteristic brush with the law – but it gave his devoted fans the opportunity to properly say, 'You'll never beat Des Walker!'

Billy Walker

Date of birth: 29 October 1897, Wednesbury, West Midlands
Died: November 1964

Nottingham Forest record:
Manager: March 1939–July 1960

Played for: Hednesford Town, Darlaston, Wednesbury Old Athletic, Aston Villa, England (18 caps)
Also managed: Sheffield Wednesday, Chelmsford City

William Henry Walker can truly be described as one of the great servants of English football, achieving success as both player and manager. In more than 20 years of leadership he guided Nottingham Forest to two promotions and a Wembley FA Cup victory before moving 'upstairs' to join the club's committee.

His father George had played at full-back for Wolves, but it was as an inside-forward that young Billy was snapped up by Aston Villa, having forged an impression in local Staffordshire football. He had turned professional in 1919 and scored both goals on his debut in a 2–1 FA Cup win over Queen's Park Rangers. This was to be a competition that would serve Billy well over the years and his introduction was spectacular, helping his side to the Final and a 1–0 success over Huddersfield Town at Stamford Bridge.

He spent 13 years at Villa Park, many as captain, and amassed more than 500 first-team outings for the club with a healthy return of almost 250 goals. Among his haul was a Football League 'first'. On 12 November 1921 against Bradford City at Villa Park, he became the first player to be credited with scoring a hat-trick of penalties in a 7–1 victory.

The previous year, the England selectors had called him up for the first time and he made his debut, against Northern Ireland at Sunderland, in October 1920. Billy crowned his first appearance with the second goal in a 2–0 victory. He went on to win a total of 18 caps for his country, three of which were as captain. Able to continue his career strike rate at the higher level, he netted nine goals in international football.

After hanging up his boots, Billy accepted the responsibility of taking over as Sheffield Wednesday's manager. Within a couple of years he had turned the fortunes of the struggling club around and taken them to third place in the First Division and then to victory in the 1935 FA Cup Final, beating West Bromwich Albion 4–2. However, off-field shenanigans forced his resignation shortly afterwards and Billy took a sabbatical from the game before returning with non-League Chelmsford City. His appetite for the game restored, he then took over at the City Ground in March 1939.

Forest survived the war years largely because of Billy Walker. With the country being urged to keep things 'as normal as possible' the Reds boss used his contacts within the game to bring many famous guest players to Nottingham, as well as concentrating on the development of the city's own footballing youngsters.

Praised for his visionary approach, Billy was always said to be preparing for the day when the hostilities would cease and the League programme would continue. His belief in young home-grown talent backfired initially, as most of his side lacked the necessary experience to succeed. Forest's resources were somewhat limited and in 1949 an inevitable relegation to the Third Division ensued. Thankfully, the board stood by Billy and he masterminded not only the return to the Second Division but also promotion to Division One as well.

Unlike so many of his contemporaries, Billy was always striving for new innovations within the game. He would constantly try and source fresh training methods and spent time speaking to top foreign coaches in order to replicate some of their methods. It was generally acclaimed that the Forest boss was one of the most knowledgeable students of the game.

His finest hour as manager of Nottingham Forest was undoubtedly the FA Cup success of 1959 – 24 years after he had guided Wednesday to the same trophy. The Cup adventure is well documented, but a key factor was Billy's faith in his best starting XI. In all nine Cup ties he was able to send out the same players. It was somewhat ironic – and totally coincidental – that his captain, Jack Burkitt, came from the same Staffordshire town as the manager.

Ill-health and common sense finally forced Billy to step down from his role at the end of the 1959–60 season. Although his popularity at the club remained untarnished he was happy to take up a position on the Forest committee, remaining loyal to the club until his death in 1964, aged 67.

Billy Walker was a truly great Forester and the only manager to lead the club to FA Cup glory at Wembley Stadium.

Neil Webb

Date of birth: 30 July 1963, Reading, Berkshire

Nottingham Forest record:
Appearances: League 176, FA Cup 20, League Cup 26, Others 7
Goals: League 50, FA Cup 4, League Cup 5, Others 4
Debut: 17 August 1985 v Luton Town (a) drew 1–1

Also played for: Reading, Portsmouth, Manchester United, Swindon Town, Grimsby Town, Exeter City, Weymouth, Aldershot Town, Merthyr Tydfil, England (26 caps)
Managed: Reading Town, Weymouth

Nottingham Forest enjoyed the best years of Neil Webb's career. At the peak of his powers he was an absolute joy to behold – a sparkling diamond in the centre of the park. The highlight of his time with the Reds came in the 1989 League Cup Final, when he scored against Luton Town – the same team he had faced when he first joined Forest.

The opening fixture of the 1985–86 season paired the Reds with a trip to Kenilworth Road. 'Luton had just had their plastic surface installed, so Cloughie took us down there on the Thursday to have a look at it. I wasn't particularly keen but managed to score a couple of days later with a free-kick which took a friendly deflection!'

Neil scored 14 goals in the League in his first season at the City Ground, including a hat-trick at home to Coventry City. 'It was a proper one, as well,' he says. 'One with the left, one with the right and a header – I've kept a set of photographs of them all.' He managed to claim the match ball as well, but that presented more of a problem the next time he scored three. 'It came at Chelsea on a hot, sunny day and everything went right. Gary Birtles then scored a couple and, when we got a penalty, I knew he'd take it. 6–2 and we'd each scored a hat-trick. I didn't fancy fighting him for the ball but then the original one was replaced, so at the end we had one each!'

During the 1987–88 season Neil earned his first international cap, against West Germany in Dusseldorf – becoming the 1000th player to appear for England. A year later the stylish midfielder was to play in his first major Wembley Final – the League Cup against Luton. Forest trailed by a single goal at the interval. 'At half-time we were expecting a right rollicking but it was all very calm and it was just emphasised that we could play much better than that.'

Forest got back on terms through a Nigel Clough penalty and then came Neil's big moment. 'Tommy Gaynor burst down the right wing – I made a run through the middle and he hit a perfect ball in. There was a shout for offside but if you look at the lines on the pitch then you can see I'm all right. My first touch was pretty good. Les Sealey then made it easy for me, sliding out sideways, and I was able to hook it over him and into the net.' Forest added a third to seal a memorable victory. 'Just going up those steps to collect the Cup was the best feeling imaginable.'

Very quickly, the Forest players were to experience a whole range of differing emotions with the tragedy of Hillsborough occurring a week later. It was then back to Wembley to clinch the Simod Cup before facing Liverpool again in the semi-final replay. 'The replay was a surreal occasion. It wasn't a sell out and we knew we couldn't win whatever happened. Everyone was saying that it had to be an all Merseyside Final after what had happened at Hillsborough.'

In July 1989 Neil left Forest to join Manchester United. 'I just saw the move as a fresh challenge at the time. I scored on my debut in a 4–1 win over the champions, Arsenal, but after just four games it all turned bad.' That was because while playing in Sweden for his country Neil snapped his Achilles tendon, ruling him out of the game for six months. He returned to feature in the FA Cup Final (and set up the winning goal in the replay) and went to Italia '90.

He went back to a relegation-threatened Forest in November 1992 but it was to be no fairy-tale comeback. 'If I'd had an inkling that Cloughie was about to retire I might not have gone back, but I returned hoping I could help get them away from the trouble they were in.'

Neil managed just a handful of appearances before his injury curse reappeared. 'My left Achilles was very sore after a match and I had to go for a scan on the Monday. It confirmed a rupture and was my last involvement of the season.'

Frank Clark replaced Cloughie as manager and Neil's involvement in the side began to dwindle. 'In my last year I hardly figured – not even as a sub. I ended up going to play a few games in Hong Kong because Frank wouldn't let me go out on loan to another English club. I'd moved back to Reading and was commuting daily. I put my house in Keyworth on the market. The manager told me I was giving up too soon, until he saw the house that is – he bought it off me!'

Despite things not going to plan during his second stint at Forest, Neil maintains that he loved his time in Nottingham and will never forget his Wembley goal. 'I can't describe how good it felt to score such an important goal and it was at the end where all the Forest fans were as well, which made it even sweeter.'

Enoch West

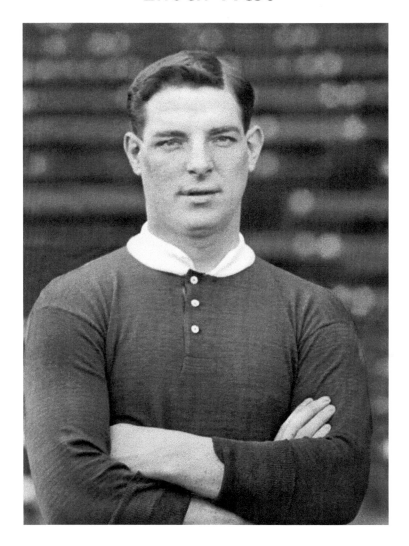

Date of birth: 31 March 1886, Hucknall, Nottinghamshire
Died: 1965

Nottingham Forest record:
Appearances: League 168, FA Cup 15
Goals: League 93, FA Cup 7
Debut: 16 September 1905 v Bury (h) won 3–2

Also played for: Hucknall Constitutionals, Sheffield United, Manchester United

Enoch West was one of the great Nottingham Forest goalscorers in the early part of the 20th century. He played for the Reds between 1905 and 1910 and notched 100 goals in just 183 appearances. In later years, after joining Manchester United, his name was blackened in the annals of football history after he was found guilty of match fixing.

Nicknamed 'Knocker', Enoch came from Hucknall and began to make a name for himself after joining Sheffield United, but somehow they allowed him to be transferred to Forest in 1905 for the paltry sum of just £5.

The Blades' loss was very much Forest's gain. He played his first couple of matches at centre-forward but then moved to inside-right and scored the only goal in a 1–0 victory over Preston North End. That was the first of the 14 he scored that year, but personal achievements were incidental in a season that ended with the disappointment of relegation.

For the task of ensuring an immediate return to the top flight, Forest signed Welsh international Grenville Morris to play alongside Enoch in attack. The pair hit it off immediately, contributing 35 goals between them as the Reds clinched the Division Two title off the back of a 17-match unbeaten run.

Although he favoured the inside-right position, Enoch was comfortable in almost any slot and played right across the forward line at some point or another for the Reds.

Happily back in the First Division, Knocker was simply unstoppable, smashing in a monumental 28 goals from just 35 appearances. Among his haul was a hat-trick in a 6–0 thrashing of Chelsea and another in a 3–3 draw at Blackburn. In both matches one of his goals had come from the penalty spot and he became one of the most consistent around, converting nine of the 10 spot-kicks he took in the League.

There were three more occasions when he hit three or more goals during his time at the City Ground. Enoch was among the three Forest players to hit hat-tricks in the record 12–0 League victory over Leicester Fosse in April 1909 – Alf Spouncer and Bill Hooper being the others. Earlier he had claimed all four goals during a 4–1 home win over Sunderland and he hit another hat-trick away at Manchester United in November 1909. Ironically, this last performance may well have convinced the United staff that Knocker could do a more than useful job for them as they stepped in and signed him the following summer.

The striker helped Manchester United to FA Cup glory in 1911 and to the First Division title a couple of years later, and he recorded a tally of 80 goals from 151 first-team appearances for them before being convicted of football's most unforgivable crime – match fixing.

The incident stemmed from a match at Old Trafford on 2 April 1915, Good Friday, between United and Liverpool at Old Trafford. Fighting to avoid relegation, the home side won the match 2–0 but observers and match officials noted an apparent lack of effort from Liverpool and a penalty miss.

Subsequently, a Football Association enquiry decided that four players from each side, Enoch among them, should be found guilty on suspicion of match fixing and banned all eight for life. Enoch vociferously protested his innocence and even sued the FA for libel, but he lost the case and the ban remained, although it was eventually lifted in 1945 when he was 59 years of age.

On several occasions since his death the FA have been approached with regards to granting Enoch a posthumous pardon for the doubt surrounding his involvement, but this has always been refused.

Although World War One would undoubtedly have brought an abrupt end to his time in the professional game, the ban tarnished a glittering playing career which ended with him having found the net 80 times for United from his 181 matches. Before that he had scored exactly 100 times for Forest and remains one of only six players to score a century of goals for the club.

Bill Whare

Date of birth:	14 May 1924, Guernsey
Died:	May 1995

Nottingham Forest record:

Appearances:	League 298, FA Cup 23, Others 1
Goals:	League 2
Debut:	23 April 1949 v Tottenham Hotspur (h) drew 2–2

Playing at right full-back in Nottingham Forest's 1959 FA Cup Final side was Bill Whare, a Channel Islander who played in almost 300 League matches for the Reds – his only club. Bill's route to the City Ground had been far from conventional. During the war he had been deported and forced to spend several years in a German internment camp. He met and became friends with Ted Malpass, who went on to play for Aston Villa. Ted knew Billy Walker, the Forest manager, and so he recommended Bill.

In May 1947 Bill joined the City Ground staff but had to learn his trade in the reserves for a couple of seasons before being handed a first-team debut. Although all of his football had been spent at right-back, his debut was played in the left-half position in a 2–2 draw at home to Spurs.

A general air of despondency hung over the club as they were relegated from the Second Division at the end of the 1948–49 season, but the team rebuilding enabled Bill to press for more regular opportunities in the side. He played in 23 of the League matches, as Forest finished fourth, and performed so consistently that the previous right-back, Geoff Thomas, could not dislodge him. Thomas later switched to left-back and the pair went on to become one of Forest's most dependable full-back partnerships of all time.

The following season, 1950–51, finally saw the Reds' fortunes improve. They won the Third Division South title by six clear points, banging in a record total of 110 goals in the process.

At just 5ft 7in tall Bill was quickly establishing himself as one of the best tacklers in the land and became a firm favourite with the City Ground regulars. They had to wait a while for him to get on the score sheet for the club, though, but almost 100 matches and three and a half years after his debut he came up with the goods by scoring the winner in a 2–1 victory at Huddersfield Town.

Bill's consistency was rewarded during the 1955–56 season when he appeared in every fixture. Ironically, injuries disrupted the following campaign, preventing him from making a full impact on a season which ended with promotion back to the top flight for the first time in 32 years.

The opportunity of playing First Division football was fully accepted by Bill and he not only rose to the challenge but excelled in the environment as well. He even notched his second and final career goal in more than a decade of service, scoring at home against Aston Villa in November 1957.

For a one-club pro like Bill, the opportunity of winning some major silverware had seemed to be little more than fanciful optimism. The FA Cup run of 1959 changed all that – even if there was almost an embarrassing early exit at the hands of Tooting and Mitcham. A replay was needed to get past the plucky non-Leaguers but four months later the same starting XI, clad in new white tracksuits, would be walking out at Wembley Stadium to confront Luton Town in Forest's first Final appearance since 1898.

There was a moment to savour for Bill when the Duke of Edinburgh stopped and chatted to him as the Royal party were introduced to the two teams. If they were discussing the match, it surely would not have included a scenario where Forest would establish an early two-goal cushion, but that is how it unfolded.

Bill and the rest of the Forest defence looked to be in for a comfortable afternoon, but Roy Dwight's injury left the side a man short and Luton seized the initiative. With half an hour still to be played, the deficit was halved.

A blow to the knee rendered Bill a hobbling passenger for a few minutes until, gloriously, the referee blew for full-time. The celebrations were a mixture of joy and relief. The long-serving Forest number two was in a better position than most to appreciate how much the success meant to the fans and to the city as a whole.

At the start of the following season Forest were brought down to earth a little when they were beaten 3–1 by the League champions, Wolves, in the Charity Shield. There was further disappointment when a specially arranged two-legged Cup-winners' affair went the way of St Mirren, the Scottish Cup holders.

Despite these two set-backs, the Wembley win ensured that 1959 had been the calendar year that Bill had craved for, so it was perhaps fitting that he would also play his final game in it. The match itself will not be fondly remembered, though: an 8–0 drubbing against Burnley at Turf Moor on 21 November.

Bill remained on Forest's books until May 1960, when he announced his retirement from the game.

Jeff Whitefoot

Date of birth: 31 December 1933, Cheadle, Greater Manchester

Nottingham Forest record:
Appearances: League 255, FA Cup 23, League Cup 4, Others 3
Goals: League 5, FA Cup 1, League Cup 1
Debut: 23 August 1958 v Wolverhampton Wanderers (a) lost 1–5

Also played for: Manchester United, Grimsby Town

Jeff Whitefoot won an FA Cup-winners' medal with Nottingham Forest to add to the League Championship he had won earlier while at Manchester United. More than half a century later, Jeff is still in the Old Trafford record books for being the youngest-ever player to play for United in a first-team match. The former 'Busby Babe' was just 16 years and 105 days old when he played in a home League match against Portsmouth in April 1950. Considering we are now in an era where outstanding youth-team players seem to get early opportunities by being blooded in 'lesser' Cup competitions, Jeff's record may not stand for much longer – but he is undeniably proud of the statistic.

The youngster's progression from the junior ranks and into the United first team had been swift, but Jeff's career as a young wing-half was then disrupted by national service with the Royal Air Force. As soon as he was able to return to the game full-time Jeff made up for lost time and received a call-up to the England Under-23 side, winning a cap against Italy in Bologna to go with those he had already won at Schoolboy level.

Although Jeff was an integral part of United's title-winning midfield, Busby began to exclude him more frequently – often in favour of the developing Eddie Colman. Forest boss Billy Walker enquired about Whitefoot but a deal could not be made and he signed for Grimsby Town instead. After just one season on the East Coast Jeff moved to the City Ground.

His debut for the Reds was not exactly auspicious – a 5–1 hammering against Wolves on the opening day of the 1958–59 season. The result was put in perspective when the men from Molineux would go on to claim the title by six clear points.

By the turn of the year Forest were comfortably entrenched in mid-table and able to turn their attention to the Cup. For Jeff, the fourth-round draw was kind, with an early reunion with the Grimsby Town side he had left just six months earlier. He relished the occasion

and netted his first goal for the Reds in a 4–0 home win.

Jeff's years at Old Trafford had added a winning mentality to the steely determination he already possessed in abundance. Often in Forest's Cup run he was able to inspire those around him and lift them to performances possibly thought beyond them. The fair-haired wing-half more than played his part as the Reds advanced to the Twin Towers and on the big day itself he ensured there would be no sagging spirits as Luton staged their late onslaught.

Following on from the immense achievement of collecting a Cup-winners' medal in his first year at the City Ground, Jeff went on to devote a decade of service to Forest. He played in the 1959 Charity Shield match against Wolves and in the first season of League Cup action 12 months later.

Not renowned for his goalscoring, Jeff popped up with the winner in a League Cup tie at Queen's Park Rangers in October 1961: this was the first time Forest had won away from home in the competition. The same month they competed in the Inter Cities Fairs Cup for the first time and Jeff played in both legs of the first-round aggregate defeat to Valencia.

He was just one of four players still at the club in 1965 when the same Spanish team returned to the City Ground to provide the opposition as Forest celebrated their centenary – the others being Peter Grummitt, Colin Addison and Bobby McKinlay.

That season Jeff played in all but one of the Reds' fixtures but a combination of injuries and the emergence of Henry Newton into the Forest ranks lessened his appearances over the next 18 months.

His final game came at Everton in December 1967, just short of his 34th birthday. Jeff remains devoted to the game and is a popular figure whenever he returns to either Old Trafford or the City Ground to catch up with his former clubs.

Sam Weller Widdowson

Date of birth: 16 April 1851, Hucknall, Nottinghamshire
Died: 9 May 1927

Nottingham Forest record:
Appearances: FA Cup 23
Goals: FA Cup 19
Debut: 16 January 1869 v Newark Town (a) drew 0–0

Also played for: Notts County, England (1 cap)

Samuel Weller Widdowson was one of football's early pioneers. A supremely gifted athlete who also played first-class cricket for Nottinghamshire, he is acknowledged to have been at the very forefront of the game as we now know it.

Christened Sam Weller after the character of the same name who appeared in Charles Dickens's *Pickwick Papers* (his father was a hugely devoted Dickensian), he first appeared for Forest in 1869. He began working in the lace industry but was in great demand as a footballer – he would occasionally turn out for Notts in some of their 'bigger' games against out-of-town sides. Forest were his team, though, and he played an important role in their early development, both as a player and as an official.

Sam was a small man, with an astonishing turn of speed. His fleetness of foot embarrassed many a defender, with the result that he was frequently – and unceremoniously – an early target for the 'professional foul'.

While nursing his sore shins one day in 1874 he happened to glance at an old pair of cricket pads and set about adapting them for football. When he next turned out for Forest he looked an unusual sight, with some buckled protection on the outside of his stockings. Sam was no fool, though: he knew the idea was practical as well as profitable, and he took out a patent on the design. Very soon most players of his generation were wearing something similar.

A keen student of the game, Sam was also responsible for a significant change in the tactical approach to football. To that point, most sides fielded something resembling a 2-2-6 formation – very attack-minded but naïve in its approach. Sam reasoned that two full-backs, three half-backs and a five-strong forward line presented a better balance. Over the next three-quarters of a century, most managers and coaches tended to agree.

In this period of the game referees and their assistants would communicate by a series of white flags. With larger crowds this was becoming increasingly more confusing. In a match featuring Forest and Sheffield Norfolk, the referee used a whistle for the first time. Sam, as Forest's captain, was asked to give his opinion on the idea and his approval helped with the speedy introduction of its widespread usage. In 1891 a Liverpool man, James Brodie, came up with the idea of attaching a net to the goal frame. Forest's Town Ground was used for a trial match, which was refereed by Sam. Again, his

thoughts afterwards were instrumental in the adoption of goal netting, as we now know it.

Another of Widdowson's inventions seemed destined to be cast aside, though. He believed that with the appropriate lighting, evening football would be popular. Using eight gas lamps he arranged a match in 1877, but with fears for public safety as well as difficulty in seeing the ball properly, the idea was abandoned until 1909 when, with electricity now in regular use, he returned to the City Ground to help adopt and install floodlighting.

Aside from his 'one-man cabaret act to improve the game', Sam was a decent player. Most of the matches he played in were friendlies, of course. The one major competition he had to demonstrate his ability in was the FA Cup. In just 23 outings he rattled in 19 goals – no Forest player has ever scored as many. Among his catalogue of scores in the competition were four in a 7–2 win over Sheffield Heeley in 1882 and a hat-trick at Rotherham Town a couple of years later.

Sam played in one full international for England, appearing at centre-forward against Scotland at Hampden Park on 13 March 1880. In what must have been a thrilling encounter between the 'Auld Enemy', the home team were victorious by five goals to four.

He combined his playing role with that of Forest's chairman between 1879 and 1884, the season in which the club reached the last four of the FA Cup competition and faced Queen's Park. The tie was drawn 1–1 at Derby and the replay took place at the Merchiston Castle ground in Edinburgh, the only occasion an FA Cup semi-final has been played in Scotland. The opposition were too strong in the rematch, winning 3–0.

In 1888 Sam was Nottingham Forest's representative as they made a bid to join the Football League, but they were not included among the original 12 founder members as they still clung to their amateur status.

That year Sam had been elected on to the FA Committee, a position he would hold for five of the next six years. Part of his duties included being a selector for the national team. At the age of 40, he left his sick bed to attend an England trial match at the Kennington Oval and, after discovering a player had not turned up, he borrowed a pair of boots and turned in an outstanding performance at left-back!

This fine servant to Nottinghamshire sport died in Beeston in 1927, aged 76, but he left behind a sport on which he had made a major impression.

Frank Wignall

Date of birth: 21 August 1939, Chorley, Lancashire

Nottingham Forest record:
Appearances: League 157, FA Cup 15, League Cup 4, Others 3
Goals: League 47, FA Cup 6
Debut: 24 August 1963 v Aston Villa (h) lost 0–1

Also played for: Horwich RMI, Everton, Wolverhampton Wanderers, Derby County, Mansfield Town, Kings Lynn, England (2 caps)
Managed: Kings Lynn, Burton Albion, Qatar (national team coach), Shepshed Charterhouse

Frank Wignall was a prolific target man for Forest during the mid-1960s, whose outstanding form for the club earned him a place among Alf Ramsey's World Cup 'wannabees'. His Forest career got off to something of a bizarre start – the manager who signed him, Andy Beattie, left the club before the season started. New boss Johnny Carey appreciated his talents, though, and reaped dividends pitching Frank alongside Colin Addison.

Twice in 1964 Frank hit hat-tricks for Forest. The first came at Bolton against the club he had supported as a youngster. 'In many ways it saddened me because they ended up getting relegated that year and took a long time to get back to the top flight. Growing up, Nat Lofthouse had been my mentor and I'd go and watch them at every opportunity.'

Of his three goals that day, Frank has clearest recollections of the third. 'John Barnwell had the ball in midfield. The Bolton defence were too square and as I ran between the full-back and the centre-half John played a perfect pass. I had time to weigh up, right or left – or bend it past the 'keeper. I ended up hitting it in at the near post with the outside of my right foot.'

Frank's second Forest triple came during a week of huge speculation. 'An England squad announcement was due and the newspapers felt that either myself or Tony Hateley of Aston Villa might get a game up front. On the Saturday we played Villa so I suppose I just wanted to try and prove I was the one to choose. I scored three times, was voted Man of the Match – and was picked to play for England!'

The national team's new centre-forward scored both Wembley goals in a 2–1 win over Wales and predictably kept this place for the next match in the Netherlands. Everything was looking rosy for Frank until the end of season County Cup match at home to Mansfield Town. 'Their centre-half whacked me on the inside of the left leg as I tried to go around him and the leg was broken.'

Although Frank returned to first-team duties by the start of the 1965–66 season, he admits he still was not fully fit and the national manager continued to look at other options. As Frank dryly comments, 'Perhaps if I hadn't broken my leg I'd have continued to be England's centre-forward – and perhaps we wouldn't have won the World Cup!'

With Joe Baker alongside him, Frank returned to his very best during the successful 1966–67 season when Forest finished as runners-up in the League

and reached the semi-finals of the FA Cup.

During that Cup run Frank made a major contribution to a game that is instantly associated with another former Forest star: the Everton tie in which Ian Storey-Moore scored a hat-trick. 'I laid a few on for him that day,' he adds modestly. 'I'll always remember the final goal. John Winfield gave the ball an almighty lump into the box. I got above Brian Labone, the Everton centre-half, and nodded it back for Ian. I think it took him three attempts to get the ball over the line but I'll never forget the roar – the atmosphere then was as good as I'd ever known at the City Ground.'

Frank had to go off injured during the semi-final defeat to Spurs – a significant blow as the side were already without Baker, who had picked up a knock in the previous round. Without the front pair, hopes of a Wembley Final were evaporated, as were any aspirations Frank may have had about adding to his tally of caps.

He did gain some further recognition, though, when he was invited to go to Montreal to play for an FA XI in a tournament to promote Expo '67. 'Bobby Moore and a few of the other members of the World Cup-winning side were involved,' explains the former striker.

In a rematch of what might have happened in 1966, Frank recalls the outcome of that tournament. 'We beat the German FA in the Final and I scored a couple!' With a strike record of 53 goals from 179 first-team appearances, Frank left Forest in March 1968 but it is a deal he has always regretted. 'I came in on a Friday morning for a light training session,' he recalls. 'I was summoned to see Tony Woods, the Chairman, who said that he'd had Wolves on the phone and they wanted to sign me to get them out of relegation trouble. It was deadline day or something, and the deal had to be done straight away. I agreed – but it's something I've always regretted. I wouldn't have gone if I'd thought about it a bit more.'

Frank severed his ties with Forest but admits they are still the club he has most affinity with. 'I won titles with Everton and Derby and won nothing at Forest – but we should have. I looked at the number of forwards they brought in over the next few seasons after I'd left and always felt I could have done a better job and wished I'd been there to do it.'

Tommy Wilson

Date of birth: 15 September 1930, Bedlington, Northumberland
Died: April 1992

Nottingham Forest record:
Appearances: League 191, FA Cup 25, Others 1
Goals: League 75, FA Cup 13, Others 1
Debut: 6 October 1951 v Luton Town (h) won 2–0

Also played for: Cinderhill Colliery, Walsall

Scorer of the decisive goal in Nottingham Forest's FA Cup Final win of 1959 was centre-forward Tommy Wilson. Although he had made his first-team debut almost eight years earlier, it had taken a while for Tommy to cement his place in the side. Nevertheless, his Wembley winner ensured him of his standing as a true Reds legend.

Tommy was taken on to Forest's books as a promising right-winger, having been spotted playing for Cinderhill Colliery. Although only around 5ft 8in in stature, he was elusive and pacy and deemed to have the necessary qualities to succeed as a flank player.

He was given his debut, on the wing, against Luton Town (appropriately enough!) in October 1951. Further first-team outings were hard to come by over the next couple of years, although there was a crumb of consolation in that he helped the reserves to win the Midland League title for three consecutive seasons.

It was clear to manager Billy Walker that Tommy had an eye for goal and possessed a decent shot with either foot, so he began the conversion by moving him to inside-forward and then centre-forward. To the delight of manager and player the move was a great success. Tommy scored his first senior goal in a 4–1 win at Middlesbrough on 8 September 1954 and then netted against the same opposition, a week later, to open his City Ground account.

In a Second Division campaign of mid-table mediocrity, Tommy's 10 goals equalled that of Jim Barrett to finish joint top scorer for the club. Against Barnsley in February 1957 the striker scored four of Forest's goals in a 7–1 home victory to become only the sixth player to achieve that feat for the club. The season would end with promotion back to the First Division.

If there were any doubts about Tommy's ability to step up to the top level they were quickly dispelled when he scored 19 League goals from 40 appearances. Incredibly, 17 of the goals came before the end of December!

For three consecutive seasons Tommy stood alone as Forest's top marksman, but any private satisfaction from that paled in significance to his Cup goals in 1959. Very few players have managed to score in every round of the competition but it looked as if he might achieve the statistic, with goals against Tooting and Mitcham, Grimsby Town, Birmingham City and then both in the 2–1 win over Bolton Wanderers in round six. The goal against Birmingham in round five is widely regarded as being the moment that Forest fans realised that fate might be conspiring to give them a Cup adventure to remember. The Reds were on their way out of the competition until Billy popped up with a last-minute header to take the tie back to Nottingham for a replay.

The sequence of scoring a goal in every round was broken at the semi-final stage, but any disappointment that Tommy might have had evaporated after just 14 minutes of the Final when he scored to put Forest 2–0 up. Billy Gray put over an inviting cross from the left and Tommy placed a well-directed header beyond the reach of Ron Baynham in the Luton goal.

That was his 27th and final goal of his most productive season ever. It did not take him long to open his account again, scoring Forest's only goal in the Charity Shield defeat to Wolves, which christened the start of the 1959–60 season.

Between 6 February and 12 March 1960 Tommy achieved the rare feat of scoring in six consecutive League matches for the Reds, although, as it turned out, these would be the final goals he would register for the club. He played one match at the start of the next season before moving to Walsall, where he scored 19 times to help them to promotion out of Division Three.

Tommy hung up his boots in 1962 and remained the last Forest player to score in an FA Cup Final until Stuart Pearce's free-kick against Spurs in 1991. He later moved to Essex and worked for the council, helping create projects for youngsters. A youth centre he helped set up in Hutton, near Brentwood, was renamed the Tommy Wilson Centre after the former Cup winner died in 1992.

John Winfield

Date of birth: 28 February 1943, Draycott, Derbyshire

Nottingham Forest record:
Appearances: League 355, FA Cup 33, League Cup 16, Others 6
Goals: League 4, FA Cup 1
Debut: 3 February 1962 v Blackpool (h) lost 3–4

Also played for: Peterborough United

Considering the amount of high-quality left full-backs that Forest have been able to call upon over the years, it is praise indeed to comment that John Winfield was up there among the very best. In a 16-year association with the club, John played in more than 400 first-team matches – a total that allows him to sit proudly in 11th position on the all-time list of appearances for the Reds.

A local lad, he graduated through the junior ranks before turning professional in May 1960, aged 17. His early football had been played in the wing-half positions, proving himself versatile enough to be comfortable on either side of the pitch.

Apart from the disappointing result his League debut was highly memorable, a thrilling encounter at home to Blackpool who ran out winners by the odd goal in seven! Playing at right-half, John scored one of the Forest goals – a collector's item as it turned out, as he only scored three more League goals in the next 354 matches!

Competition for first-team places was fierce. John had to bide his time and learn his trade as Calvin Palmer and Henry Newton claimed seniority for the half-back berths and the likes of Billy Gray and Denis Mochan were given preference in the number-three jersey. One match in which John did start (and probably wished he had not) was the infamous 2–9 defeat against Tottenham Hotspur at White Hart Lane in September 1962, in which Jimmy Greaves bagged four of Spurs' goals.

Andy Beattie had been in charge of the Reds when John first became involved, but it was under Johnny Carey that he was given an extended run in the side after fully converting to left-back. With Peter Hindley occupying the right-back position, the pair formed a tight and consistent cornerstone of the Reds' back-line for six years and more than 200 matches. It was very rare for either of them – let alone both – to be absent from any match between 1966 and 1972.

Standing at 6ft tall, John was a difficult opponent. Strong in the air, physically imposing and a resolute tackler, he was unlucky not to have any senior international caps to add to those won at Under-23 level. He played in all but two of the matches during the 1966–67 season when Forest finished as runners-up in the League to Manchester United and reached the FA Cup semi-finals. Over the next four years he missed only another three games – a rare level of consistency, although he would not come as close again to landing any major silverware.

Second in the League guaranteed Forest a spot in the UEFA Cup and John played in all four of the matches in the autumn of 1967, appearing in the two victories over Eintracht Frankfurt as well as the aggregate defeat to FC Zurich of Switzerland. A year later he was playing for Forest on the day the main stand caught fire and burned down during a home League match against Leeds United. The defender later claimed that it was one of the saddest sights during his time with the club.

In January 1969 Matt Gillies succeeded Johnny Carey as Forest manager – the third boss that John had played under at the City Ground – and later he served under both Dave Mackay and briefly Allan Brown.

It was under Brown's reign that John – and Forest – experienced another lengthy FA Cup run in 1974 that eventually saw them eliminated in controversial fashion after three matches against Newcastle United – none of which were played in Nottingham. His final match in the Garibaldi colours was a League game at Aston Villa on 24 April 1974, although in recognition of his outstanding service to the club he was granted a testimonial match a few weeks later and Leicester City provided the opposition.

John Barnwell, a former Forest teammate, was manager of Peterborough United and persuaded John to sign for him there, but he only spent one season at London Road before deciding to finally hang up his boots for good.

One of Forest's most successful home-grown talents later became a newsagent and has been a frequent and popular guest whenever he has returned to the City Ground to watch his former club in action.

Peter Withe

Date of birth: 30 August 1951, Liverpool, Merseyside

Nottingham Forest record:
Appearances: League 75, FA Cup 11, League Cup 8, Others 5
Goals: League 28, FA Cup 3, League Cup 5, Others 3
Debut: 25 September 1976 v Carlisle United (h) won 5–1

Also played for: Skelmersdale, Southport, Barrow, Port Elizabeth City (South Africa), Arcadia Shepherds (South Africa), Wolverhampton Wanderers, Portland Timbers (US), Birmingham City, Newcastle United, Aston Villa, Sheffield United, Huddersfield Town, Evesham United, England (11 caps)
Managed: Wimbledon, Thailand (national team manager), Indonesia (national team manager)

It is somewhat ironic that the defining moment of Peter Withe's footballing career was the winning goal in a European Cup Final. Withe left Forest after playing a major role in helping the Reds to their League Championship triumph of 1977–78, moving on before Clough's side went on to even greater accomplishment on the continent.

Peter Withe's travels took him near and far as he searched for the ideal home for his uncompromising style of forward play. Leaving behind his Merseyside roots, he journeyed via the north-west non-League and lower League scenes, and incorporated spells in South Africa and the US before eventually rising to prominence in the Midlands.

Brian Clough signed him from Birmingham City in September 1976, aware that he had purchased a striker out of the box labelled 'Battering Ram'. Second Division Forest were already six matches into the new season – but with only one win to their name – when their new target man arrived at the City Ground. His acquisition complemented the slightly more cultivated style of some of those around him but, make no mistake, Peter knew his craft. Possessed with a good first touch and excellent distribution skills, he quickly endeared himself to fans and teammates alike.

He scored on his debut and continued to find the net with pleasing regularity to help maintain a position of close proximity to the other promotion challengers. An additional bonus came by way of success in the Anglo-Scottish Cup; although he did not find the net in the two-legged Final victory over Orient, Peter had played his part by netting goals in both legs of the semi-final win over Ayr United. The club could do no better than a third-place finish in the table, but they had done enough to return to the top flight on the back of a season which had brought Peter 19 goals for the club.

The new campaign began in spectacular style with three consecutive victories – Peter scoring in each match. His form was eye-catching and his finishing deadly. On 4 October 1977 he scored all of Forest's goals in a 4–0 home win over Ipswich Town – the first Reds player to score four in a League match since Tommy Wilson 20 years earlier.

As with the previous campaign, Cup success went hand in hand with League victories and Forest advanced to their first League Cup win, beating Liverpool in a replay. Peter had weighed in with five goals en route, scoring against West Ham in round two, Villa in round four and three against Leeds United in the semis – two of them in the first leg win at Elland Road. His League Cup-winners' medal soon had a companion as the Reds swept to their maiden top-flight championship – Peter again contributing 19 goals during the season.

His final goal for Forest came at Wembley in the 5–0 Charity Shield win over Ipswich Town in August 1978. A few days later he was gone – signing for Newcastle United for £200,000 after scoring 39 goals in 99 outings for the Reds.

Peter's next transfer brought him even further success and international recognition. He left St James' Park for Aston Villa in May 1980 for a club-record fee of £500,000. The investment reaped dividends as Peter won his second League title in three years before going on to enjoy the type of success he may have experienced had he remained a Forest player.

He picked up the first of his 11 international caps for England when he played against Brazil at Wembley in May 1981 and helped his club side to their greatest achievement when he scored the only goal of the 1982 European Cup Final against Bayern Munich in Rotterdam.

Peter wound down his playing days before accepting the assistant manager's job and then the reserve-team coach's role at Villa Park. He later spent most of the 1991–92 season as boss of Wimbledon, but in recent years has rekindled his nomadic existence with spells as national team coach of both Thailand and Indonesia.

Ian Woan

Date of birth: 14 December 1967, Heswall, Merseyside

Nottingham Forest record:
Appearances: League 221, FA Cup 21, League Cup 18, Others 13
Goals: League 31, FA Cup 6, League Cup 1, Others 2
Debut: 2 January 1991 v Norwich City (a) won 6–2

Also played for: Runcorn, Barnsley, Swindon Town, Columbus Crew (US), Shrewsbury Town

Ian Woan had a 'wand' of a left foot that served Forest admirably for a decade. Selected in the 1991 FA Cup Final team, he also played his part in two successful promotion campaigns for the Reds.

'Woany' had signed for Brian Clough from non-League Runcorn in March 1990. 'I'd done well in my first year in the Conference and had agreed to join Bournemouth, but then I was told of Forest's interest. I went and met Alan Hill and Ronnie Fenton and it was clear they needed a left-sided player. I signed without them having seen me play!'

He had to wait until the following January – when he came on as a sub in a 6–2 win at Norwich – before making his first-team bow. 'It was a bit frustrating waiting that long for my chance but I realise now it was necessary for me to adapt to Forest's way of doing things. Coming on at Norwich was great because my dad, Alan, used to play for them!' His first goal for the Reds came against Chelsea, on a day when the whole team turned on the style to trounce the Blues 7–0. 'It sticks out because it was with my right peg – a bit of a collector's item.'

At the end of his first full season with the club, and having played only around 15 matches, Ian was included in the starting line up for the FA Cup Final against Spurs. 'I'd played in the semi-final and had scored a few goals leading up to the Final, but it was still a big surprise to be selected. We'd all got on the bus after training and Cloughie just handed a folded piece of paper to Pearcey for him to read out.' Apart from the disappointing outcome, the day itself was very memorable for the young winger. 'I suppose really it came too early in my career to appreciate it fully, but meeting Charles and Diana [the Prince and Princess of Wales] was very special and my whole family were there to enjoy the day as well.'

Ian still feels that Paul Gascoigne was fortunate to escape a red card for his two reckless lunges early in the game. 'Rules are rules and he got the sympathy vote, but we still thought the whole of the first half had gone well for us.'

Spurs' fightback was doubly demoralising for Ian, who was substituted after 68 minutes and did not get the opportunity to play at the national stadium again. 'I was left out of the League Cup Final side the following year – that was one of the real lows of my career, not to even make the bench. Despite that, I've nothing but the highest of regards for Cloughie. I only worked under him for the last couple of years of his career and it's clear that they weren't his best.'

The relegation from the Premiership at the end of the 1992–93 season marked the end of an era but an up-turn in Ian's fortunes. 'When Frank Clark took over he assembled a really good side and it suited my strengths. Stan Collymore could win games for you that nobody else could so it was important to get the ball in quickly for him.'

Whipping in crosses was not Ian's sole contribution to the Forest cause. He always maintained a decent strike rate for a wide player and even finished as the club's top scorer in the 1995–96 campaign. Additionally, most of his goals were eye-catching. 'I never used to get tap-ins because I was always trying to catch up with play,' he laughs. 'If I had to pick out my favourites they would be against Liverpool, a goal that cost them the title, against Newcastle in the FA Cup and a goal against Arsenal. I beat David Seaman from a long way out but it was the year before Sky's coverage began so it never gets shown!'

Ian has always remained good friends with his former teammate Steve Stone, despite often getting abused because of him! 'Steve was an exceptional talent. Great credit to him to come back from three broken legs and a ruptured patella. He always made me look dreadful because he would be working busily on the right-hand flank, running about like a wasp in a bottle, whereas I had a different style – every game we'd get compared and some fan would call me a "lazy Scouse git"!'

After playing more than 250 first-team games for the Reds, Ian was allowed to leave on a free transfer to join Barnsley but did not remain at Oakwell long before he was taken on by Swindon Town. A short stint in Major League Soccer preceded a move to Shrewsbury Town, whom he helped to some FA Cup giantkilling acts in 2003.

Moving into coaching, Ian worked for a while at Rushden & Diamonds with ex-Foresters Paul Hart and Ian Bowyer before returning to his old club to help develop the young talent within the Forest Academy.

Tony Woodcock

Date of birth: 6 December 1955, Nottingham

Nottingham Forest record:

Appearances:	League 133, FA Cup 14, League Cup 21
Goals:	League 36, FA Cup 10, League Cup 12
Debut:	24 April 1974 v Aston Villa (a) lost 1–3

Also played for: Lincoln City (loan), Doncaster Rovers (loan), Arsenal, Cologne (Germany), England (42 caps)

Managed: Fortuna Cologne (Germany)

Tony Woodcock was one of the 'hidden talents' on Forest's books, who blossomed into a European champion and a full England international. The young striker had appeared in the final two matches of the 1973–74 season but then disappeared back into the reserves for a couple of years. Loan spells at Lincoln City and Doncaster Rovers brought a few goals and some invaluable experience, and they gave Tony some confidence to approach Brian Clough with. 'I knew a few clubs were interested in signing me so I asked Cloughie to either play me or let me go. I think he realised I'd got a bit of talent and asked me where I wanted to play!'

Finally given his chance, 'Woody' scored 17 goals to help the club win the Anglo-Scottish Cup and also an unexpected holiday bonus. 'We'd finished our season before some of the other clubs and were flying to Majorca while some matches were still in progress. I can remember the pilot saying, "We have Nottingham Forest on board and I hope we can give them some good news when we land." Obviously, when we heard that we'd been promoted it set us up for a great week's holiday!'

When the new season's fixtures were announced, Tony made a point of looking for one away fixture in particular. 'I was a big Denis Law fan as a kid and always hoped I'd get the chance to play at Old Trafford. I'd gone there once before, with Forest's reserves, and played at left-back. I still managed to score twice and afterwards the ref asked me to autograph his programme, saying, 'Can you sign this please because one day you'll play for England!'

By the time of the United fixture Forest were top of the table and on their way to the League title. The record books credit the opening goal that afternoon against United defender Brian Greenhoff, with Woodcock (two) and Robertson doing the rest of the damage in a 4–0 rout. 'I've always claimed a hat-trick that day,' says Tony. 'My first shot hit him as it crossed the line!'

The next couple of years were memorable as Tony picked up a League title, a European Cup win, the first of his 42 England appearances and a couple of League Cup triumphs, which included the fulfilment of a boyhood dream. 'Like all youngsters I'd always hoped to score at Wembley in a Cup Final.' Tony realised that ambition in the 1979 League Cup Final against Southampton. 'There were lots of things I remember about that day. The pitch

wasn't great – every time you played the ball big chunks of the Wembley turf were dislodged. Also, we played with a brand new ball which we all felt was much lighter than the one we used every week.'

Whatever the reasons, Forest were out of sorts in the first period. 'We'd gone in at the break trailing 1–0 and we really hadn't played very well. You might expect Cloughie to have started ranting and raving but he was all nice and calm. He just emphasised, "All you have to do is give it to a red shirt!" We began the second half as we'd been asked and pretty soon the confidence returned.'

A brace of goals from Garry Birtles turned the game around for Forest and the win was all but sealed when Tony added a third. 'The ball was being played around the edge of their box. Archie Gemmill chipped it back in and I managed to get on the end of it and lift it, right-footed, over the 'keeper.'

In the following season's competition Tony hit a hat-trick against Middlesbrough, which even the record books confirm. 'The good thing about that performance was that the next morning I'd agreed to go in and have a meeting with Cloughie about my new contract. He just said, "That was a good way to start negotiations."'

A month later Tony signed for Cologne, a club who had clearly monitored his progress since the two sides had met in the previous season's European Cup. 'There were rumours that a lot of European clubs liked my style of play and I think Cologne had been chasing me for a while. They were a big club, with 16 or 17 full internationals on their staff. When I'd first started playing I'd always thought that I'd like to try my hand abroad and this was the perfect opportunity to give it a go.'

Tony left behind a side that went on to win the European Cup for the second season in succession and he feels that should have been recognised. 'I scored a couple of goals in the early rounds and should have qualified for a medal but they didn't give out as many as they do nowadays and I still haven't got one!'

Recently, Tony was given a reminder of his early days at the City Ground. 'I met up with Tommy Gemmell again – the former Celtic great. He had a brief spell at Forest in the early 1970s and as part of my apprenticeship I used to clean his boots. I was surprised when he said that he's always told people that "Tony Woodcook used to clean my boots"!'